Women's Words

Women's Words

The Feminist Practice
of Oral History

Edited by
Sherna Berger Gluck
and Daphne Patai

Routledge
New York and London

Published in 1991 by

Routledge
An imprint of Routledge, Chapman and Hall, Inc.
29 West 35 Street
New York, NY 10001

Published in Great Britain by

Routledge
11 New Fetter Lane
London EC4P 4EE

Judith Stacey's article "Can There Be a Feminist Ethnography?" is reprinted, with some alterations, from *Women's Studies International Forum,* Vol. 11, no. 2 (1988) Pergamon Press.

Library of Congress Cataloging in Publication Data

Women's words : the feminist practice of oral history / [edited by]
  Sherna Berger Gluck and Daphne Patai.
    p.   cm.
    Includes index.
    ISBN 0-415-90371-8.—ISBN 0-415-90372-6 (pbk.)
    1. Women—Historiography. 2. Oral   history. 3. Women's   studies—
Methodology.   I. Gluck, Sherna Berger, 1935–   II. Patai, Daphne, 1943-.
HQ1121.W886 1990
305.4'0722—dc20
90-48234

British Library Cataloguing in Publication Data

Gluck, Sherna Berger, 1935–
  Women's words : the feminist practice of oral history.
  1. Feminism. Oral history
  I. Title   II. Patai, Daphne, 1943–
  305.4207
  ISBN 0-415-90371-8
  ISBN 0-415-90372-6 pbk

Contents

Introduction

A casual announcement made at the founding conference of the National Women's Studies Association in 1977 brought almost two dozen feminists together for an early morning breakfast meeting where we shared our enthusiasm for the new, uncharted work that we were doing collecting women's oral narratives.[1] It had become increasingly clear to all of us that traditional oral history methodology did not serve well the interests of women's oral history.[2] This methodology did not address the basic insights that grew out of the women's liberation movement, including the notion that the personal is political and the conviction that women's experiences were inherently valuable and needed to be recorded.

Present at that early morning meeting were community activists committed to uncovering women's history both as part of consciousness raising and as a way to inform organizing; academicians from a variety of disciplines who were beginning to think of oral narratives as an avenue for understanding and documenting women's culture and history; and young students eager to be a part of the new feminist scholarship that was less than a decade old.

This meeting gave the first hint of the numbers and range of women across the country who, in isolation, were developing projects that, broadly speaking, constitute the field of feminist oral history. What united us was our fascination with the possibilities afforded by the technique of recording women's words: their oral narratives, testimonies, and life histories. We were not yet a network, and we had no literature to guide us.[3] At the same time, other scholars throughout the country were independently discovering oral history's extraordinary potential as a tool of feminist research.

The editors of this volume came to oral history through these two paths and represent, in effect, two generations of feminist oral historians. Each was driven by a sense of urgency to recover women's words. Sherna Gluck, angered by the invisibility of women in the writing of U.S. history, began her work in 1972. She has been involved in the field of women's oral history since its inception as a distinct area linking women's studies to history, anthropology, and sociology—disciplines in which the collection of oral narratives has been an important method. Daphne Patai, a critic of Brazilian literature, became concerned about all the women whose "texts" were nowhere to be found and began recording Brazilian women's stories in 1981.

The appeal of oral history to feminists is easy to understand. Women doing oral histories with other women in order to recover their stories and revise received knowledge about them have seen their work as consistent with the principle of feminist research later codified in the phrase "research by, about, and for women."[4] This conviction generated an enormous volume of women's oral history, making available in accessible forms the words of women who had previously been silenced or ignored. On radio, in community auditoriums, in classrooms, and in bookstores, women from all walks of life were being introduced as agents whose very presence transformed our understanding of the social world.

This immense literature, in addition to its inherent significance, also provided a body of material that could in turn become the object of critical analysis. In fact, when examined through the lens of the expanding feminist scholarship of later years, women's oral history revealed itself to be more problematic than we had imagined.

Most striking, in retrospect, were the innocent assumptions that gender united women more powerfully than race and class divided them, and that the mere study of women fulfilled a commitment to do research "about" women. Although we had questioned the value of traditional androcentric methodology, not all of us had yet learned to be skeptical of the claims for a single feminist methodology. Our assumptions had the effect of foregrounding gender while obscuring the possible centrality of other factors—race and class, in particular—in the identity of our narrators. To define feminist scholarship as work done by, about, and for women had seemed simple. Experience, however, demonstrated that these three little words positioned the scholar within a complex web of relationships, loyalties, and demands.[5]

Because it involves at least two subjectivities, that of the narrator and that of the interviewer, oral history adds a new dimension to the concept of work "by" women. A story or statement that, in its oral form, is "by" the speaker very often reaches the public in the form of a text "by" the scholar, whether as a life history or as excerpts used by a scholar to illustrate a line of argument.

It is, of course, the case that narrators frequently shape their narratives according to their own sense of direction, often in the face of considerable interference from single-minded interviewers.[6] It is also true that the telling of the story can be empowering, validating the importance of the speaker's life experience. This, indeed, is one of the reasons that oral history work with women was assumed to be inherently feminist. On the other hand, narrators typically are not true partners in the process. Whatever control they exercise during the interview, when they are able to negotiate the terrain, usually ends once the session is completed.[7] This shift in control over the narrative reveals the potential for appropriation hiding under the comforting rationale of empowerment. Although narrators are occasionally consulted prior to publication, and at times even share in some of the material benefits of publication, the scholar/interviewer typically returns to her life and her scholarly enterprise, having transformed women's words into various written forms, but having also walked away—usually for good—from the situation that led her to her subject in the first place.

Ironically, it is precisely at this moment, when the individual narrator's power over the process recedes, that the feminist scholar is most actively engaged in fulfilling her sense of obligation that her research be "for" women. Through our work of framing, presenting, interpreting, analyzing, and making the work public, we have believed, simply and finally, that we were contributing to the larger collectivity of women—making a kind of return. By documenting women's representations of their own reality, we were engaging in advocacy. We felt that our work was, indeed, political and that it was for women.

But as scholars have continued to examine the different moments in the production of oral history, the real separation between narrator and interviewer has become ever more apparent. It was no longer possible to ignore the distinct imbalances in power and privilege that characterize most women's oral history projects. Perhaps we were merely discovering on our home turf and from the perspectives of our own disciplines what some ethnographers have considered to be the pitfalls of their fieldwork.

Anthropology is by no means the only discipline that offered valuable insights to those collecting oral narratives, although it is the field that has produced the greatest body of work of immediate relevance to understanding the intricacies of interviewing across cultural boundaries. The fields of speech communication and linguistics helped us recognize the importance of analysis of women's speech patterns and of the interview as a linguistic event; folklore emphasized narration as a type of performance. From psychology we gained an awareness of the more subtle dynamics of the interview process and the importance of subjectivity and memory in shaping narratives. On the other hand, sociology alerted us to the ways in which narrators are constrained by and at the same time contest their social environments. History contributed an understanding of the dynamic interaction between continuity and change. Contemporary literary theory—challenging the older historian's tendency to see oral history as a transparent representation of experience—made us aware that the typical product of an interview is a text, not a reproduction of reality, and that models of textual analysis were therefore needed.

The contributions of the different disciplines often overlap, revealing the artificiality of the academic division of knowledge. But it was the specific addition of feminist scholarship, frequently transforming these fields and dissolving their boundaries, that led to the multidisciplinary perspective characterizing the essays prepared for this volume.

These essays reflect some of the recurring problems with which feminist scholars have grappled in the practice of oral history as we have moved beyond celebration of women's experience to a more nuanced understanding of the complexities of doing feminist oral history. Ironically, it is the feminist emphasis on the personal, which is criticized by several of our contributors, that also enables these authors to be reflexive and analytical of their own practice. By focusing on themselves and their own experiences, they have been able to expose the flaws of existing models, including the prevailing feminist ones.

Originally trained in anthropology, history, folklore, literature, psychology, sociology, linguistics, and speech communication, all our contributors draw on their experience in a variety of national and international contexts. As each of them guides the reader along the paths followed in her own oral history work, the authors indicate, sometimes in bold strokes, at other times in tentative outline, the problems they confronted and the solutions they have devised as they collect, interpret, and use women's words.

Notes

1. We are using "oral narratives" to mean the material gathered in the oral history process, typically utilizing a tape recorder. These narratives take a variety of forms, including life history, topical interviews, and testimonies. "Oral history," in contrast, refers to the whole enterprise: recording, transcribing, editing, and making public the resulting product—usually but not necessarily a written text.

2. Traditional oral history methodology was outlined in such early sources as the 1966 pamphlet by William G. Tyrell, *Tape Recording Local History,* and the 1969 booklet, *Oral History for the Local Historical Society,* both published by the American Association for State and Local History (AASLH); and the 1973 book by Gary L. Shumway and William G. Hartley, *An Oral History Primer,* produced by the California State University, Fullerton program. It was not until the publication in 1978 of Paul Thompson's *The Voice of the Past: Oral History* (New York: Oxford University Press) that a general work on oral history methodology became available, one that was helpful to those engaged in social history, including women's oral history. Many early articles are collected in the more recently published volume by David K. Dunaway and Willa K. Baum, *Oral History: An Interdisciplinary Anthology* (Nashville, Tenn.: AASLH and the Oral History Association [OHA], 1984). Even today there are stark contrasts between the practices of oral history followed by social historians, anthropologists, and other researchers in the human sciences, on the one hand, and the practices of the more traditional historians and political scientists, on the other. One example of this is the recent debate within the Oral History Association on the issue of anonymity. Anonymity is anathema to some historians and political scientists, trained above all to value verifiability and specified sources. But it is a necessity to people using oral narratives in social history and other disciplines, who have learned that identifying one's sources may drastically restrict the type of material with which a researcher is likely to be entrusted.

3. The first major body of literature on women's oral history appeared in late 1977 in a special issue of *Frontiers: A Journal of Women's Studies.* This ground-breaking issue served as the key reference in women's oral history for many years, and the suggested outlines for women's oral history interviews that appeared at the back of the journal were xeroxed, dittoed, and mimeographed by women in communities and classrooms around the country. In 1983 a new collection of articles was gathered, resulting in another special issue of *Frontiers:* "Women's Oral History, II." Since then, a number of journals have published special issues predominantly or exclusively on women's oral history.

4. For a discussion of the criteria for feminist scholarship, see, especially, Joan Acker, Kate Barry, and Joke Esseveld, "Objectivity and Truth: Problems in Doing Feminist Research," *Women's Studies International Forum* 6 (1983):423–35; and Sandra Harding, "Introduction: Is There a Feminist Method?" in *Feminism and Methodology,* ed. Sandra Harding (Bloomington, Ind.: Indiana University Press, 1987), pp. 1–14.

5. Concern with connection and collaboration emerges as a clear theme of the feminist oral history work that is presented in this volume. Women's attraction to the techniques of oral history may well be due to the opportunity it affords for interaction with other women in a setting that both overlaps and transcends the usual private sphere. The phenomenon of feminist oral history may thus provide support for Carol Gilligan's hypothesis that women's moral development in this society (and perhaps in other Western societies) leads them to value "attachment that creates and sustains the human community" rather than separation and detachment, as men characteristically do. See Carol Gilligan, *In a Different Voice: Psychological Theory and Women's Development* (Cambridge, Mass.: Harvard University Press, 1982), p. 156.

6. We are thankful to Michael Frisch for his forceful description of this process during the dialogue with the audience at the roundtable discussion, "Empowerment or Appropriation: Oral History, Feminist Process, and Ethics," at the Oral History Association meeting in Baltimore, Maryland, October 1988.

7. Rendering the oral narrative into an accessible form for public consumption requires considerable intervention on the part of the researcher/editor. The literal transcription is usually edited into a continuous narrative, in the process of which choices are constantly made about how to translate the spoken word into the written word. Because the final product is in most cases a text that is to be read, it must conform, to a greater or lesser extent, to literary expectations. Punctuation is added, repetitions are deleted, words and passages are discarded, highlighted, and/or taken out of sequence. In short, conventional editorial considerations come into play. Typically, the speaker is consulted, if at all, only once the editing process is completed.

I

Language and Communication

Oral history begins with talk. Because feminists, like social historians, were initially attracted to oral history as a way of recovering the voices of suppressed groups, they tended to ignore the problematic dimension of language as the basis of oral history. But as the thirst for information about women's lives began to be assuaged, it became apparent that attention had to be given to the very medium and process through which this information was being made available. The three essays in this section all focus on language and communication, and on the ways in which they are shaped by gender.

Coming from the discipline of history, many of the early feminist scholars collecting oral narratives were impeded by traditional historical methodology, above all by the belief that their main task was to ask the right questions in order to uncover new data about women's lives and activities. Kathryn Anderson and Dana Jack urge interviewers to abandon this stance, discard their protocols and presuppositions, and, instead, truly attend to narrators' self-evaluative comments, meta-statements, and the overall logic of the narrative.

The active nurturing of the interview process is further elaborated by Kristina Minister, who argues that gender itself should become a basic unit of analysis in oral history methodology. Evoking an imaginary video of a group conversation, she explores how women's style of communication structures women's verbal and nonverbal interaction, and urges that we draw on these resources and abandon patriarchal models of communication.

Gwendolyn Etter-Lewis demonstrates the need for specific studies of the language and communication patterns of different groups, arguing that black women in the United States cannot be understood if their talk is examined using models created for white women. Analyzing the speech patterns of a group of Afro-American women and delineating three distinct narrative styles in their talk, Etter-Lewis shows how language shapes the representation of self.

Together, these essays move us beyond earlier prescriptions for women's oral history. They make us realize that women interviewing women is not an unproblematic activity. Taping a woman's words, asking appropriate questions, laughing at the right moment, displaying empathy—these are not enough. What is missing from this list is the realization that the interview is a linguistic, as well as a social and psychological, event, one that can be better understood by taking into account the specific characteristics and styles of the group being studied.

1

Learning to Listen:
Interview Techniques and Analyses

Kathryn Anderson and Dana C. Jack

Oral history interviews provide an invaluable means of generating new insights about women's experiences of themselves in their worlds. The spontaneous exchange within an interview offers possibilities of freedom and flexibility for researchers and narrators alike. For the narrator, the interview provides the opportunity to tell her own story in her own terms. For researchers, taped interviews preserve a living interchange for present and future use; we can rummage through interviews as we do through an old attic—probing, comparing, checking insights, finding new treasures the third time through, then arranging and carefully documenting our ~~results.~~ *discoveries*

Oral interviews are particularly valuable for uncovering women's perspectives. Anthropologists have observed how the expression of women's unique experience as women is often muted, particularly in any situation where women's interests and experiences are at variance with those of men.[1] A woman's discussion of her life may combine two separate, often conflicting, perspectives: one framed in concepts and values that reflect men's dominant position in the culture, and one informed by the more immediate realities of a woman's personal experience. Where experience does not "fit" dominant meanings, alternative concepts may not readily be available. Hence, inadvertently, women often mute their own thoughts and feelings when they try to describe their lives in the familiar and publicly acceptable terms of prevailing concepts and conventions. To hear women's perspectives accurately, we have to learn to listen in stereo, receiving both the dominant and muted channels clearly and tuning into them carefully to understand the relationship between them.

How do we hear the weaker signal of thoughts and feelings that differ from conventional expectations? Carolyn Heilbrun urges biographers to search for the choices, the pain, the stories that lie beyond the "constraints of acceptable discussion."[2] An interview that fails to expose the distortions and conspires to mask the facts and feelings that did not fit will overemphasize expected aspects of the female role. More important, it will miss an opportunity to document the experience that lies outside the boundaries of acceptability.

To facilitate access to the muted channel of women's subjectivity, we must inquire whose story the interview is asked to tell, who interprets the story, and with what theoretical frameworks. Is the narrator asked what meanings she makes of her experiences? Is the researcher's attitude one of receptivity to learn rather than to prove preexisting ideas that are brought into the interview? In order to learn to listen, we need to attend more to the narrator than to our own agendas.

Interview Techniques: Shedding Agendas—
Kathryn Anderson

My awareness of how both personal and collective agendas can short-circuit the listening process developed while scanning oral histories for the Washington Women's Heritage Project. This statewide collaborative effort received major support from the National Endowment for the Humanities and the Washington Commission for the Humanities to develop educational workshops and to produce a traveling exhibit documenting women's lives in interviews and historical photographs. The first stage of the project involved training dozens of interviewers in a series of oral history workshops held throughout the state. A typical workshop provided information on equipment, processing tapes, interviewing techniques, and a crash course in the new women's history scholarship. Prospective interviewers left with a manual, which included Sherna Gluck's "Topical Guide for Oral History Interviews with Women."[3]

To select excerpts for the exhibit, we reviewed dozens of interviews produced by project staff and workshop participants along with hundreds of interviews housed in archives and historical societies. We found them filled with passages describing the range and significance of activities and events portrayed in the photographs. To our dismay and disappointment, however, most of them lacked detailed discussions of the web of feelings, attitudes, and values that give meaning to activities and events. Interviewers had either ignored these more subjective dimensions of women's lives or had accepted comments at face value when a pause, a word, or an expression might have invited the narrator to continue. Some of us found discrepancies between our memories of interviews and the transcripts because the meaning we remembered hearing had been expressed through intense vocal quality and body language, not through words alone.

We were especially confused that our interviews did not corroborate the satisfactions and concerns other historians were discovering in women's diaries and letters, or the importance of relationships social scientists were uncovering in women's interviews. To understand why, I scrutinized the interviews with rural women that I had done for the project, paying special attention to interview strategies and techniques. My expectations that the interviews would give rural women a forum to describe their experiences in their own terms and to reflect on their experiences as women in the specific context of Washington state were thwarted to some extent by three factors: the project's agenda to document women's lives for the exhibit; an incomplete conversion from traditional to feminist historical paradigms; and the conventions of social discourse.

While the project's general goal was to accumulate a series of life histories, my special task was to discover women's roles in northwest Washington farming communities. Project deadlines and the need to cover a representative range of experiences combined to limit interviews to no more than three hours. In retrospect, I can see how I listened with at least part of my attention focused on producing potential material for the exhibit—the concrete description of experiences that would accompany pictures of women's activities. As I rummage through the interviews long after the exhibit has been placed in storage, I am painfully aware of lost opportunities for women to reflect on the activities and events they described and to explain their terms more fully in their own words.

In spite of my interest at the time in learning how women saw themselves as women in specific historical contexts, the task of creating public historical documents as well as the needs of the project combined to subvert my personal interests and led to fairly traditional strategies. As a result, my interviews tended to focus on activities and facts, on what happened and how it happened. They revealed important information about the variety of roles women filled on Washington farms, and how they disguised the extent and importance of their contributions by insisting that they were just "helping out" or "doing what needed to be done." Left out, however, was the more subjective realm of feelings about what made these activities fun or drudgery, which ones were accompanied by feelings of pride or failure. The resulting story of what they did tells us something about the limitations under which they operated but less about the choices they might have made. My interests were not incompatible with the project's goals but my methods often failed to give women the opportunity to discuss the complex web of feelings and contradictions behind their familiar stories.

My background included both women's history and interpersonal communication, but no specific training in counseling. My fear of forcing or manipulating individuals into discussing topics they did not want to talk about sometimes prevented me from giving women the space and the permission to explore some of the deeper, more conflicted parts of their stories. I feared, for good reasons, that I lacked the training to respond appropriately to some of the issues that might be raised or uncovered. Thus, my interview strategies were bound to some extent by the conventions of social discourse. The unwritten rules of conversation about appropriate questions and topics—especially the one that says "don't pry!"—kept me from encouraging women to make explicit the range of emotions surrounding the events and experiences they related. These rules are particularly restrictive in the rural style I had absorbed as a child on an Iowa farm. In a context where weather, blight, pests, and disease were so crucial to productivity and survival, conversation often tended toward the fatalistic and pragmatic; we certainly did not dwell on feelings about things beyond our control. As I interviewed rural women, the sights, sounds, and smells of a farm kitchen elicited my habits of a rural style of conversation and constrained my interview strategies.

Another interviewer experienced tensions between project goals and rules of conversation in a different context for different reasons. As she interviewed Indian women from various Washington tribes, she felt torn between a need to gather specific information and an awareness of appropriate relationships between yound and old: the rules she had learned as an Indian child prohibited questioning elders, initiating topics, or disagreeing in any form, even by implying that a comment might be incomplete. When, as in these instances, interviewer and narrator share similar backgrounds that include norms for conversation and interaction, interview strategies must be particularly explicit to avoid interference.

Although I approached the interviews with a genuine interest in farm women's perceptions of themselves, their roles, and their relationships in the rural community, I now see how often the agenda to document farm activities and my habit of taking the comments of the farm women at face value determined my questions and responses. Both interfered with my sensitivity to the emotionally laden language they used to describe their lives. My first interview with Elizabeth illustrates a lost opportunity to explore her discussion of the physical and mental strains of multiple roles.[4] We had been talking about her relationships with her mother and half-sister when she offered the following:

> I practically had a nervous breakdown when I discovered my sister had cancer, you know; it was kind of like knocking the pins [out from under me]—and I had, after the second boy was born, I just had ill health for quite a few years. I evidently had a low-grade blood infection or something. Because I was very thin, and, of course, I kept working hard. And every fall, why, I'd generally spend a month or so being sick—from overdoing, probably.

Instead of encouraging further reflection on the importance of her relationship with her sister or on the difficulties of that period in her life, my next question followed my imperative for detailing her role on the farm: "What kind of farming did you do right after you were married?"

Elizabeth was a full partner with her husband in their dairy farm and continued to play an active role as the farm switched to the production of small grains. Her interview has the potential of giving us valuable information about the costs incurred by women who combined child-rearing and housework with the physical labor and business decisions of the farm. It also suggests something of the importance of relationships with family and close friends in coping with both roles. The interview's potential is severely limited, however, by my failure to encourage her to expand upon her spontaneous reflections and by my eagerness to document the details of her farming activity. Not until later did I realize that I do not know what she meant by "nervous breakdown" or "overdoing." The fact that other farm women used the same or similar terms to describe parts of their lives alerted me to the need for further clarification. I now wish I had asked her to tell me in her own words of the importance of the relationship with her sister and why its possible loss was such a threat.

Later in the same interview I was more sensitive to Elizabeth's feelings about the difficulty of combining roles, only to deflect the focus from her experience once again. She was telling me how hard it was to be a full partner in the field and still have sole responsibility for the house:

> This is what was so hard, you know. You'd both be out working together, and he'd come in and sit down, and I would have to hustle a meal together, you know. And that's typical.

> *How did you manage?*

> Well, sometimes you didn't get to bed till midnight or after, and you were up at five. Sometimes when I think back to the early days, though, we'd take a day off, we'd get the chores done, and we'd go take off and go visiting.

> *Was that typical? Neighbors going to visit each other after the chores were done?*

While Elizabeth was telling me how she managed, I was already thinking about patterns in the neighborhood. My first question had been a good one, but, by asking about what other people did, my next one told her that I had heard enough about her experience. The two questions in succession have a double message: "Tell me about your experience, but don't tell me too much." Part of the problem may have been that even while I was interviewing women I was aware of the need to make sense of what they told me. In this case, the scholar's search for generalizations undermined the interviewer's need to attend to an individual's experience. Ideally, the processes of analysis should be suspended or at least subordinated to the processes of listening.

If we want to know how women feel about their lives, then we have to allow them to talk about their feelings as well as their activities. If we see rich potential in the language people use to describe their daily activities, then we have to take advantage of the opportunity to let them tell us what that language means. "Nervous breakdown" is not the only phrase that I heard without asking for clarification. Verna was answering a question about the relationship between her mother and her grandmother when she said:

> It was quite close since my mother was the only daughter that was living. My grandmother did have another daughter, that one died. I didn't know it until we got to working on the family tree. My mother was older than her brother. They were quite close. They worked together quite well when it would come to preparing meals and things. They visited back and forth a lot.

Her answer gave several general examples of how the closeness was mani-
fested, but what did Verna mean when she described a relationship as "close"
twice in a short answer? What did her perception of this relationship mean
to her? My next question asked, instead, for further examples: "Did they
[your grandparents] come to western Washington because your parents were
here?"

Even efforts to seek clarification were not always framed in ways that encouraged the interviewee to reflect upon the meaning of her experience. Elizabeth was answering a question about household rules when she was a child
and commented: "My mother was real partial to my brother because, of
course, you know that old country way; the boy was the important one." My
question "How did her partiality to the brother show?" elicited some specific
examples, but none of a series of subsequent questions gave her an opportunity
to reflect upon how this perception affected her understanding of herself and
her place in the family.

A final example from Verna's interview illustrates the best and the worst
of what we are trying to do. Her statement is a powerful reflection upon her
role as a mother; the subsequent question, however, ignores all the emotional
content of her remarks:

> Yes. There was times that I just wished I could get away from it all. And
> there were times when I would have liked to have taken the kids and left
> them someplace for a week—the whole bunch at one time—so that I wouldn't
> have to worry about them. I don't know whether anybody else had that
> feeling or not, but there were times when I just felt like I needed to get away
> from everybody, even my husband, for a little while. Those were times when
> I would maybe take a walk back in the woods and look at the flowers and
> maybe go down there and find an old cow that was real gentle and walk up
> to her and pat her a while—kind of get away from it. I just had to, it seems
> like sometimes . . .
>
> *Were you active in clubs?*

As the above portion of her remarks indicates, Verna was more than willing
to talk spontaneously about the costs of her choice to combine the roles of
wife, mother, and diligent farm woman. Perhaps she had exhausted the topic.
If not, my question, even though it acknowledged the need for support at
such times, certainly did not invite her to expand upon the feelings that both
she and I knew might contradict some notion of what women ought to do
and feel. She was comfortable enough to begin to consider the realities beyond
the acceptable facade of the female role, but my question diverted the focus
from her unique, individual reflections to the relative safety of women's clubs
and activities, a more acceptable outlet for such feelings. In this case, my
ability to listen, not Verna's memory, suffered from the constraints of internalized cultural boundaries. Until we can figure out how to release the brakes

that these boundaries place on both hearing and memory, our oral histories are likely to confirm the prevailing ideology of women's lives and rob women of their honest voices.

What I learned by listening carefully to my interviews is that women's oral history requires much more than a new set of questions to explore women's unique experiences and unique perspectives; we need to refine our methods for probing more deeply by listening to the levels on which the narrator responds to the original questions. To do so we need to listen critically to our interviews, to our responses as well as to our questions. We need to hear what women implied, suggested, and started to say but didn't. We need to interpret their pauses and, when it happens, their unwillingness or inability to respond. We need to consider carefully whether our interviews create a context in which women feel comfortable exploring the subjective feelings that give meaning to actions, things, and events, whether they allow women to explore "un-womanly" feelings and behaviors, and whether they encourage women to explain what they mean in their own terms.

When women talk about relationships, our responses can create an opportunity to talk about how much relationships enriched or diminished life experiences. When women talk about activities or events, they might find it easy to take blame for failures, but more sensitive responses may also make it possible to talk about feelings of competence or pride, even for women who do not consider such qualities very womanly. When women talk about what they have done, they may also want to explore their perceptions of the options they thought they had and how they feel about their responses. We can probe the costs that sometimes accompany choices, the means for accommodating and compensating for such costs, and how they are evaluated in retrospect. We can make it easier for women to talk about the values that may be implicit in their choices or feelings. When women reveal feelings or experiences that suggest conflict, we can explore what the conflict means and what form it takes. We can be prepared to expect and permit discussions of anger. If our questions are general enough, women will be able to reflect upon their experience and choose for themselves which experiences and feelings are central to their sense of their past.

The language women use to explore the above topics will be all the richer when they have ample opportunity to explain and clarify what they mean. When they use words and phrases like "nervous breakdown," "support," "close," "visiting," and "working together," they should have an opportunity to explain what they mean in their own terms. With letters and diaries we can only infer what individuals mean by the language they use; with oral interviews we can ask them. As they discuss examples, the particularities of their experiences often begin to emerge from behind the veil of familiar and ambiguous terms.

As a result of my discussions with Dana, a trained therapist, I have developed a new appreciation for oral history's potential for exploring questions of self-concept and -consciousness, for documenting questions of value and meaning in individuals' reflections upon their past. Important distinctions remain between oral history and therapeutic interviews, but as we shed our specific agendas the women we interview will become freer to tell their own stories as fully, completely, and honestly as they desire.

Interview Analyses: Listening for Meaning—
Dana Jack

I have been using oral interviews in research on depression among women and on moral reasoning among practicing attorneys.[5] In broad terms, both studies examine the interactions among social institutions, social roles, and women's consciousness. The women I interviewed are grappling with ideas about relationships, self-worth, career, and personal integrity in the context of society-wide changes in women's roles. As I listened to a woman's self-commentary, to her reflection upon her own thoughts and actions, I learned about her adaptation to her particular relationships and historical circumstances, especially her adaptation to the ideals of "good lawyer," "good wife," "good woman," to which she tried to conform.

I listened with an awareness that a person's self-reflection is not just a private, subjective act. The categories and concepts we use for reflecting upon and evaluating ourselves come from a cultural context, one that has historically demeaned and controlled women's activities. Thus, an exploration of the language and the meanings women use to articulate their own experience leads to an awareness of the conflicting social forces and institutions affecting women's consciousness. It also reveals how women act either to restructure or preserve their psychological orientations, their relationships, and their social contexts. This was true for two very different studies and populations—depressed women and practicing lawyers.

The first, and the hardest, step of interviewing was to learn to listen in a new way, to hold in abeyance the theories that told me what to hear and how to interpret what these women had to say. Depressed women, for example, told stories of the failure of relationships, an inability to connect with the person(s) with whom they wanted to experience intimacy. These were the expected stories, predicted by existing models, and the temptation was to interpret the stories according to accepted concepts and norms for "maturity" and "health." Because psychological theories have relied on men's lives and men's formulations for these norms, they explain women's psychological difference as deviant or "other."[6] The interview is a critical tool for developing new frameworks and theories based on women's lives and women's formulations. But we are at an awkward stage: old theories are set aside or under suspicion and new ones are still emerging. We must therefore be especially attentive to the influences that shape what we hear and how we interpret. How do we listen to an interview when we have rejected the old frameworks for interpretation and are in the process of developing new ones? How can an interview pull us beyond existing frameworks so that we stretch and expand them?

First, we must remember that the researcher is an active participant in qualitative research. My initial training was as a therapist, and the practice of listening to others while also attending to my own response to them has helped in conducting interviews. Theodore Reik calls this quiet involvement of the self "listening with the third ear."[7] As a researcher, I have learned that critical areas demanding attention are frequently those where I think I already know what the woman is saying. This means I am already appropriating what she says to an existing schema, and therefore I am no longer really listening to *her*. Rather, I am listening to how what she says fits into what I think I already know. So I try to be very careful to ask each woman what she means by a certain word, or to make sure that I attend to what is missing, what literary critics call the "presence of the absence" in women's texts—the "hollows, centers, caverns within the work-places where activity that one might expect is missing . . . or deceptively coded."[8]

And what is it that is absent? Because women have internalized the categories by which to interpret their experience and activities, categories that "represent a deposit of the desires and disappointments of men,"[9] what is often missing is the woman's own interpretation of her experience, or her own perspective on her life and activity. Interviews allow us to hear, if we will, the particular meanings of a language that both women and men use but that each translates differently. Looking closely at the language and the particular meanings of important words women use to describe their experience allows us to understand how women are adapting to the culture within which they live. When their behavior is observed from the outside, depressed women are called passive, dependent, masochistic, compliant, and victimized by their own learned helplessness. Yet, when I listened to the women's self-reflection, what became clear was that behind the so-called passive behavior of depressed women was the tremendous cognitive activity required to inhibit both outer actions and inner feelings in order to live up to the ideal of the "good" woman, particularly the good wife. Statements such as "I have to walk on eggshells in dealing with my husband," and "I have learned 'don't rock the boat' " show awareness of both their actions and their intended effects: not to cause discord.[10]

How do we listen to interviews without immediately leaping to interpretations suggested by prevailing theories? The first step is to immerse ourselves in the interview, to try to understand the person's story from her vantage point. I found that three ways of listening helped me understand the narrator's point of view. The first was to listen to the person's *moral language*. In the depression study, I heard things like: "I feel like I'm a failure," "I don't measure up," "I'm a liar, a cheat, and I'm no good." In the lawyer study, when lawyers were describing fulfilling the obligations of role, we heard statements such as:

"It's like being forced into a sex relationship you didn't anticipate. It's a screw job. It feels horrible to do something that you wouldn't do normally." Or "I have to contradict myself depending on what role I'm taking . . . it's sort of professional prostitution." Or finally, "Sometimes you feel almost like a pimp or something. . . . [I]t felt sleazy to cut the truth that finely."

Although very different in tone, these moral self-evaluative statements allow us to examine the relationship between self-concept and cultural norms, between what we value and what others value, between how we are told to act and how we feel about ourselves when we do or do not act that way. In a person's self-judgment, we can see which moral standards are accepted and used to judge the self, which values the person strives to attain. In the depression study, this was the key to learning about gender differences in the prevalence and dynamics of depression. Negative self-judgment affecting the fall in self-esteem is considered to be one of the key symptoms of depression. Research by Carol Gilligan and her colleagues indicates that women and men often use differing moral frameworks to guide their perception and resolution of moral problems.[11] Listening to the moral language of depressed women illuminated both the standards used to judge the self and the source of their despair. The women considered the failure of their relationships to be a *moral* failure; their sense of hopelessness and helplessness stemmed from despair about the inability to be an authentic, developing self within an intimate marriage while also living up to the moral imperatives of the "good woman."

Attending to the moral standards used to judge the self allows the researcher to honor the individuality of each woman through observing what values she is striving to attain. An oral interview, when structured by the narrator instead of the researcher, allows each woman to express her uniqueness in its full class, racial, and ethnic richness. Each person is free to describe her idiosyncratic interaction between self-image and cultural norms. Each person can tell us how she comes to value or devalue herself. During the interview, the researcher's role is to preserve and foster this freedom, and to restrict the imposition of personal expectations. When the woman, and not existing theory, is considered the expert on her own psychological experience, one can begin to hear the muted channel of women's experience come through.

In analyzing the depression study, for example, I heard how women use the language of the culture to deny what, on another level, they value and desire. A key word for depressed women is "dependency." Psychologists consider depressed women to be excessively dependent upon their relationships for a sense of self and self-esteem. But when I looked at how depressed women understand dependence, and how their negative evaluation of themselves as dependent affects their self-perception and their actions, the concept was cast in a new light.

In a first interview with a thirty-three-year-old depressed woman, the issue of dependence was central and problematic: "You know, I'm basically a very dependent person to start with. And then you get me married and tied down to a home and start not working. . . ."

Asked what she meant by dependent, she responded:

I like closeness. I like companionship. I like somebody, an intimate closeness, even with a best friend. And I've never had that with my husband. . . . Sometimes I get frustrated with myself that I have to have that, you know.

I look at other people that seem so self-sufficient and so independent. I don't know—I just have always needed a closeness. And maybe I identified that as dependency.

. . . [S]ince I've been married I realize it's kind of a negative thing to be that way. I've tried to bury that need for closeness. And so I guess that has also contributed to a lot of my frustrations.

Saying that she "had been feeling that my need for intimacy and my need for that kind of a deep level of friendship or relationships with people was sort of bad," this woman began "to believe there was something the matter with me." In her attempt to bury her needs for closeness, she revealed the activity required to be passive, to try to live up to self-alienating images of "today's woman."

This interview contains an implicit challenge to prevalent understandings of dependence. Looking closely, we are able to see how this woman has judged her feelings against a dominant standard that says to need closeness makes one dependent, when one should be able to be self-sufficient and autonomous. Further, she reflects upon her own experience, her capabilities, and her needs not from the basis of who she is and what she needs but in terms of how her husband and others see her. Her capacity for closeness and intimacy goes unacknowledged as strength. Rather than a failure of the husband's response, the problem is identified as her "neediness." If a researcher went into this interview with the traditional notion of dependence in mind, s/he would find the hypothesis that depressed women are too dependent confirmed. But if one listens to the woman's own feelings about dependence, her confusion about what she knows she needs and what the culture says she *should* need, one begins to see part of the self-alienation and separation from feelings that is a key aspect of depression.

The second way of listening that allowed me to hear the voice of the subject instead of my own preconceptions was to attend to the subject's *meta-statements*. These are places in the interview where people spontaneously stop, look back, and comment about their own thoughts or something just said.

For example, in the lawyer study, a woman is answering the question, "What does morality mean to you?":

. . . [I]t seems to me anything that raises to mind hurting other people or taking things away from other people or some sort of monetary gain for oneself. . . . And I suppose just how we interact with each other, if there's a contentiousness or bad feelings or bad blood between some people, that raises some moral issues because I guess I see us all as having a bit of a moral obligation to be nice to each other and to get along. *So—do I sound much like a litigator?*

Meta-statements alert us to the individual's awareness of a discrepancy within the self—or between what is expected and what is being said. They inform the interviewer about what categories the individual is using to monitor her thoughts, and allow observation of how the person socializes feelings or thoughts according to certain norms.[12] Women lawyers made many more meta-statements than men, indicating they were "watching" their own thinking. Because women have come into a legal system designed by men, for men, and because they still face discrimination, it is easy for them to develop an "onlooker" attitude of critical observation toward themselves.[13] This woman looks at herself being looked at in law and notices the difference. Second, these remarks show how powerfully a stereotypic image of the successful, adversarial lawyer divides them from their personal experience and makes some women, early in their careers, question their ability within law. Finally, such comments reveal the lack of public validation of frameworks that women use to understand and value their own feelings and experiences.[14]

The third way of listening was to attend to the *logic of the narrative,* noticing the internal consistency or contradictions in the person's statements about recurring themes and the way these themes relate to each other. I listened to how the person strings together major statements about experience so I could understand the assumptions and beliefs that inform the logic and guide the woman's interpretation of her experience.

A woman I call Anna, age fifty-four, hospitalized twice for major depression, provides an example of a contradiction within the logic of her narrative, a contradiction that points to conflicting beliefs. Anna says:

I was telling my daughter-in-law, "I guess I was just born to serve others." But we shouldn't be born to serve other people, we should look after ourselves.

Anna constructs the most important issues in her life—how to balance the needs of her self with the needs of others—as an either/or choice that presents her with loss on either side. The choice is either loss of self or loss of other. Such dichotomous thinking leaves Anna with feelings of hopelessness about how to resolve the conflicts in her relationships, and restricts her perception of choice.

On the surface, Anna's statement simply pits the traditional female role against the new "me first" ethic of self-development. But, looking more deeply, one sees that she describes two visions of relationship: either isolation or subordination. Through Anna's construction of her possibilities in relationship, one gains a glimpse of how specific historical ideas about women's roles and women's worth affect her own depression. Anna's vision of her self in relationship as either subordinated or isolated is profoundly influenced by a social context of inequality and competition. When unresolved personal issues intersect with conflicting social ideals that limit women's lives, that intersection increases the difficulty of forming a positive and realistic vision of self toward which one can strive.

Rather than conclude, as do cognitive theories of depression, that cognitive errors "cause" depression, observing this dichotomous thinking led me to see how the female social role is structured in thought and works to constrict women's perceptions of their relationships and their choices. Such logic of the narrative allowed me to see how a woman deals with conflicting cultural ideals, and how easy it is to feel depression as a personal failure rather than to recognize its social and historical aspects.

Conclusion

The process of sharing and critiquing our interviews has helped us sharpen our listening skills and improve our interviewing methods so that narrators feel more free to explore complex and conflicting experiences in their lives. Because of our divergent disciplinary interests, we have changed in different ways. The historian has become more alert to the subjective dimensions of events and activities; the psychologist has gained greater awareness of how the sociohistorical context can be read between the lines of a woman's "private" inner conflict. Both are more determined to discover how individual women define and evaluate their experience in their own terms.

Realizing the possibilities of the oral history interview demands a shift in methodology from information gathering, where the focus is on the right questions, to interaction, where the focus is on process, on the dynamic unfolding of the subject's viewpoint. It is the interactive nature of the interview that allows us to ask for clarification, to notice what questions the subject formulates about her own life, to go behind conventional, expected answers to the woman's personal construction of her own experience. This shift of focus from data gathering to interactive process affects what the researcher regards as valuable information. Those aspects of live interviews unavailable in a written text—the pauses, the laughter—all invite us to explore their meaning for the narrator. The exploration does not have to be intrusive; it can be as simple as "What did that [event] mean for you?"

This shift in focus, from information (data) gathering to interactive process, requires new skills on the researcher's part. In our view, it stimulates the development of a specific kind of readiness, the dimensions of which have been sketched in this paper. As Anderson has suggested, its most general aspects include an awareness that (1) actions, things, and events are accompanied by subjective emotional experience that gives them meaning; (2) some of the feelings uncovered may exceed the boundaries of acceptable or expected female behavior; and (3) individuals can and must explain what they mean in their own terms. Jack described three ways of listening during the interview that sharpen the researcher's awareness of the feelings and thoughts that lie behind the woman's outwardly conventional story: (1) listening to the narrator's moral language; (2) attending to the meta-statements; and (3) observing the logic of the narrative. Incorporating these insights has helped us learn how to remain suspended and attentive on a fine line between accomplishing our research goals and letting the subject be in charge of the material in the interview.

While by no means conclusive or inclusive, the following points suggest further ways to sharpen our attentiveness to the interactive process of the interview:

A. Listening to the narrator
 1. If the narrator is to have the chance to tell her own story, the interviewer's first question needs to be very open-ended. It needs to convey the message that in this situation, the narrator's interpretation of her experience guides the interview. For example, in the depression study, Jack started with, "Can you tell me, in your own mind what led up to your experience of depression?"
 2. If she doesn't answer the interviewer's question, what and whose questions does the woman answer?
 3. What are her feelings about the facts or events she is describing?
 4. How does she understand what happened to her? What meaning does she make of events? Does she think about it in more than one way? How does she evaluate what she is describing?
 5. What is being left out, what are the absences?

B. Listening to ourselves
 1. Try not to cut the narrator off to steer her to what our concerns are.
 2. Trust our own hunches, feelings, responses that arise through listening to others.
 3. Notice our own areas of confusion, or of too great a certainty about what the woman is saying—these are areas to probe further.
 4. Notice our personal discomfort; it can become a personal alarm bell alerting us to a discrepancy between what is being said and what the woman is feeling.

Oral history interviews are unique in that the interaction of researcher and subject creates the possibility of going beyond the conventional stories of women's lives, their pain and their satisfactions, to reveal experience in a less culturally edited form. But despite the value of this focus on the oral history interview in its dynamic, interactive form, we must offer one word of caution. The researcher must always remain attentive to the moral dimension of interviewing and aware that she is there to follow the narrator's lead, to honor her integrity and privacy, not to intrude into areas that the narrator has chosen to hold back.[15] This is another part of the specific kind of readiness the researcher brings to the interview: a readiness to be sensitive to the narrator's privacy while, at the same time, offering her the freedom to express her own thoughts and experiences, and listening for how that expression goes beyond prevailing concepts.

Notes

Public discussion of this collaborative work began at the National Women's Studies Association Conference held in Seattle, Washington, in June 1985 and continued with coauthors Susan Armitage and Judith Wittner in the *Oral History Review* 15 (Spring 1987): pp. 103–27.

1. See Shirley Ardener, ed., *Perceiving Women* (New York: John Wiley and Sons, 1975), pp. xi–xxiii. In that volume, see also Edwin Ardener, "Belief and the Problem of Women," pp. 1–27, and Hillary Callan, "The Premise of Dedication: Notes Towards an Ethnography of Diplomats' Wives," pp. 87–104.
2. Carolyn Heilbrun, *Writing a Woman's Life* (New York: W. W. Norton and Company, 1988), pp. 30–31.
3. "Women's Oral History Resource Section," *Frontiers* 2 (Summer 1977): pp. 110–18.
4. Kathryn Anderson and others, interviews for the Washington Women's Heritage Project, Center for Pacific Northwest Studies, Western Washington University, Bellingham, Washington. In the following account, two interviews from the collection are cited: interview with Elizabeth Bailey, 1 July 1980; interview with Verna Friend, 31 July 1980.
5. Dana C. Jack, "Clinical Depression in Women: Cognitive Schemas of Self, Care and Relationships in a Longitudinal Study" (unpublished doctoral dissertation, Harvard University, 1984); and Dana C. Jack, "Silencing the Self: The Power of Social Imperatives in Female Depression," in *Women and Depression: A Lifespan Perspective,* ed. R. Formanek and A. Gurian (New York: Springer Publishing Co., 1987). The lawyer study is in Rand Jack and Dana C. Jack, *Moral Vision and Professional Decisions: The Changing Values of Women and Men Lawyers* (New York: Cambridge University Press, 1989).
6. Carol Gilligan, *In a Different Voice* (Cambridge, Mass.: Harvard University Press, 1982).
7. Theodore Reik, *Listening with the Third Ear* (New York: Farrar Straus Giroux, 1948).
8. Carolyn Heilbrun and Catharine Stimpson, "Theories of Feminist Criticism: A Dialogue," in *Feminist Literary Criticism,* ed. Josephine Donovan (Lexington, KY.: The University Press of Kentucky, 1975), pp. 61–73.
9. Karen Horney, *Feminine Psychology,* ed. Harold Kelman (New York: W. W. Norton and Company, 1967), p. 56.
10. Jack, "Clinical Depression in Women," p. 177.
11. Gilligan, *In a Different Voice.* See also C. Gilligan, J. Taylor, and J. Ward, eds., *Mapping the Moral Domain* (Cambridge, Mass.: Harvard University Press, 1989).
12. See Arlie Russell Hochschild, "Emotion Work, Feeling Rule, and Social Structure," *American Journal of Sociology* 85 (November 1979): pp. 551–75.
13. The onlooker phenomenon is described by Marcia Westkott, *The Feminist Legacy of Karen Horney* (New Haven, Conn.: Yale University Press, 1986).
14. Jean Baker Miller, *Toward a New Psychology of Women* (Boston: Beacon Press, 1976), writes: "When . . . we can think only in terms given by the dominant culture, and when that culture not only does not attend to our own experiences but specifically denies and

devalues them, we are left with no way of conceptualizing our lives. Under these circumstances, a woman is often left with a global, undefined sense that she must be wrong" (p. 57).

15. The American Psychological Association (APA) has adopted ethical standards for the treatment of research subjects that provide some guidelines for thinking through issues of researcher intrusiveness. A copy of the APA Ethical Principles may be obtained from the APA Ethics Office, 1200 17th Street NW, Washington, DC 20036.

2

A Feminist Frame for the
Oral History Interview

Kristina Minister

Despite the present great migration of women from the private to the public sphere, androcentrism maintains a tenacious grip on society, as evidenced by the inequality between women's and men's wages and domestic work. One not commonly understood explanation for this lid on the status of women can be traced to a largely hidden process that sustains differential treatment of the sexes—our gender-based communication system. After direct physical force, communication is the means for "doing" power. We all frequently negotiate power by our verbal and nonverbal communication with others. Both those who exercise the power and those who yield it do so without being consciously aware that the socially constructed communication patterns that individuals carry with them substantially determine the balance of power in specific situations.

Many individuals learn unconsciously—and a few learn by direct study—various strategies for tolerating, adapting to, or outmaneuvering others who attempt to gain control with the help of gendered, i.e., socially acquired, verbal and nonverbal signs. The young woman student learns how to suppress feminine signals during conferences with a male professor, while he learns that sympathy for her must be confined to verbal communication; the female executive takes up habits associated with authority, such as occupying more space, smiling less, and using a particular system of eye contact. Although many individuals remain unwitting victims of the gendered communication codes they acquired early in life, thus providing fodder for the perseveration of sexual stereotypes by advertisers, others do cut those bonds and move toward individuality. It is not easy, but it is possible to manage the gendered signs of synchronous communication, those verbal and nonverbal signs humans compose and construe from moment to moment in specific situations.

Even the strongest individuals, however, are relatively helpless in certain kinds of communication situations that are validated by tradition. These diachronic genres of communication—for example, sales talk, preaching, and interview talk—are the accretion of communication processes that have worked effectively in the past and thus are imitated and passed on. Eventually the successful forms are regarded as universal formulas and are prescribed. Erving Goffman calls this kind of social interpretive act a "frame," which "allows its user to locate, perceive, identify, and label a seemingly infinite number of concrete occurrences defined in its terms."[1] Once understood and accepted by the participants, the frame regulates the situation and the latitude of what the participants do and say within it. Although such diachronic communication rituals are modified over the years by succeeding generations of persons whose values are different from the founders of the forms, the very communication forms themselves conserve the values of their originators. Such is the case for standard oral history interviewing methods.

My purpose in this essay is simple: to justify for oral history method the kind of interviewing that women intuitively would like to use when talking with women. First, I will describe oral history method from a performance perspective. Second, I will explain and define a general female sociocommunication subculture. Third, I will recommend appropriate and productive feminist methods for interviewing women who do not communicate the way men communicate.

So that we can feel the dilemma posed by oral history method for women who do not use male communication strategies, assume with me temporarily the point of view of persons being approached for the first time about contributing to an oral history project. "What is oral history?" potential narrators ask. When answering, experienced oral historians learn not to sabotage their projects by alluding to the controlling journalistic conventions and highly edited interviews published on television.[2] These are false models for the actual talk and action of interviews. What potential narrators are really asking is "What are the rules and rituals in the oral history situation, and what is it that I'm supposed to do there?" Once the purpose of the project is explained, including the standard disclosures and legal agreement, narrators make an accurate inference about one thing that goes on in oral history: they are going to have to display a respectable degree of speaking competence. This supposition contributes to the hesitation of all kinds of narrators to participate. "All right," most finally agree, "but you'll have to ask the questions." What that means is, "I trust you to guide me through this thing, whatever it is." I have stopped being surprised at finding narrators, especially females, in more formal costumes and with freshly coiffed hairdos when I arrive on the appointed interview day, regardless of whether the recording mode is audio or video. These nonverbal signs are clear: narrators know this is going to be a public performance.

When narrators are plunged into the interview, they see the interviewer's body poised toward them and, as they hear the first question, they note how the interviewer's facial expression turns into an expectant audience gaze. Narrators now realize that they are expected to "take the floor." The oral history interview frame has been offered and accepted. This frame will determine to a large extent how meaning is proposed, modified, and interpreted in this situation. First, it is apparent that contradictory verbal and nonverbal signs fill the oral history frame. We see a dyad talking earnestly together, apparently using turn-taking conversation form, yet each knows that the narrator is expected to "take the floor." The participants pretend that a tape recorder or a video camera and recorder just a few feet away does not exist and that a "live" microphone is not making what ordinarily is ephemeral into a repeatable audio- or videotape that may be listened to or watched by strangers. The conversants' behavior indicates no apparent concern that the electronic record eventually may be reduced to print and made available to the eyes of strangers. The interviewer occasionally leans toward the equipment to check its operation, but both pretend this activity is not happening. Perhaps the interviewee, beginning to toy with the microphone, will be signaled by the interviewer's back-channel gesture to stop interfering with the recording mechanism that both parties have agreed does not exist.

These are just a few of the conventions peculiar to the oral history frame. In short, it is a performance for a ghostly audience. Every successful field-worker accepts these conventions and works hard for years to master them, even though, as David Dunaway notes, "The theoretical issues of oral history-as-performance have . . . not received wide attention."[3] Methodology handbooks only implicitly recognize the audience. Oral history method, so centered on interviewers' needs to elicit and to present new or profound information for various audiences, is designed to control the flow of information. Oral historians should well note the admonition of sociolinguists Gunther Kress and Roger Fowler: "In the hands of an experienced practitioner, the devices for control granted to the interviewer by the format and situation of the interview itself constitute a formidable armoury."[4]

Why is it that many North American and British women are not used to speaking in public? Feminist research points to the cause: postagrarian culture has assigned women to the private sphere.[5] The general public appearance of women as full-time wage earners at all levels of organizations and in all kinds of work, as full-time entrepreneurs and business owners, graduate students, students in professional schools, and holders of political office, is so recent that it has had little effect upon the way women speak and the way in which persons in positions of power expect women to speak. Changes in gender presentation lag far behind societal changes. One has but to turn to an evening television newscast for confirmation that a woman may speak to large mixed audiences if she is conventionally attractive and if she enthusiastically displays traditional feminine, i.e., stereotypical, gender signs. Deeply embedded habits feed the stereotypical values of those who hold power and who manage the media in our consumer-driven society. These habits are not only perpetuated through institutions; they are learned anew by each individual born into the culture and thus conserve women's and men's elaborately differentiated communication processes.

Anthropologist Ray Birdwhistell maintains that the low degree of human sexual differentiation in relation to all species creates the opportunity for humans to invent a wide and varied range of sexual differentiation on the behavioral level.[6] Anthropologists Daniel Maltz and Ruth Borker observe:

> [the rules women and men have learned for conversation] . . . were learned
> not from adults but from peers, and . . . they were learned during precisely
> that time period, approximately age 5 to 15, when boys and girls interact
> socially primarily with members of their own sex.[7]

North American women and men, Maltz and Borker argue as they scrutinize the literature of ethnic and interethnic communication, come from distinct sociolinguistic subcultures. Girls, who are relatively more closely supervised by adults than boys, use speech "(1) to create and maintain relationships of closeness and equality, (2) to criticize others in acceptable ways, and (3) to interpret accurately the speech of other girls."[8] Boys, left to their own devices for group regulation in relatively unsupervised environments outside the home, display quite a different use of speech: "(1) to assert one's position of dominance, (2) to attract and maintain an audience, and (3) to assert oneself when other speakers have the floor."[9] Thus, for girls, communication is the opportunity for establishing equality and intimacy in relatively small and private groups; for boys, communication is the site for contesting dominance in hierarchically structured groups that are public and relatively large. Girls negotiate their ever-changing friendships indirectly; boys negotiate their hierarchies openly. These strikingly different communication domains are the primary classrooms for learning greatly elaborated and differentiated ways of displaying culturally acquired, stereotypical femininity and masculinity. Although the genetic communication differences between the sexes are minimal, amounting to variations in vocal pitch only (and that difference overlapping rather than discrete),[10] sex-specific communication lessons are learned early, and they are not forgotten. This is why adults tend to remain gender-communication perseverators, that is, they use the same speech and nonverbal behavior learned from their same-sex childhood peers.

Many women are not yet comfortable speaking in public. Not only are they not used to public speaking, their public discourse has been rigorously proscribed, and their silence and quiet attentiveness are valued most highly. Cheris Kramarae, examining books published over the past 150 years that recommend how and where women may talk, finds these traditional prescriptions not merely historically interesting; high school and university students in a 1977 study listed essentially these same communication traits as typical of women's speech.[11] The myths about women's talk are tenacious: women talk more than men, don't talk about significant things, can't tell jokes, are weak and less capable speakers than men, and cannot speak logically. One may conclude that women's speech generally has been devalued for a very long time. The speech communication profession has only recently begun to investigate women's speech *per se,* and the few female orators who have been admitted to the canon of public address, as communication scholars Carole Spitzack and Kathryn Carter assert, "can easily support the presumption that the *majority* of women cannot rival male accomplishments."[12] When one lacks realistic gender models and when self identity and social identity have been trimmed to ladylike size, anxiety floods one's public speaking, especially in appearances before mixed-sex and large audiences. Indeed, a formidable double bind ties women's tongues in the oral history situation, posing a contradiction between expectations that they will seek out and name their meaningful life experience and that they will do so in a public context.

Oral history blossomed in the 1940s in a strongly androcentric society and now flourishes in a society that continues to assume androcentrism in its public, institutionalized forms—for example: religion, media, law, and sports. Although oral historians are at present cutting across class and ethnic lines in a new commitment to publish the voices of those who were once silent or silenced in the larger human community, oral history method continues to rest upon the assumption that interviewers will conduct interviews the way men conduct interviews. This means that women who do not participate in the male sociocommunication subculture will remain as invisible as most of their white, middle- and upper-class sisters were until relatively recently.[13]

The male sociocommunication subculture is assumed to be the norm for social science interviewing,[14] and, as devoted as oral history is to its unique objective of eliciting recollected experience, men's forms of communication also are assumed to be the norm for oral history interviewing.[15] If women aspire to become approved oral historians, they must learn to control topic selection with questions, must make certain that one person talks at a time, and must encourage narrators to "take the floor" with referential language that keeps within the boundaries of selected topics. Men, even those not used to public speaking, will feel relatively comfortable using talk and gesture that refer to acts and events; women, skilled at talk and gesture that refer to personal relationships, are relatively disadvantaged by the oral history frame. A wide range of social science research and ethnographic studies verify that women traditionally refer to personal and family matters, and to relationships with others. Stewart, Cooper, and Friedley conclude: "Women traditionally talk to each other about personal and affiliative issues that reflect *who they are;* men traditionally talk about task and power issues that reflect *what they do.*"[16] The oral history interview that hosts a clash of communication form with persons who have not practiced that form not only will preclude topics that are central to the narrators' lives, such interviews will also increase the chances of introducing unreliable and invalid information. What needs to be altered for women's oral history is the communication frame, not the woman.

Oral history interviewing, influenced by its ties to academic history and by the practice of interviewing in general, has developed in the context of the male sociocommunication system. Because in an androcentric world male speaking is the norm, any other kind of speaking is subnormal or, as Dale Spender wryly observes, "minus male."[17] Although some women narrators have adapted well to this male interviewing system that female oral historians must acquire, we will not hear what women deem essential to their lives unless we legitimate a female sociocommunication context for the oral history situation. As Sue Armitage says, "We will learn what we want to know only by listening to people who are not accustomed to talking."[18] We will not be able to hear and to interpret what women value if we do not know how to watch and how to listen and how to speak with women as women. We first need to know consciously how women do communicate privately and with each other.

To pragmatically review and integrate the disparate body of research about women's communication, we will first scrutinize a hypothetical videotape featuring a group of women who meet regularly for discussion. Although the individual women come from the range of ethnic, race, class, and age subgroups of North America and exhibit dialect, intonation, and body language specific to their respective subgroups, we are interested in the common features of speech, voice, and body movement that they display to one another and use to interpret one other. Provided that these common communication attributes that the women collectively know and use are not the same communication features commonly known and used by men's groups, we can have confidence that we have isolated some of the major components of the North American female sociocommunication subculture.

For your initial review of the tape the sound is turned off so that you may first isolate the group's nonverbal behavior. You note that every woman is seated so that she can see each of the others. Because each woman visually tracks speakers as well as the responses of everyone in the situation, eye-contact binds these women into a communal embrace. Women not speaking nod their heads frequently at the speakers and sometimes at each other as they interpret and anticipate speakers' meaning with raised eyebrows, tilted heads, and considerable smiling, and sometimes mirror speakers' movements, facial expressions, posture, and gestures. By these gestures the women show how they invest effort in decoding, i.e., interpreting, one another, and that they take care to demonstrate to the speakers an active gestural encouragement and understanding. You realize that this kind of communication nurturing is in general more active than men's decoding behavior.[19]

At times several persons speak simultaneously to the speaker or to nonspeakers, and sometimes an individual calls across the room to another individual. The speaker continues speaking throughout these occasional free-for-alls, although no one seems disturbed by the confusion. Occasional touching on hands and arms can be seen. It becomes obvious that the group is conducting an elaborate, meaningful, and pleasurable ritual. Monitoring only the visible nonverbal behavior tells you that these women are masters at creating their own spoken and gestured conversational process, a process that obviously is highly esteemed.

You rewind the tape to play it through again, turning the picture to black and turning on the sound slightly, not loud enough to perceive speech clearly, but loud enough to hear the paralanguage—the voiced nonverbal characteristics of the group. Laughter is prominent. Encouraging minimal responses, principally the phoneme "m" uttered with a falling melody and "uh huh," punctuate the conversation frequently.[20] Most pervasive are intonation melodies, dynamic variations of pitch and volume overlaid on utterances. If you could listen only to intonation, with speech and fundamental pitch masked, you would identify these tunes as typical of English-speaking North American women from a range of cultural groups and classes.[21] Men's pitch is more restricted in range and changes more slowly and less frequently.[22] The women's melodies vary from loud to soft, high to low pitch, fast to slow rate. Combined with such voice qualities as articulation control, rhythm, tempo, and resonance,[23] the women's communal intonation orchestrates an interconnecting musical pattern.

When you rewind the tape and turn up the sound so that you can hear the women's speech, you note a general concern for maintaining politeness and showing empathy.[24] Some women apologize as they begin and end speaking; many times explicit acknowledgment is given to previous speakers; quiet women are invited to contribute; and conflict is resolved indirectly, including rotating leadership to prevent dominance by any one person.[25] Such personal and inclusive pronouns as "you," "we," "our," and "let's" are common.[26]

There is an abundance of laughter and joking, but these are not jokes used competitively; they are humorous anecdotes and personal narratives, some of them self-deprecating.[27] The jokes seem to reinforce communal bonds.[28] You realize that women enjoy telling jokes for women in private contexts, but women's jokes don't necessarily develop by formula to the "normal" punch line.

Despite this abundant evidence of politeness and concern for everyone, you are surprised to observe that the group consistently ignores the politeness rule about taking turns at speaking. Simultaneous speech is prominent, sometimes "seeming free-for-alls; and more frequently, cases of several people being 'on the same wave length.' "[29] Quite unlike the male monologic ritual, one or several women may take a turn while another speaker holds the floor. Frequently one woman initiates a sentence and another woman takes it to completion. One speaker's side comment augments another speaker's turn, sometimes in succession and often by interruption and overlap. You realize that this supportive and interactive work accounts for the often brief and unfinished nature of individuals' specific utterances. Questions, comments, and encouraging remarks run throughout individual speakers' descriptions and narrations. These interruptions, however, are welcomed by everyone, for they seem to be motivated as much to support speakers as to clarify topics. "Intersupport" is a better word, one that has not been necessary in an androcentric world where utterances from those not possessing the floor are regarded as attempts to take it over.

As you monitor the group through several sessions over an extended time period you come to realize how uniquely the women develop their stories. Performed stories with a familiar beginning, development to a precipitating action, and a culminating "point" are the exception. Anecdotes are more common. These women sometimes develop their stories by reference to one member's prior story that becomes a collectively owned "kernel."[30] The kernel usually is but a brief reference to a phrase in a longer story told previously. At the mention of the kernel, another kernel story emerges out of the conversational context, further cementing the group's feelings and relationships. The point of the story, already established in communal memory, need not be stated.[31] For example, one member of the group relates an incident occurring in an automobile with her intimate male friend. In response to her query about some contested matter between them, he lapses into nonresponsiveness. Explaining how she suppressed her habitual verbal encouragement to respond, she tells her group: "I would have rolled my tongue up in the car window rather than beg him to speak." The group now possesses this creative kernel as a conversational resource that is utilized by other members of the group to develop other anecdotes and stories over an extended period of time.[32]

The foregoing hypothetical observation of the collaborative, participatory, and inclusive process women together use to discover themselves prepares the way for general conclusions about what women discuss privately, the referential axis of communication. Many of women's stories and jokes are not particularly remarkable; in fact, they are about commonplace matters and mundane experience, and are valued for their very typicality.[33] Few of the stories are self-aggrandizing, and many narrators do not even feature themselves as central characters.[34] Often they define themselves in terms of their roles and relationships to others.

In summary, women's same-sex topics are inseparable from their deeply gendered communication context. Women speaking together encounter one another for the purpose of searching for and collaboratively constructing both personal and female cultural identity. Because women "cannot draw upon a shared history at the institutional level when that history is particularized, depreciated, regulated, and silenced," Langellier and Peterson reason, women collaboratively seek out and discover "culturally interesting materials for women's experience."[35] Women talking with women use a unique dialectical choice of words coordinated with a unique nonverbal system for the purpose of exploring and naming issues unique to women. Women engage in the process of self and gender construction, and they do so protected and sustained within their own sociocommunication system. Women from the ghetto, the suburb, and the farm may not mingle as often and as intimately as our hypothetical group, but women meeting typically in homogeneous social groups enjoy a doubly intense encounter as players in gendered and in other highly elaborated and particular subcultural communication forms.

Because of the intense intersubjective nature of North American women's same-sex communication, members of this sociocommunication system do not need to compose nor do they value explicit, "well-formed" verbal comments and monologic, chronologically developed stories about attention-getting events, although some women demonstrably can perform as effectively as men in men's genres and styles.[36] Women's groups readily interpret, modify, and enhance the contributions of individual members. Their conversational process, nourished and groomed by its complex nonverbal ritual, ripens over time and holds rich resources for eliciting, developing, and elaborating individuals' speech. Communication form and content, how women speak and what they speak about, grow tightly interdependent within women's protected and private places of encounter.

The standard oral history frame—topic selection determined by interviewer questions, one person talking at a time, the narrator "taking the floor" with referential language that keeps within the boundaries of selected topics—denies women the communication form that supports the topics women value. Historian Kathryn Anderson, questioning oral history's poor record in obtaining subjective accounts from women, confesses:

> My own interviews and those of others show a definite preference for questions about activities and facts and a conspicuous lack of questions about feeling, attitudes, values, and meaning. Traditional historical sources tell us more about what happened and how it happened than how people felt about it and what it meant to them.[37]

Women who do not participate in the male sociocommunication subculture do not usually want to talk about activities and facts, and they are unused to developing topics without a high degree of collaboration from other women. Without abundant collaboration from other women, they are rendered nearly speechless in a situation demanding speech. The following are my recommendations for framing the oral history interview with women's communication patterns.

First, women should do the interviewing, for obviously they know how to utilize women's communication patterns. However, it is less obvious that sex is no more a guarantee of a gender-neutral attitude than are institutionally sanctioned codes for equality. It is how individuals communicate in particular situations that reveal their assumptions about gender.

Furthermore, it is necessary to be aware, in general, of other socially constructed variables that both parties bring to the interview, variables that strongly condition the kind of frame that will influence meaning in particular interview situations. Remember that from childhood women value equality and are not comfortable with hierarchical same-sex systems. Gluck, Oakley, and Langellier and Hall take a close look at the contradiction between women's culture and the typical social science interview, and recommend various compromises.[38] In brief, field-workers can analyze the hierarchial system brought to specific interview situations, asking themselves, "How can I equalize the power inherent in the differences between my narrator's and my age, class, ethnic affiliation, and education?" Experienced oral historians will be aware of such differences because they do not attempt interviews until they have studied the social and historical contexts of narrators' lives, and thus they learn subtly to adapt their own linguistic performance to narrators' linguistic performance. Some sensitive field-workers adjust differences between themselves and narrators nonverbally—for example, by matching apparel and demeanor—just as polite and sensitive persons adapt to all kinds of cross-class situations. Feminist interviewers can do more.

Prior to the initial meeting, interviewers can discard their own research-oriented time frame in favor of narrators' temporal expectations. Taking time to know another means more than a preliminary interview; it entails meeting for an extended session or more. Congruent with good oral history practice, researchers take the opportunity to solicit narrators' comments and suggestions about the project, including names of potential narrators, other resource persons, and sources for photos, artifacts, and written materials. However, the purpose of the initial contact is not just a preliminary interview to obtain data; the meeting is an opportunity to promote collegiality and to engage in mutual self-disclosure. For feminist researchers, questions flow both ways. Narrators have the opportunity to interrogate interviewers about the research project and about the interviewer herself.

After the interview, so that narrators will not be led into researchers' interpretations, the interviewer can reveal her personal investment in the project and discuss project issues. At the conclusion of the project, narrators can become involved again in a variety of formal and informal ways, such as contributing to field notes and commenting on researchers' interpretations.

Before oral history can build subjective records of women's lives, interviewers must position themselves subjectively within the discourse. Once narrators are free to take some responsibility for the project, and once researchers have explicitly placed themselves in a subjective position within the project, chances improve for the dialogic relationships that can support examination and disclosure of narrators' life experiences as women. Feminist oral history is intersubjective oral history.

Next, the feminist oral historian needs to wipe clean her slate of expectations about the form of oral history discourse. Oral history practice recommends that interviewers take to the interview a list of topics derived from research on project issues and a compilation of narrators' biographies. Consider the assumptions grounding such a list. First, its chronological nature reflects the interviewer's analytical thinking, which probably will bear little resemblance to narrators' recollected life experiences. Worse, a list tempts one to control interview topics, a hallmark of the male interviewing norm. Worse yet, as the interview proceeds on its inevitably unique career, its resemblance to the topic list decreases, and the interviewer's dismay increases about the loss of her ideal interview. What emerges and develops through dialogue are issues—the chaotic and problematic process of two humans thinking and communicating.[39] It is this rich dialogue that holds ontological priority, not an impoverished list. Topic lists double-bind oral historians and deafen them to emergent meanings and to opportunities to draw out narrators' experience, an experience that has not yet been examined linguistically. To prompt one's memory, an open-ended random scattering of potential issues over a sheet of paper can be checked off, amended, and linked with circles and lines as the discussion develops.

Although feminist interviewers will invite women unused to public speaking to take increasing responsibility for the oral history project, they will not expect narrators to lead in taking responsibility for interview performance. If narrators do take this responsibility, that is all to the good of the project, but I have outlined in the present essay why North American women in general will not perform in a public setting in the manner and style in which men perform. Thus, feminist interviewers will not expect or try to elicit a repertoire of attention-getting monologic narratives, especially narratives that originated in previous communication contexts and are well-polished from repeated rehearsals. Jokes with punch lines, stories with dramatic points, and stories featuring the narrator as the central character will not be expected. On the other hand, feminist interviewers will expect that narrators' stories and descriptions will exhibit an unfinished or incomplete quality and will not conform to the plot and action structures of publicly performed pieces. Again, if well-polished stories are offered—and most persons have ready a few rehearsed self-narratives—they will be welcome, but feminist interviewers know that these stories are typical of men. A feminist oral history frame will nurture and assist in the interpretation of stories by women for women.

In general, feminist interviewers will expect women who do not perform as men perform to be relatively dependent upon the interviewer's collaboration. One might, for example, start with an inquiry about the narrator's typical topic as discovered during the preliminary meetings, and offer frequent overt and nonverbal expressions of understanding. Verbal intersupport work, although less frequent than nonverbal collaboration, might take the form of short overlapping remarks and even completion of the narrator's unfinished remarks. All of the verbal and nonverbal attributes described in the present essay will be appropriate, and will be specified in the following explanation, but all interviewer contributions must be authentic components of the interviewer's personal female communication style. It would not be appropriate to portray or suggest the feminine stereotype spuriously based on myths about women's "weak," "gabby," or "illogical" communication.

Because nonverbal communication usually precedes verbal communication, the feminist interviewer begins with the basic posture and eye-contact of women in women's groups, positioning herself so that each individual can observe the other fully and without effort. She uses her own habitual intonation to support her opening remark. For a model of a woman who uses her own habitual female intonation pattern professionally, listen to Susan Stamberg, who has successfully legitimated women's intonation for news and magazine formats during her long career with National Public Radio. Stamberg never sacrifices content or form; her female intonation is the appropriate vehicle for her professionally executed stories.

Feminist interviewers are aware that questions function differently in the female and the male subcultures, and that cross-cultural misunderstanding can be the source for women's "inept" response to direct questions. Women use questions to maintain and enhance conversation, men interpret questions as requests for information.[40] For women who do not speak as men speak, requests for information can be worded indirectly, as polite and inclusive imperatives: "Let's talk about your young married life now." Declaratives, such as "You worked a long time at the post office," followed by a long pause and an expectant facial expression, are another indirect means to avoid direct questions. Gradually, the interviewer can resort to the standard open-ended "why" and "how" questions that work so well because interviewers give up some control by their use.

Keeping in mind the explicit vitality of women's nonverbal communication reinforcement, feminist interviewers let their natural communication encouragement work by uttering positive vocal minimal responses, tempering a monotonous "uh huh" with equivalent facial expressions and nods. Verbal reinforcement abounds as interviewers anticipate narrators' thoughts, occasionally cause an overlap with their own words, and at times link and fill in incomplete thoughts. This kind of work does not interrupt narrators; it supports them. One would put interviews with men at risk with such intersupport work, for some men would interpret the intended help as interruption.

Without condescending, feminist interviewers occasionally explicitly acknowledge narrators' previous utterances. "Oh, now I understand," and "I know what you mean." This metalinguistic "talk about talk," long used by seasoned oral historians in general, slows the pace of the transaction, introduces more collaboration, and simultaneously encourages both speakers to reflect upon and savor the conversation *per se*. The interview context now supports and supplements narrators' contributions. The pleasurable and familiar collaboration of women is underway. Interviewer self-disclosure is sanctioned in this environment. Although narrators do most of the speaking, interviewers offer anecdotes to narrators' extended descriptions, thus contributing their own subjective self-reflection to the project. To repeat, in woman talk, reflexivity is not only legitimate, it is inseparable from the process. Feminist interviews are not a radical departure from the most meaningful kind of oral history; they simply make the self-reflexivity inherent in the experience of the interview[41] explicit and part of the performance record.

For extremely shy women, and where salient class, age, and cultural distinctions between interviewers and narrators are likely to inhibit disclosure, group interviews more closely resemble natural language situations than do feminist oral history dyads. I have arranged interviews with groups of three to five women. One woman volunteers to be featured as the others ask questions and briefly offer comparisons with their own experiences. I am somewhat prominent at first, showing the group how a dyad maneuvers through an interview. Gradually I recede into a moderator's role. The collaboration can become quite spontaneous and intensely involving. Even very shy women grow eager for their turns, because, as Barbara Myerhoff discovered with her venerable group,[42] they long to validate their lives. Individuals have voluntarily told me that listening to their colleagues stimulates their own recall of events long dormant or never before considered worthy of being spoken.

As in the early meetings between narrators and interviewers, feminist interviewers adopt their narrators' time frame, shifting gradually to new issues only after old ones have been developed generously. The leisurely pace frees interviewers for the kind of demanding listening that nourishes inferences about what issues may be waiting to be born and examined for the first time. When these issues are close to term, interviewers will need a peculiar mixture of determination and tact to validate narrators' public naming of buried or previously only whispered experiences. Do not underestimate female narrators' communication skills. They are as robust as women themselves. Since childhood, women have struggled with conflict linguistically, and they are well prepared to join interviewers in the search for women's culture.

Susan Armitage asks, "Is there really a female subculture in all times and places, and does it really function as a defense against male dominance?"[43] I have proposed, justified, and described the existence of a vigorous female sociocommunication subculture. This system might function as a defense against male dominance; more important, its ongoing process, created and maintained through communication, flourishes in its own right. If examined in contexts similar to its natural context, women's construction of self and gender can be recorded, analyzed, and interpreted so that it will reconstruct human history.

Feminist oral historians interviewing women who do not communicate as men do have learned to discard idealized, androcentric concepts of the effective oral history interview, the assumption that a universal method can successfully be applied to situated and particular oral history encounters. Interviewers who validate women by using women's communication are the midwives for women's words.

Notes

1. Erving Goffman, *Frame Analysis* (New York: Harper, 1974), p. 21.
2. In 1987 a state Arts and Humanities Council revealed to the proposers of an oral history project the following professional television consultant's recommendations: "If this proposal is to come to life, the producers must develop a *phantom dialog script.* . . . The phantom is a prewritten, nearly word for word proposed response of the interviewees (*before* they are interviewed). [Footnote: *Yes,* you do script interviews!] It is the framework used by the interviewer to guide the interviewee into a predetermined answer pattern. While it is obvious that each interviewee's response will never be verbatim according to script, a skillful inter-

viewer, schooled in tape manipulation, can lead an interviewee to speak naturally pre-scripted lines without knowing it. . . . *This does demand carefully crafted work*. . . . It's hard work, it can be done and it's far more rewarding than relying on, 'let's see what we'll get' ad libs—then writing the script. Polishing this 'good stuff' is a pleasure."

3. David Dunaway, "Field Recording Oral History," *Oral History Review* 15 (Spring 1987): 36. But note Edward Ives's insistence upon the active presence of field equipment in *The Tape-Recorded Interview: A Manual for Field Workers in Folklore and Oral History* (Knox-ville, Tenn.: University of Tennessee Press, 1980).

4. Gunther Kress and Roger Fowler, "Interviews," *Language and Control,* ed. Roger Fowler et al. (Boston: Routledge, 1979), pp. 63–64.

5. Joan Kelly, "The Social Relation of the Sexes: Methodological Implications of Women's History," in idem, *Women, History and Theory: The Essays of Joan Kelly* (Chicago: Univer-sity of Chicago Press, 1984), pp 1–18.

6. Ray L. Birdwhistell, "Masculinity and Femininity as Display," in idem, *Kinesics and Con-text: Essays on Body Motion Communication* (Philadelphia: University of Philadelphia Press, 1970), pp. 39–46.

7. Daniel Maltz and Ruth Borker, "A Cultural Approach to Male-Female Miscommunica-tion," in *Language and Social Identity: Studies in International Sociolinguistics,* ed. John J. Gumperz (Cambridge: Cambridge University Press, 1982), p. 203.

8. Maltz and Borker, "Male-Female Miscommunication," p. 205.

9. Ibid., p. 207.

10. Sally McConnell-Ginet, "Intonation in a Man's World," in *Language, Gender, and Society,* ed. Barrie Thorne, Cheris Kramarae, and Nancy Henley (Rowley, Mass.: Newbury, 1983), pp. 69–88.

11. Cheris Kramarae, *Women and Men Speaking: Frameworks for Analysis* (Rowley, Mass.: Newbury, 1981).

12. Carole Spitzack and Kathryn Carter, "Women in Communication Studies: A Typology for Revision," *Quarterly Journal of Speech* 73 (1987): 405. Italics in original.

13. According to Susan Geiger, women offer the largest population for field study because "literacy is a very recent possibility, and of the one-quarter of the total population that remains illiterate, nearly 70 percent is female." From "Women's Life Histories: Method and Content," *Signs: Journal of Women in Culture and Society* 11 (1986): 335.

14. Ann Oakley, "Interviewing Women: A Contradiction in Terms," *Doing Feminist Research,* ed. Helen Roberts (New York: Routledge, 1981), pp. 30–61.

15. Sherna Gluck, "What's So Special about Women? Women's Oral History," *Frontiers, a Journal of Women Studies* 2, no. 2 (1977): 8; and Kristin M. Langellier and Deanna L. Hall, "Interviewing Women: A Phenomenological Approach to Feminist Communication Research,"in *Doing Research on Women's Communication: Perspectives on Theory and Method,* ed. Carole Spitzack and Kathryn Carter (Norwood, NJ: Ablex, 1989).

16. Lea P. Stewart, Pamela J. Cooper, and Sheryl A. Friedley, *Communication Between the Sexes: Sex Differences and Sex-Role Stereotypes* (Scottsdale, Ariz.: Gorsuch Scarisbrick, 1986), p. 100. Italics in original.

17. Dale Spender, *Man Made Language,* 2d ed. (Boston: Routledge, 1985), p. 3.

18. Susan Armitage, "The Next Step," *Frontiers* 7, no. 1 (1983): 5.

19. Stewart, Cooper, and Friedley, *Communication Between the Sexes,* pp. 67–68.

20. Paula A. Treichler and Cheris Kramarae, "Women's Talk in the Ivory Tower," *Communica-tion Quarterly,* 31, no. 2 (1983): 120.

21. Provided English is their first language.

22. McConnell-Ginet, "Intonation in a Man's World," p. 75.

23. Elizabeth C. Fine, *The Folklore Text: From Performance to Print* (Bloomington, Ind.: Indiana University Press, 1984), pp. 116–18.

24. Mercilee MacIntyre Jenkins, "The Story Is in the Telling: A Cooperative Style of Conversa-tion among Women," in *Gewalt durch Sprache: die Vergewaltigung von Frauen in Ge-*

sprächen, ed. Senta Tromel-Plotz (Frankfurt am Main: Fischer Taschenbuch-Verlag, 1982) (ERIC Document Reproduction Service No. ED238083).

25. Kristin M. Langellier and Eric C. Peterson, "Spinstorying: A Communication Analysis of Women's Storytelling," Speech Communication Association Convention, Chicago, Illinois, November 1984, forthcoming in *Performance, Culture, and Identity,* ed. Jean Haskell Speer.

26. Treichler and Kramarae, "Women's Talk in the Ivory Tower," p. 120.

27. Susan Kalčik, " '. . . like Ann's gynecologist or the time I was almost raped': Personal Narratives in Women's Rap Groups," *Journal of American Folklore* 88 (1975): 5–6; Jenkins, "The Story Is in the Telling," p. 7.

28. Carol Mitchell, "Some Differences in Male and Female Joke-Telling," *Women's Folklore, Women's Culture,* ed. Rosan A. Jordan and Susan J. Kalčik (Philadelphia: University of Pennsylvania Press, 1985), p. 167.

29. Carole Edelsky, "Who's Got the Floor?" *Language in Society* 10 (1981): 391.

30. Kalčik, " '. . . like Ann's gynecologist,' " pp. 7–8. Kernel stories are not exclusive to women; rather, their function may be strategically specific to women's groups, according to Langellier and Peterson, "Spinstorying," pp. 12–13.

31. Karen Baldwin, " 'Woof!' A Word on Women's Roles in Family Storytelling," in Jordan and Kalčik, eds., *Women's Folklore,* pp. 149–62.

32. This tongue-rolled-up-in-the-car-window kernel emerged from and lives in the communal memory of the spring 1989 course in Women and Communication, Arizona State University West. Janine Campo is the creator of this kernel.

33. Langellier and Peterson, "Spinstorying"; Mitchell, "Male and Female Joke-Telling"; and Kristin M. Langellier, "Performing Women's Personal Narratives," Speech Communication Association, Chicago, Illinois, November 1986.

34. Jenkins, "The Story Is in the Telling," pp. 14–18.

35. Langellier and Peterson, "Spinstorying," pp. 28 and 21.

36. Kristina Minister, "Rehearsing for the Ultimate Audience: Ila Harrison Healy's Narrated Self," in Speer, ed, *Culture, Performance, and Identity.*

37. Kathryn Anderson, Susan Armitage, Dana Jack, and Judith Wittner, "Beginning Where We Are: Feminist Methodology in Oral History," *Oral History Review* 15:108–9. See also the essay by Anderson and Jack in this volume.

38. Sherna Gluck, "What's So Special about Women?" pp. 3–13; Ann Oakley, "Interviewing Women," pp. 30–61; Kristin M. Langellier and Deanna L. Hall, "Interviewing Women: A Phenomenological Approach to Feminist Communication Research," in Spitzack and Carter, eds., *Doing Research on Women's Communication.*

39. "The construction of meaning will be a by-product of the understanding and interpretation of both interviewer and interviewee as they perform the linguistic possibilities within the situation," E. Culpepper Clark, Michael J. Hyde, and Eva M. McMahan, "Communication in the Oral History Interview: Investigating Problems of Interpreting Oral Data," *International Journal of Oral History* 1 (1980): 30–31. See also Eva M. McMahan, "Communicative Dynamics of Hermeneutical Conversation in Oral History Interviews," *Communication Quarterly* 31, (1983): 3–11.

40. Pamela Fishman, "Interaction: The Work Women Do," in Thorne, Kramarae, and Henley, eds., *Language, Gender, and Society,* pp. 89–101; Maltz and Borker; "Male-Female Miscommunication"; and Treichler and Kramarae, "Women's Talk in the Ivory Tower."

41. Ronald J. Grele, *Envelopes of Sound: The Art of Oral History,* 2d ed. (Chicago: Precedent, 1985), Chapter VIII.

42. Barbara Myerhoff, *Number Our Days* (New York: Dutton, 1978).

43. Susan Armitage, "The Next Step," p. 6.

3

Black Women's Life Stories: Reclaiming Self in Narrative Texts

Gwendolyn Etter-Lewis

Oral narrative offers a unique and provocative means of gathering information central to understanding women's lives and viewpoints. When applied to women of color, it assumes added significance as a powerful instrument for the rediscovery of womanhood so often overlooked and/or neglected in history and literature alike. Specifically, articulation of black women's experiences in America is a complex task characterized by the intersection of race, gender, and social class with language, history, and culture. It is oral narrative that is ideally suited to revealing the "multilayered texture of black women's lives."[1] The resulting information is not a mere compilation of idiosyncratic recollections only interesting to a specialized audience; rather, black women's life stories enrich our understanding of issues of race and gender. To this end, I select, from my own study of older black women, narratives that exemplify the perils and triumphs of being black and female in America. In particular, I focus on sociolinguistic representations of a black female self and the power of language to transform experiences into words. While these narratives reveal experiences common to all women, the black female self emerges as a variation of several unique themes.

Oral Narrative as Feminist Methodology

The search for self in many contemporary scholarly studies by and about women often proves to be fruitless for women of color. Usually what is found in research on women is the "mythical male norm,"[2] or, in more current research, the white female norm, as the standard by which all others are judged. The narrative self that is defined by the "mythical male norm" is the center of the universe and is empowered by the notion that the individual is more important than the group.[3] As a result, views of self that differ from this norm are judged to be deviant or deficient. Furthermore, as Doris Sommer has suggested, the very manner in which we perceive personal narratives reflects the trappings of Western thought.[4] Readers habitually identify with a single center or voice that usually is seen as autonomous and singlehandedly in control of the direction of his life. We must question not only the validity of positing one "center" or self as a model for all life experiences, but also the expectation that a single male voice has the power and authority to represent others, regardless of race or gender.

On the other hand, the white female experience as norm presents its own set of problems. To take a white, middle-class female's experience as a given and generalize to all other women ignores the experiences of women of color and working-class women. It establishes an elitism within the heart of much feminist research. As Hazel Carby has observed, "White female critics continued to perpetrate against black women the exclusive practices they condemned in white male scholarship by establishing the experience of white middle-class women as normative within the feminist arena."[5] The effect of this practice is to establish a new canon with white female experience at its core. The distinct experiences of women of color in general, and black women in particular, are, by definition, excluded. Their concerns can find no voice in a white female self.

The point is this: existing norms of self in narrative texts have failed to account for black female life experiences. Self-images of black women cannot be determined by a prescribed norm based on male and/or white middle-class values and experiences. Instead, multiple and differing images of a black female self must be anchored to culturally relevant constructs. Nellie McKay provides a fitting example in her analysis of Zora Neale Hurston's autobiography. According to McKay, Hurston viewed herself as part of a group of rural southern black Americans, and a "self-appointed cultural interpreter for the community from which she came."[6] Therefore, Hurston's self-image, no matter how elusive, is intimately connected to her home community. In order to understand Hurston, one must also understand her community. In essence, race is not a hidden quality that surfaces only in connection with external events, it is an essential component of existence imposed by a prejudiced society upon the daily lives of black Americans.

Feminist research design and methodology, as well as analytical approaches to the data, must be sensitive to the cultural diversity present in the larger population. Sensitivity, however, must go beyond simple tokenism to fair and accurate representation. Applied to oral narrative, this means inclusion rather than exclusion, and that *all* women must tell their own stories in their own words.

Language and Narrative Texts

Language is the invisible force that shapes oral texts and gives meaning to historical events. It is the primary vehicle through which past experiences are recalled and interpreted. Attention to language, its variations and categorical forms, enriches narrative text analysis beyond strictly linguistic concerns.

On a most fundamental level, language is the organizing force that molds oral narrative according to a narrator's distinct style. Styles vary as widely as individuals,[7] but recurring patterns indicate more than speakers' personal quirks. Speech patterns inherent in oral narrative can reveal status, interpersonal relationships, and perceptions of language, self, and the world.[8] In the case of black women, we must ask what their narrative patterns reveal about their lives. How do their unique experiences influence the manner in which they tell their own life stories?

To explore this issue, I have collected oral narratives of older black women professionals who held positions traditionally occupied by whites and/or males in the period between 1920 and 1940. Most of the women were college-educated, and many held advanced degrees in their respective fields. While one could argue that it is educated black women who are most capable of articulating their own life stories, slave narratives and early autobiographies by black women indicate that it was not necessarily education but rather opportunity that determined whether or not a black American's story was printed. Financial backing from a group or an individual insured publication regardless of the author's educational background. Furthermore, only a few of the black women educated during the postslavery period found willing publishers or readers for their life stories. In the 1960s and 1970s, studies of the black community, particularly sociolinguistic studies, concentrated on the poor and uneducated. Although the majority of the subjects of the language studies was male, it was black poor and working-class who had the greatest access to the media. Thus, the speculation cannot be fully supported. Educated black women did not necessarily have the advantage in publishing their life stories.

In my analysis of black women's oral narratives, I find that experiences of the kind I recorded have not previously appeared in existing oral narratives. This information provides a more complete account of black women's lives, and their narrative styles supply us with much needed and traditionally over-looked female perspectives. An additional benefit is that sociolinguistic information makes a connection between the narrator's verbal performance and her views of self and the world.

For women of color, this opens a virtually unexplored avenue of knowledge. With this type of fine-grained focus on language, their suppressed and often censored viewpoints can be brought to the surface. In my study,[9] I found at least three distinct oral narrative styles in unedited narrative texts:

I. Unified:
Contiguous parts of a narrative fit together as a whole, usually in the form of an answer to a particular question. Words and phrases all are related to a central idea. Example:

Q: *How did you become interested in foreign languages?*

A: In the early days it became fashionable . . . I guess in all cities and in all social circles for uh . . . adults to study a foreign language. There were French clubs and Spanish clubs and German clubs. And my parents were members of that kind of a society and they studied French and . . . uh . . . enjoyed it very much. And they also studied Spanish.

And then in their schooling they had taken German. Cleveland was kind of a center of German activities. And so all of us grew up in the family speaking a little bit of French, a little bit of Spanish, a little bit of German. And so forth. And we would be told to sit down in German or get up and go to the piano in French. Or study something in Spanish. And we even made up our own language, a Cleveland language we called it. And I think that was what sparked my interest in foreign languages. Also, my mother was studying Spanish, she tells me, at the time I was conceived. So who knows?[10]

Notice that with the exception of pauses (e.g., uh), each utterance is related to the central idea of the question/answer—interest in foreign languages. The narrator supports her answer as completely as possible by providing several relevant examples. The result is a stretch of discourse unified by its focus on a particular topic.

II. Segmented:
Contiguous parts of a narrative characterized by a diverse assortment of seemingly unrelated utterances. Example:

Q: *What made you decide to go back to school?*

A: Look at me, I quit school to go find knowledge. Well, you need knowledge . . . I . . . to find knowledge. You gotta know where to search for knowledge. That's why I guess it took me so long. . . . I was forty years old when I had that vision, but I said . . . I wrote home to my folks and I said, "You know they tell me that life begins at forty and I have not yet begun to live. I'm just now beginning." So I went back to school and finished high school. Well, I didn't finish there but I got back to school right then in Kentucky, Louisville. And then I came home. In 1954 I went to California. So I enrolled in high school there and got my degree in the adult night school. Then I went on to college.[11]

The narrator seems to digress at the very beginning of her answer when she starts to discuss her search for knowledge. However, placing this information first may also be a strategy for expressing both the importance of her quest for knowledge and, thus, the motivation first for leaving, then for returning to school. The middle section answers the question, and the last part appears to be additional information not necessarily crucial to understanding the answer as a whole. The chronological ordering of the last few utterances suggests that the narrator's segmented style may be due to shifts in focus on topics of varying importance. Initially the narrator appears to be concerned with the significance of her decision to return to school, and, as her answer unfolds, switches to ordering events sequentially.

III. Conversational:

A contiguous part of a narrative identified by the reconstruction of conversations as they probably occurred in the past. Conversational elements are used to illustrate an idea or event. The narrator modifies voice, tone, and pitch in order to represent different speakers and different emotions (e.g., high pitch for anger or surprise). Example:

Q: *Did anything in your life ever happen or not happen solely because you were a woman?*

A: When I went to City College I remember, I'm not going to call any names, a young man uh . . . friend of mine said, "I don't have any time. Will you uh . . . will you do this paper for me?" And I said, "No!" I didn't mind doing anything for anybody, but I . . . I . . . isn't it funny how you are? I said, "No, I'm sorry, I can't do that. You have to do it yourself." He looked at me. You know, he gives me this dirty look. He did his paper because *nobody* [i.e., none of the other girls in the class] would do it for him. And he got an A. If I had done it for him, he would have gotten a B. (laughs) Isn't it funny how people are? It's an interesting thing.[12]

The narrator does not directly answer the question. Instead, she provides a conversational example of an affirmative answer. In fact, the narrator's conversational style throughout her narrative allowed her to answer questions regarding issues of sex and race in an indirect manner, by repeating past conversations. Perhaps conversation can function as a buffer to screen out uncomfortable emotions that accompany painful experiences. On the other hand, one could argue that conversation acts as a magnifying glass through which details can be highlighted. Whatever the reasons, conversation embedded in a narrative account of a particular experience or event often means more than words explain.

On the whole, oral narrative style is significant in revealing the meaning of words and phrases beyond the printed page. Categorizing narratives according to styles allows us to "read between the lines," where deep-seated feelings are hidden and disguised. For women of color, this is especially crucial in that their voices are usually not heard or deemed important. As long as women of color suffer double discrimination, understanding the texts of their lives will require a close reading of the styles or patterns through which their life stories unfold.

Specifically, these oral narrative styles produced by black female narrators generally indicate that large units of discourse such as question/answer segments or "frames"[13] assume a specific pattern according to a narrator's unique style of speaking. However, such styles are not exclusive to black women; all narrators exhibit distinct patterns of speaking. Neither are styles necessarily discrete, for a single narrator may use more than one style in developing the whole of her life story. Yet the fact remains that the speech patterns of oral narratives provide additional information about an individual's life and perceptions. Further sociolinguistic research could reveal which variables (e.g., sex, race, social class, etc.) most influence a speaker's style preference and whether or not the experience of oppression influences narrative style.

On a different level, the hidden meaning of words is especially important in black American speech. Wideman observes that multiple meanings can be found in a single speech act.[14] He explains that black speakers have a highly developed system of signifying how they feel about what they're saying. As a case in point, my study of older black professional women uncovered some interesting uses of diminutive terms. An eighty-one-year-old attorney who received her law degree in 1930 made the following comment about one of her cases:

> So I promptly got out attachment papers on all the costumes and sets and then filed her claim for the wages and they came across. And that little case was written up in the newspapers and I got a little publicity and I . . . I was really . . . very happy over that one.[15]

Similarly, a seventy-eight-year-old historian who earned her doctorate in 1946 reminisced:

> Yeah. They were keen. That was a keen class. The professors would always say no . . . not a class that's come through in . . . in there . . . in a high school class like that. Ah . . . you know . . . we were handling *heavy* debates and subjects, and writing our *little* essays. Like college people.[16]

Notice the opposition of heavy/little in the historian's comment. Not only is a diminutive term used to describe some very important work but, in the context of the whole utterance, it contradicts the description of the complexity of the work previously established by the use of "heavy."

Use of the diminutive term "little" confirms other researchers' previous findings. Several scholars have noted that women's oral narratives and autobiographies often are characterized by frequent understatements, avoidance of first-person point of view, rare mention of personal accomplishment, and disguised statements of personal power.[17] Many of these features are present in the foregoing examples. In fact, there appears to be a compounding of features in a single utterance. Understatement is enhanced by use of the term "little" in the description of an important achievement. The narrators tend to refer to noteworthy achievements in a manner that diminishes the significance of these achievements. This compounding could represent an interaction of the variables sex and race in that both black Americans and women are discouraged from publicly expressing pride and confidence in oneself. Or it could mean that gender overrides other variables in this instance, and produces an understatement that is characteristic of women's language in general. Either option is a reasonable conjecture. Without a doubt, causal relationships are not single and unidirectional. Instead, one cause can create several effects, and one effect can be generated by several causes acting in concert. Further discussion of the matter will be undertaken briefly in the concluding section of this essay.

Language and Social Class

Discussion of sociolinguistic variables would not be complete without some mention of social class. What impact, if any, does social class have on the construction of oral narratives? How does the narrator's social class influence the perception and telling of her own life story? These questions are not easily answered fully, but several ideas warrant consideration.

First and foremost, statistics from the U.S. census indicate that although there have been some gains, black Americans continue to lag behind whites in most areas (e.g., income, education, home ownership, employment, investments, etc.).[18] Thus, any serious discussion of social class must recognize this fundamental reality of American life: black and white communities are not on parallel socioeconomic tracks.

Another important issue to consider is that indices of social class are usually based on white communities,[13] which are regarded as the norm. These indices have failed, however, to show reliability and accuracy when applied without modification to the black community. In other words, the condition of being working-class or middle-class is not identical for blacks and whites. Some scholars claim that education, rather than income, is one of the most important factors in delineating the social structure of black America.[20] Although education is not the only factor that makes a difference, it is a primary element in establishing social class groupings within the black community.

For black women, as for any other group of women, social class operates in a wide range of ways. On the one hand, early historical and social trends in black America generated numbers of college-educated black women who were dedicated to "racial uplift."[21] They were encouraged to obtain an education in order to contribute to racial progress. Teaching, of course, was the most acceptable career choice for these women. On the other hand, the pattern by which poor black women stay poor and middle-class black women continue to make gains is often played out in the black community.[22] The pattern can, however, be broken, and, in most cases, such a break is due to education. In the final analysis, black women's social status must be evaluated in the context of a variety of factors. Even though there are middle-class and working-class divisions among black Americans, social class in and of itself may not be the single most important determinant of the course of a black woman's life.

When applied to oral narrative research, we must recognize that women's life stories need to be told regardless of social class. All of us can benefit from learning of the experiences of women from various strata of society. Yet the question remains: How, if at all, does class status influence the oral narratives of working-and middle-class black women?

My study of black professional women contained a small subsample of working-class women. All of the women, regardless of social class, experienced racism and sexism to some degree. In addition, working-class women also experienced the elitism of others. They were denied access to authority, service, and even respect because of their lower-class status. For most of these women, their socioeconomic condition translated into fewer choices and greater risks. A seventy-year-old interviewee described her childhood days as one would a job:

> I had to stay there an' keep house at home. An . . . an' cook for the children. See it was a heap of us. An' I had to stay there an' keep house an' cook for the children. I was the oldes'. An' I had to make them boys, you know . . . to keep yards clean an' paper an' rubbers, an' keep wood stove an' stuff. When my mom get there all she had to do was res' an' supper an' everything be already ready . . . [23]

When she grew up, the same interviewee worked as a domestic, then as a cook. Her mother also had been a cook, although she gave the credit to her grandmother: "I even thank and praise God for my granma which was——— [name deleted]. She the one learn me how to work, cook, tell the truth, don't tell a lie for no one!"[24]

Work outside of the home was not a choice but a necessity. More often than not, it was grueling and unrewarding, as explained by a sixty-seven-year old who eventually became self-employed:

> I would take my husband on these jobs. I took my husband to this one job and he was a butler and think of it, we got sixty dollars for the two of us, and I was work . . . I was washing twenty-one shirts a week and all that, cooking for thirty . . . that's just like slavery, it really was uh . . . [25]

Life for these women and their families seemed to be a series of struggles that promised to continue indefinitely. They experienced some pleasures and joys along the way, but inevitably they were faced with channeling all of their energies into bare survival in a very hostile world. Some overcame the limitations of poverty while others succumbed. The majority of women in my study who rose from a lower social class to a higher one had the support of their families. Many times the support was not financial, but moral and spiritual.

Although few generalizations can be drawn from such a small subsample, some characteristics of working-class black women's oral narratives are striking. The vernacular known as black English is immediately noticeable. It varies according to both level of education and intensity of experience. Women who had obtained an education beyond elementary school exhibited fewer instances of black English than women who had not. Black English also functioned as a means of expressing intense emotions or emphasizing an important event, regardless of the educational attainment of the narrator. The seventy-year-old interviewee previously discussed tended to place the most important information at the end of her responses to questions. In that same concluding utterance she would produce more black English than earlier in her response.

The self-image present in working-class black women's oral narratives is likely to reflect a disconnected self. The bonds or ties that normally exist between family members, for example, are severed for various reasons such as death, abuse, divorce, or some other misfortune. As with many of the life stories in my study, the young girl who stayed at home to care for younger siblings developed a sense of self disconnected from childhood. She had to assume the duties of an adult caretaker, and thereby exchanged childhood experiences for adult responsibilities. A narrator can also be disconnected from the literate world, as was the case of one of the older black women in the Buss study who had not learned to read and write.[26] Work in the cotton fields beginning at age nine prevented her from attending school for more than two months a year. Finally, she gave up and quit school, never having learned the basics. The double X she used as a signature symbolized the difficulties of her exile from a literate society. Furthermore, there can be other breaks, such as the crucial disconnection from family described by Josephine from the Buss study:

> It was hard to feel my family loved me when I was little. I didn't know, when I'd wake up in the morning, if I was going to sleep in the house with them that night. . . . My family never gave me anything. I never knew what it was to have a nickel in my hand to go to the store to buy an ice cream cone or a piece of candy. . . . Things stayed hard and as I grew older I seen the other children having more. If I'd been a boy I could have run away but I couldn't.[27]

As a young girl, Josephine realized the contradictions in her life. After her mother's premature death, the relatives who were left to care for the two children acted like unconcerned strangers while a godmother performed the role of caring grandmother. Added to those mismatched realities was the fact that her brother ran away to escape the negligent home environment. Yet Josephine clearly understood that such an option was not available to her simply because she was a girl.

Disconnections from childhood, family, and the literate world may not be unique to black women. There are numerous ways that the self-image of any person can be modified by various life experiences. However, the struggles of working-class Americans, as reported in oral narratives, suggest that there is likely to be some sort of break or gap in relationships fundamental to daily living. This human condition is reflected in oral narratives as a disconnected or detached sense of self. For black women, the disconnection from family is most damaging.

Clearly, the language that shapes texts also shapes images of self. Sociolinguistic studies indicate that speech is an act of identity.[28] It singles out speakers both as unique individuals and as members of particular social groups. For black American women, these issues of language and identity are intricately connected to the sociohistorical forces that influence their lives.

The black female self in oral narrative texts is particularly difficult to define because black women are rarely the subjects of sociolinguistic research. Usually, studies of women's language exclude women of color, and studies of black English exclude women. From a different although equally important perspective, expression and definition of the black female self is not merely a matter of speaking one's mind. As has been previously discussed, racist and sexist constraints often force women and black Americans to alter their self-images. A telling example can be found in Andrews's work, which indicates that, historically, black autobiographers were forced to invent devices and strategies that would endow their stories with the appearance of authenticity. This was perhaps the greatest challenge to the imagination of the Afro-American autobiographer. The reception of his narrative as truth depended on the degree to which his artfulness could hide his art.[29] A narrator could not appear to be too skillful in the telling of her/his own life story. It was not possible to deviate far from the black stereotype without risking alienating the white audience.

A similar condition exists for black women. They are constantly expected to *prove* that their situations are radically different from those of white women. If not, then their lives are considered unremarkable. Several readers who have reviewed the narrative accounts in my descriptive study of black professional women commented that these women seemed to be just like white middle-class women. I have then been advised to undertake a comparative analysis of professional black and white women's oral narratives in order to establish "genuine" differences between the two. In the readers' minds, black women must earn credibility by claiming features unique to their own embedded sub-group. Otherwise they are viewed merely as white women in black face. Such attitudes are uniformed and counterproductive. Whether or not black women measure up to such superficial standards has little to do with the reality of their struggles and the quality of their lives. While grouping all women together may produce a collective strength, it also creates a convenient fiction that allows issues of race and ethnicity to be categorically ignored.

In Search of the Black Female Self

The black female self-image, like any other, is complex and cannot be reduced to a single experience. However, several different aspects of this self-image are prominent in oral narratives. The issue of self in relation to the group, for example, is a recurring theme in black women's lives. McKay acknowledges that several scholars have noted that the black self is "conceived as part of a group."[30] She explains that "community identity" is essential for at least two reasons: (1) it allows for the rejection of bankrupt self-images "imposed by the dominant culture," and (2) it permits "marginalized individuals to embrace alternative selves constructed from more positive (and more authentic) images of their own creation."[31] This distinguishing feature appears to be present in both oral and written narratives of black male and female narrators. The black professional women I interviewed revealed this same attitude. A seventy-five-year-old administrator for self-help organizations described her community connection:

> I knew that if I wasn't able to find something to help the whole race, helping myself wouldn't do any good. Because my brother was heavyweight champion of the world and uh . . . he couldn't help the race.[32]

She offered a moving statement of commitment to the mission of racial uplift. In spite of difficulties at that point in her life, the narrator remained concerned about her progress in relation to the entire race of black Americans.

Even in a crisis, black women demonstrated their focus on the group as a whole rather than on their own personal well-being. Another narrator recalled a racist incident in which a dean warned only the black female students to "be as unobstrusive as possible" since black students were not welcome on the university campus. The female students responded as a group representing the whole rather than as self-centered individuals:

> We immediately met with the young [black] men on the campus and told them about it and we all decided that we were going out for everything. That everybody in that freshman class is gonna come away with some distinction. . . . And we all did . . .[33]

Thus, a critical component of the black female self is her tie to the Afro-American community. In many instances she is simultaneously a stabilizing force from within the community and an agent of change. Afro-American history is replete with examples of black women who often were the first on the picket line and the last to close school doors.

Attachment to the black community generated a binding force that united all black Americans on the basis of their common experiences with racism. Professional black women who entered nontraditional fields such as law and medicine were especially vunerable to discrimination and bigotry. However, they were not intimidated, nor were they surprised by the seemingly inevitable confrontation with racism. A seventy-five-year-old composer of music exemplified this attitude through her philosophical view of racism:

> Yeah . . . now racism . . . oh, it's one of those things you . . . you . . . you know is going to be there. . . . [O]ne . . . experience I had that was very, very, ah . . . poignant was the fact that I had been selected for a national award and they didn't know, when I had written this [musical composition] that I was black, and when they found it out, then the award was no longer available. . . . I try to forget things like that because I . . . I just don't think bitterness is going to help us get anywhere.[34]

Although she described the situation in very cautious terms, her disappointment was clearly a part of the "poignancy" of the experience. Perhaps the word "poignant" functions here as a euphemism for deeper feelings or deeper hurt. In addition, notice the identification with the black community in her last utterance. There is even some implication that the narrator's philosophical view may have occurred in retrospect: "I try to forget things like that" is a statement made in the present rather than at the time of the actual experience. For other women, strong doses of racism were encountered early in life. A seventy-two-year-old medical researcher whose family was the only black family in town vividly recalled a childhood incident that alerted her to the harmful effects of prejudice:

> This was at the Seventh Day Adventist school where this happened and I had this very good [white] friend named——— and one day she came to school and she told me she couldn't play with me any longer . . . she said she couldn't play with me any longer and so I said well why can't you play with me and so she took my hand and told me it was because I was black, was why she couldn't play with me. I said, "Oh, I'll fix that." I said, "When I go home I'll ask my mother to wash me real clean."[35]

This situation contained all the essential ingredients for an identity crisis. The pain that accompanied the discovery of stigma associated with being black, and the loss of a best friend at the same time, had the potential to turn innocence into bitterness. Instead, when the black child asked her mother to wash the darkness from her skin, the mother helped her child understand the beauty of being black. Thus, many of the black women in my study developed a self-concept endowed with the power to regenerate the self-esteem naturally lost through repeated assaults by a racist society. Sometimes this ability to restore a damaged self-image was learned from the family. At other times it was acquired from the sheer repetition of daily living. Whatever the source, a regenerated self-image served as an antidote for the self-hatred that could develop as a by-product of racism.

Although the black female self is strongly linked to the black community, she does not disappear into the group. Rather, a powerful voice of self-determination also emerges from black professional women's oral narratives. The seventy-five-year-old composer learned early in life the benefits of self-determination:

On the other hand, I was at the piano . . . I started off taking violin lessons, and then piano lessons and I liked both but then ah . . . the piano was a solo instrument whereas if you played violin you always have to get someone to accompany you. So, I forgot the violin. I stayed with the piano. . . . And when I was eleven, I won the . . . district [competition] for piano.[36]

A seventy-eight-year-old history professor recognized the necessity for self-determination in her desire to be different from other students in graduate school:

They all had to pass a French and German . . . um . . . you know, language [exam]. But that's just ordinary reading, that's kind of simple. . . . But, to go abroad to study, it required working in another language . . . so I went to Heidelberg.[37]

She then developed the habit of directing her career away from paths ordinarily chosen by others. This kind of decision-making served her well and allowed her to attain prominence in her field and in local politics. The black professional women in my study reported that awareness of their own need for self-determination usually occurred between childhood and early adulthood. That is, their feelings of being different were due in part to their drive or need to do things their own way. Usually such an attitude fueled their parents' concerns, but ultimately the strong will to choose for themselves guided these women to lives of distinction.

Transformation and Change

Scholarly representations of the black female self must be directed by a sense of black women's sociohistorical roots. As members of two oppressed groups, that of black Americans and that of women, their life stories cannot be isolated from their distinct perspectives, values, and roles. This means that scholarly treatment of black women's lives and viewpoints also must be distinct in its conception, methodological approach, and analysis. Unless and until there is an organic transformation in the way we think and write about black women's lives, we will continue to be unwitting victims of our own ignorance.

Several alternatives for including women and minorities in "mainstream" scholarly research have been proposed, but few have resulted in any serious or enduring changes. There is frequent dialogue about expanding "the canon" to embrace women and minorities. This approach to scholarly research and pedagogy is viewed as a viable remedy for white male dominance in education and the professions. However, expanding any canon within any discipline is a stopgap procedure. In essence, it is treating the symptom and not the disease. It is important to realize that the concept of a canon fits appropriately within what Schaef refers to as a "white male system."[38] This system is characterized in part by "dualistic thinking": "Things have to be either this way or that. One must be either superior or inferior."[39] This type of thinking is especially pervasive in the academy, the wellspring of scholarly research. As is evident in Gates's words, the canonical versus the noncanonical is "the ultimate opposition."[40] It is not, however, the only possible opposition. In fact, there does not have to be an opposition at all. Options do not have to be competitive. Alternatives need not be limited to adversarial stances. Oral narrative, for example, reflects a multiplicity of experiences and worldviews. As a result, it is fundamentally resistant to any form of canonical structuring. Therefore, if scholars are really committed to *transforming* rather than *revising* the system, a canon, as such, is out of place. It is antithetical to the process of change and can only serve to maintain the status quo.

Specifically, Patricia Hill-Collins suggests that we must confront the male system "not piecemeal, but root and branch."[41] She argues that we must reject dualistic constructs of the white male system, and "train ourselves to think of interlocking matrixes of relationships."[42] In other words, we must replace male standards within our previous research paradigms with more equitable, realistic, and culturally appropriate measures. We must cease to view the world around us in terms of duality and/or opposing pairs.

Similarly, we must contest the male tendency to organize information in terms of separability and discreteness. The notion that a single cause creates a single effect is inadequate. Black women's experiences, for example, are influenced by their multiple social roles, which are acted out simultaneously. They do not have the privilege of *only* being women, or of *only* being black Americans in particular situations. Instead, their roles are melded. Usually they must wear both hats at the same time. The merger or blending of roles/variables confirms Patricia Hill-Collins's contention that multiple, interconnecting variables are more representative of real life experiences.

Problems/issues in feminist research will not be resolved by simply rejecting previous ideas. There needs to be a reciprocal process of building and growth that involves women from a diversity of backgrounds and viewpoints. In fact, whether or not black women's life stories become a focus of feminist research will be a telling indication of our ability to progress beyond short-lived revisions. One thing is certain, positive thoughts and good intentions are not enough. We must act with deliberation and commitment in order to ensure that all women have a voice and an audience for the telling of their lives.

Notes

This research was made possible in part by a grant from the Ford Foundation.

1. Gloria Hull, Patricia Bell Scott, and Barbara Smith, eds., *All the Women Are White, All the Blacks Are Men, But Some of Us Are Brave: Black Women's Studies* (Old Westbury, N.Y.: The Feminist Press, 1982), p. 17.
2. Patricia Hill Collins, "Critical Questions: Two Decades of Feminist Scholarship." Paper

presented at the Eleventh Annual National Women's Studies Association Conference, Towson, Maryland, 14–18 June 1989 (personal notes).

3. See Jeanne Noble, "The Higher Education of Black Women in the Twentieth Century," and Linda Perkins, "The Education of Black Women in the Nineteenth Century," in *Women and Higher Education in American History,* ed. John Mack Faragher and Florence Howe (New York: W. W. Norton, 1988), pp. 88 and 66.

4. Doris Sommer, " 'Not Just a Personal Story': Women's *Testimonios* and the Plural Self," in *Life/Lines: Theorizing Women's Autobiography,* ed. Bella Brodzki and Celeste Schenck (Ithaca, N.Y.: Cornell University Press, 1988), p. 118.

5. Hazel Carby, *Reconstructing Womanhood: The Emergence of the Afro-American Woman Novelist* (New York: Oxford University Press, 1987), p. 11.

6. Nellie McKay, "Race, Gender, and Cultural Context in Zora Neale Hurston's *Dust Tracks on a Road,*" in Brodzki and Schenck, eds., *Life/Lines,* p. 182.

7. See R. A. Hudson, *Sociolinguistics* (New York: Cambridge University Press, 1980), p. 120.

8. See Jennifer Coats, *Women, Men and Language* (New York: Longman, 1986), and Jennifer Coates and Deborah Cameron, eds., *Women in Their Speech Communities* (New York: Longman, 1988), pp. 12 and 13–14.

9. Over thirty oral narratives of black professional women between the ages of sixty and ninety-five form the basis of my book in progress. All of the women were college educated and held positions in the decades between 1920 and 1940 that were traditionally occupied by males and/or whites.

10. Interview with Dr. S. P. by Gwen Etter-Lewis, 18 August 1986, Charlotte, North Carolina, tape #3, Gwen Etter-Lewis's (hereafter GEL) personal collection.

11. Interview with E.B. by Gwen Etter-Lewis, June 1986, West Point, Georgia, tape #4, GEL personal collection.

12. Interview with E.H. by Gwen Etter-Lewis, June 1986, Ann Arbor, Michigan, tape #5, GEL personal collection.

13. Deborah Tannen, "What's in a Frame? Surface Evidence for Underlying Expectations," in *New Directions in Discourse Processing,* ed. Roy Freedle (Norwood, N.J.: Ablex, 1979).

14. John Wideman, "The Black Writer and the Magic of the Word," *New York Times Book Review,* 24 January 1988, pp. 1 and 28–29.

15. Interview with H.A. by Gwen Etter-Lewis, 17 June 1988, Silver Spring, Maryland, tape #36, side #2, GEL personal collection.

16. Interview with H.E. by Gwen Etter-Lewis, 23 April 1988, Kalamazoo, Michigan, tape #30, side #3, GEL personal collection.

17. See Estelle Jelinek, ed., *Women's Autobiography: Essays in Criticism* (Bloomington, Ind.: Indiana University Press, 1980); Lenore Hoffman and Margo Culley, eds., *Women's Personal Narratives: Essays in Criticism and Pedagogy* (New York: Modern Language Association, 1985); and Brodzki and Schenck, eds., *Life/Lines.*

18. U.S. Department of Commerce, Bureau of the Census, 1980 Census of Population, Chapter C: General Social and Economic Characteristics, vol. 1, pt. 1, December 1983, pp. 21, 31, 55, 101, and 249.

19. Andrew Billingsley, *Black Families in White America* (Englewood Cliffs, N.J.: Prentice-Hall, 1968), p. 122.

20. James Blackwell, *The Black Community* (New York: Dodd, Mead, and Co., 1975), p. 73.

21. Perkins, "The Education of Black Women," p. 66; Noble, "The Higher Education of Black Women," p. 88.

22. Paula Giddings, *When and Where I Enter* (New York: Bantam Books, 1984), p. 205.

23. Interview with N.B. by Gwen Etter-Lewis, 26 July 1987, Atlanta, Georgia, tape #13, side #2, GEL personal collection.

24. Ibid.

25. Interview with N.O. by Gwen Etter-Lewis, 7 August 1987, Detroit, Michigan, tape #7, side #2, GEL personal collection.

26. Fran Leeper Buss, *Dignity: Lower Income Women Tell of Their Lives and Struggles* (Ann Arbor, Mich.: University of Michigan Press, 1985), p. 113.

27. Ibid., pp. 23–24 and 26.

28. R. B. Le Page et al., "Further Report on the Sociolinguistic Survey of Multilingual Communities: Survey of Cayo District, British Honduras," *Language in Society* 3 (1974): 1–32; R. A. Hudson, *Sociolinguistics* (New York: Cambridge University Press, 1980), p. 120; and Jennifer Coates, *Women, Men and Language* (New York: Longman, 1986), p. 161.

29. William Andrews, *To Tell a Free Story: The First Century of Afro-American Autobiography, 1769–1865* (Urbana, Ill.: University of Illinois Press, 1986), p. 2.

30. Nellie McKay, "Race, Gender, and Cultural Context," p. 176.

31. Ibid., p. 175.

32. Interview with E.B. by Gwen Etter-Lewis, June 1986, West Point, Georgia, tape #4, side #1, GEL personal collection.

33. Interview with H.A. by Gwen Etter-Lewis, 17 June 1988, Silver Spring, Maryland, tape #36, side #1, GEL personal collection.

34. Interview with Z.P. by Gwen Etter-Lewis, 6 July 1987, Wilberforce, Ohio, tape #27, side #3, GEL personal collection.

35. Interview with V.W. by Gwen Etter-Lewis, 23 May 1988, Wilmette, Illinois, tape #29, GEL personal collection.

36. Interview with Z.P. by Gwen Etter-Lewis, 6 July 1987, Wilberforce, Ohio, tape #27, GEL personal collection.

37. Interview with H.E. by Gwen Etter-Lewis, 23 April 1988, Kalamazoo, Michigan, tape #30, side #2, GEL personal collection.

38. Anne W. Schaef, *Women's Reality* (San Francisco: Harper and Row, 1985), p. 12.

39. Ibid.

40. Henry Louis Gates, Jr., "Writing 'Race' and the Difference it Makes," in idem, ed., *"Race," Writing, and Difference* (Chicago: University of Chicago Press, 1986), p. 2.

41. Patricia Hill-Collins, 1989, personal notes.

42. Ibid.

II

Authority and Interpretation

As we move from the problems of interviewing to those of interpretation of the resulting text, the oral history process seems progressively to efface the original narrator and diminish her control over her own words. Once the tape has been converted into a text, what at first may have appeared to be an immediately accessible account of a life or an episode, with the speaker as the ultimate authority, becomes a site of interpretive conflict. The essays in this section address three moments in the process by which meaning and signification come to be assigned to oral narratives. They also, incidentally, reveal the culture-specific quality of oral narratives gathered in three different countries: the United States, France, and Guatemala.

Katherine Borland explores the potential for interpretive conflict in a project on oral narrative that she conducted with her grandmother, Beatrice Hanson, in Maine. Borland suggests a model of continuing negotiation about meaning and import—a model that respects the speaker's "ownership" of her words as well as the researcher's commitments to scholarship. Her essay thus focuses on those stages after the interview when the researcher is delicately poised between the text she is producing, on the one hand, and her relationship with the speaker, on the other.

At a further remove from her narrators, Marie-Françoise Chanfrault-Duchet focuses on texts she produced from interviews she herself conducted. Starting from the premise that facts and events, as recounted in the life story, take their meaning from the narrative structure in which they are embedded, she elaborates a multifaceted interpretive model that combines the analyses of narrative structures, social context, and symbolic representations. This model is illustrated by examining the stories of two Frenchwomen whose lives had taken a similar course but who produced very different narratives.

Claudia Salazar, positioning herself entirely outside the process of oral history production, attempts a critique of that very process as she explores the well-known book, I . . . Rigoberta Menchú. In an endeavor to appropriate the text both for its narrator and as a political document, Salazar places this narrative within the larger context of material and textual relations of power, including those relations that undergird the production and translation of such texts.

Borrowing from contemporary theory in a number of fields, these essays offer fruitful examples of the ways in which scholars can avoid treating oral histories either as unmediated and disembodied texts or as authoritative statements that preclude questioning and analysis. Negotiation thus proceeds on several fronts at once—between narrator and researcher, researcher and text, and text and reader.

4

"That's Not What I Said": Interpretive Conflict in Oral Narrative Research

Katherine Borland

In the summer of 1944, my grandmother, Beatrice Hanson, put on a pale, eggshell-colored gabardine dress with big gold buttons down the side, a huge pancake-black hat, and elbow-length gloves—for in *those* days ladies dressed *up* to go to the fair—and off she went with her father to see the sulky (harness) races at the Bangor, Maine, fairgrounds. The events that ensued provided for a lively wrangle between father and daughter as they vied to pick the winner. Forty-two years later Beatrice remembered vividly the events of that afternoon and, in a highly structured and thoroughly entertaining narrative, recounted them to me, her folklorist-granddaughter, who recorded her words on tape for later transcription and analysis. What took place that day, why it proved so memorable, and what happened to the narrative during the process of intergenerational transmission provide a case study in the variability of meaning in personal narrative performances. This story, or, better said, these stories, stimulate reflexivity about our scholarly practice.

Let me begin with the question of meaning and its variability. We can view the performance of a personal narrative as a meaning-constructing activity on two levels simultaneously. It constitutes both a dynamic interaction between the thinking subject and the narrated event (her own life experience) and between the thinking subject and the narrative event (her "assumption of responsibility to an audience for a display of communicative competence"[1]). As performance contexts change, as we discover new audiences, and as we renegotiate our sense of self, our narratives will also change.

What do folklorists do with the narratives performed for/before us? Like other audience members, we enjoy a skillfully told tale. But some of us also collect records of the performance in order to study them. Oral personal narratives occur naturally within a conversational context, in which various people take turns at talk, and thus are rooted most immediately in a web of expressive social activity. *We* identify chunks of artful talk within this flow of conversation, give them physical existence (most often through writing), and embed them in a new context of expressive or at least communicative activity (usually the scholarly article aimed toward an audience of professional peers). Thus, we construct a second-level narrative based upon, but at the same time reshaping, the first.

Like the original narrator, we simultaneously look inward toward our own experience of the performance (our interpretive shaping of it as listeners) and outward to our audience (to whom we must display a degree of scholarly competence). Presumably, the patterns upon which we base our interpretations can be shown to inhere in the "original" narrative, but our aims in pointing out certain features, or in making connections between the narrative and larger cultural formations, may at times differ from the original narrator's intentions. This is where issues of our responsibility to our living sources become most acute.

Years ago, scholars who recorded the traditions, arts, and history of a particular culture group gave little thought to the possibility that their representations might legitimately be challenged by those for and about whom they wrote. After all, they had "been in the field," listening, taking notes, and witnessing the culture firsthand. Educated in the literate, intellectual tradition of the Western academy, these scholars brought with them an objective, scientific perspective that allowed them, they felt, to perceive underlying structures of meaning in their material that the "natives," enmeshed in a smaller, more limited world, could not see. Therefore, it is not surprising that general ethnographic practice excluded the ethnographic subject from the process of post-fieldwork interpretation, nor that folklorists and anthropologists rarely considered their field collaborators to be potential audiences for their publications. More recently, some researchers sensitive to the relationships of power in the fieldwork exchange have questioned this model of the scholar as interpretive authority for the culture groups he/she studies.[2]

For feminists, the issue of interpretive authority is particularly problematic, for our work often involves a contradiction. On the one hand, we seek to empower the women we work with by revaluing their perspectives, their lives, and their art in a world that has systematically ignored or trivialized women's culture.[3] On the other, we hold an explicitly political vision of the structural conditions that lead to particular social behaviors, a vision that our field collaborators, many of whom do not consider themselves feminists, may not recognize as valid. My own work with my grandmother's racetrack narrative provides a vivid example of how conflicts of interpretation may, perhaps inevitably do, arise during the folklore transmission process. What should we do when we women disagree?

To refrain from interpretation by letting the subjects speak for themselves seems to me an unsatisfactory if not illusory solution. For the very fact that we constitute the initial audience for the narratives we collect influences the way in which our collaborators will construct their stories, and our later presentation of these stories—in particular publications under particular titles—will influence the way in which prospective readers will interpret the texts. Moreover, feminist theory provides a powerful critique of our society, and, as feminists, we presumably are dedicated to making that critique as forceful and direct as possible. How, then, might we present our work in a way that grants the speaking woman interpretive respect without relinquishing our responsibility to provide our own interpretation of her experience?

Although I have no easy answer to this question, I believe that by reflecting on our practice we can move toward a more sensitive research methodology. In the spirit of reflexivity I offer here a record of the dispute that arose between my grandmother and myself when I ventured an interpretation of her narrative. First, I will summarize the narrative, since the taped version runs a full twenty-five minutes. Then I will present her framing of the narrative in performance and my reframing during the interpretive process. Finally, I will present her response to my interpretation. While I have already "stacked the deck" in my favor by summarizing the story, reducing it through my subjective lens, my grandmother's comments powerfully challenge my assumption of exegetical authority over the text.[4]

Beatrice began her story with a brief setting of the scene: in the grandstand, she finds herself seated directly behind Hod Buzzel, "who," she states, "had gotten me my divorce and whom I *hated* with a passion." Hod is accompanied by his son, the county attorney (who, Beatrice says, "was just as bad as his father in another way—he was a snob"). Beatrice's father knows them both very well.

Beatrice, the narrator, then explains the established system for selecting a horse. Observers typically purchase a "score card" that lists the past records of horses and drivers, and they evaluate the horses as they pace before the grandstand. Beatrice's personal system for choosing a horse depends most heavily on her judgment of the observable merits of both horse and driver. She explains:

> And if I could find a *horse* that right pleased me, and a driver that pleased me that were together . . . *there* would be my choice, you see? So, this particular afternoon . . . I *found* that. Now that didn't happen all the time, by any means, but I found . . . perfection, as far as I was concerned, and I was absolutely *convinced* that *that* horse was going to win.

Beatrice decides to bet on Lyn Star, an unknown horse driven by a young man. She knows that this young man's father is driving another horse in the race. Her father and the Buzzels select Black Lash, a horse with an established reputation for speed.

The subsequent action exhibits an inherent potential for narrative patterning. Sulky races, in which a driver sits behind the horse in a two-wheeled, single-seat carriage, are presented in a series of three heats. In other words, the same group of horses races against each other three times during the afternoon, alternating with three groups of horses who race against one another in the same fashion. Normally, drivers act on their own, competing individually against their opponents, but the appearance of a father and son in the same race suggests to Bea the possibility that these two may collaborate with one another in some way. Each heat, from the perspective of the audience, involves three stages: selecting a horse and placing a bet, observing the race proper, and collecting on one's winning tickets. With regard to the particular race narrated, an additional structural element is provided by the repetitive strategy employed by the father and son upon whom Bea has placed her hopes.

In each heat, the father quickly takes the lead and sets a fast pace for the other horses while the son lopes along behind. As the horses turn into the second lap and start their drive, the father moves over to let his son through on the rail (the inside lane of the track) thereby forcing Black Lash, the next-to-front runner, to go out and around him. Dramatic tension is produced by the variable way in which this strategy is played out on the course. In the first heat, Lyn Star wins by a nose. In the second, he ties in a photo finish with Black Lash. In the third, the father's horse, worn out by his previous two performances, drops back behind the others, leaving Lyn Star and Black Lash to really race. But because of the way the races have been run, Lyn Star's driver had never really had to push his horse. He does so this time and leaves Black Lash half a length behind.

As a superlative narrator, Beatrice recognizes and exploits the parallels between the observed contest and the contest between observers who have aligned themselves with different horses. She structures her narrative by alternating the focus between a dramatic reenactment of events in the grandstand and a description of the actual race as it unfolds before the observers. Within this structure, the cooperation between the father and son on the racecourse provides a contrast to the conflict between father and daughter in the grandstand.

Before the first heat, Bea's father asks her, "D'you pick a horse?" And she responds that, yes, she has chosen Lyn Star. At this, her father loudly denounces her choice, claiming that the horse will never win, she'll lose her money, and she should not bet. Beatrice puts two dollars on the horse. When Lyn Star wins, Bea turns triumphantly to her father. Undaunted, he insists that the race was a fluke and that Bea's favorite horse will not win again. Nevertheless, Beatrice places six dollars on Lyn Star in the next heat. By now, though, her father is irate and attempts first to trade horses with her so that she won't lose her money, and then, when she declines this offer, he refuses altogether to place her bet. Young Buzzel, who has become an amused audience of one to the father-daughter contest in the grandstand, offers to take her money down to the betting office. Since Bea has never placed her own bets, she accepts.

With the third heat Beatrice's father catapults their private argument into the public arena, as he asks his daughter, "What are you going to do this time?" Beatrice is adamant, "I am *betting on my horse* and I am betting *ten bucks* on that horse. It's gonna win!" At this, Beatrice, the narrator, explains, "Father had a fit. *He* had a fit. And he tells everybody three miles around in the grandstand what a fool I am too. . . . *He* wasn't gonna take my money down!" So Beatrice commandeers young Buzzel to place her bet for her again. When Lyn Star wins by a long shot, Bea's father is effectively silenced:

> And *I* threw my pocketbook in one direction, and I threw my gloves in another direction, and my score book went in another direction, and I jumped up and I hollered, to everyone, "You see what know-it-all said! *That's* my father!" And finally one man said to me . . . no, he said to my father, "You know, she *really* enjoys horse racing, doesn't she?"

To understand how Bea frames her narrative, we must return to a consideration of her initial description of how a horse is chosen. This prefatory material orients the audience to a particular point of view, emphasizing that the race should be understood as an opportunity for racegoers to exercise their evaluative skills in order to predict an eventual outcome. Indeed, the length and detail of this portion of the narrative emphasizes the seriousness, for Beatrice, of this preliminary evaluative activity. This framing of the story gains significance if one considers that Bea's knowledge of horses was unusual for women in her community. Emphasizing the exceptionality of her knowledge, she explained to me that her father owned and raced horses when Bea was a child and "though I could not go *fishing* with my father on Sundays, or *hunting* with him on any day of the week, for some strange reason, he took me with him, mornings" to watch his horses being exercised.[5]

Additionally, in her framing of the narrative, Beatrice identifies the significance of the event narrated, its memorability, as the unique coming together of a perfect horse and driver that produced an absolute conviction on her part as to who would win the contest. Since this conviction was proved correct, the narrative functions to support or illustrate Bea's sense of self as a competent judge of horses within both the narrative and the narrated event. In effect, her narrative constitutes a verbal re-performance of an actual evaluative performance at the track.[6]

What do I as a listener make of this story? A feminist, I am particularly sensitive to identifying gender dynamics in verbal art, and, therefore, what makes the story significant for me is the way in which this self-performance within the narrated event takes on the dimension of a female struggle for autonomy within a hostile male environment. Literally and symbolically, the horse race constitutes a masculine sphere. Consider, racing contestants, owners, and trainers were male (although female *horses* were permitted to compete). Also, while women obviously attended the races, indeed, "ladies dressed up" to go to the races, they were granted only partial participant status. While they were allowed to sit in the grandstand as observers (and, having dressed up, one assumes, as persons to be observed), they were not expected to engage as active evaluators in the essential first stage of the racing event. Notice that even at the very beginning of the story Bea's father did not want her to bet.

Betting is inherently a risk-taking activity. Men take risks; women do not. This dimension of meaning is underscored in the second heat when Beatrice, the narrator, ironically recounts that her father was going to be "decent" to her, in other words, was going to behave according to the model of gentlemanly conduct, by offering to bear his daughter's risk and bet on her horse for her.

Significantly, as the verbal contest develops, Beatrice displays greater and greater assertiveness as a gambler. Not only does she refuse to align herself with the men's judgment, she also raises the ante by placing more and more serious bets on her choice. From an insignificant bet in the first heat—and here it bears recalling that in racing parlance a two-dollar bet is still called a "lady's bet"—she proceeds in the second and third heats to bet six and ten dollars, respectively.

In portraying the intensification of the contest, Beatrice, the narrator, endows Beatrice, the gambler, with an increasingly emphatic voice. Her tone in addressing her father moves from one of calm resolution before the first and second heats—"That's the horse I'm betting on," and "No, I'm gonna stay with that horse"—to heated insistence before the third heat—"I am *betting on my horse!*" (each word accentuated in performance by the narrator's pounding her fist on the dining-room table).

Finally, if one looks at Beatrice's ost-heat comments, one can detect a move from simple self-vindication in ᴜne first heat to a retaliatory calumniation of her father's reputation delivered in a loud disparaging voice—"You see what know-it-all said! *That's* my father!" Thus, at the story's end, Beatrice has moved herself from a peripheral feminine position with respect to the larger male sphere of betting *and* talk, to a central position where her words and deeds proclaim her equal and indeed superior to her male antagonist. Symbolically underscoring this repudiation of a limiting feminine identity, Bea flings away the accessories of her feminine costume—her gloves and her pocketbook.

If on one level the story operates as a presentation of self as a competent judge of horses, on another it functions to assert a sense of female autonomy and equality within a sphere dominated by men. From yet another perspective, the verbal contest between father and daughter results in a realignment of allegiances based on the thematic contrasts between age and youth, reputation and intrinsic merit, observable in the contest between the horses Black Lash and Lyn Star. When her father (tacitly) refuses to place her bet before the second heat, young Buzzel, whom Bea has previously described as an antagonist, and who has been betting with the older men, offers to place her bet for her. In effect, he bets on Beatrice in the contest developing on the sidelines.[7]

Furthermore, with regard to the narrator's life experience, one can view the narrative as a metaphor for a larger contest between Beatrice and her social milieu. For in the early 1930s Beatrice shocked her community by divorcing her first husband. This action and her attempt to become economically independent by getting an education were greeted with a certain amount of social and familial censure. For instance, Beatrice recalls, when her mother entered the date of the divorce in the family bible, she included the note: "Recorded, but not approved." It also forced Beatrice to leave her two young daughters in the care of their paternal grandparents for the five years she attended college, a necessity that still saddens and troubles her today.[8]

My grandparents agree that, in the ideology of marriage at that time, "you weren't supposed to be happy." My grandfather relates that his grandmother suffered severe psychological strain during menopause, was committed to a psychiatric hospital, and, while there, crossed her name off her marriage certificate. In a slightly more active form of resistance, Beatrice's grandmother, after injuring herself while doing heavy farm work, took to her bed for several years. However, as soon as her son married, she got up, moved in with him, and led a normal, active life, becoming the strong maternal figure of Bea's own childhood. Bea's mother separated herself psychologically from both her husband and her family by retreating into a strict, moralistic, and, in Bea's view, hypocritical religiosity. For Bea's predecessors, then, a woman's socially acceptable response to an unhappy marriage was to remove herself from the marriage without actually effecting a formal, public separation. Although Bea's first husband was tacitly recognized by the community as an unfit husband—irresponsible, alcoholic, a spendthrift and a philanderer—Beatrice was expected to bear with the situation in order to protect her own reputation and that of her family.

By divorcing her first husband Beatrice transgressed middle-class social decorum and was branded "disreputable." The appearance in the present narrative of the divorce lawyer and Bea's negative reaction to him leads me to link Beatrice's performance and status at the races to her previous loss of reputation in the larger village society.[9] In both instances Beatrice had to prove in the face of strong opposition the rightness of not playing by the rules, of relying on her own judgment, of acting as an autonomous individual. I would suggest, then, that the latent associations of this narrative to circumstances critical to the narrator's life, even if not consciously highlighted in the narrative, may reinforce its memorability.

What is essential to emphasize, however, is that this is *my* framing of the racetrack narrative informed by contemporary feminist conceptions of patriarchal structures, which my grandmother does not share. Moreover, after reading an initial version of this interpretation, Beatrice expressed strong disagreement with my conclusions. I quote a portion of the fourteen-page letter she wrote to me concerning the story:

> Not being, myself, a feminist, the "female struggle" as such never bothered me in my life. It never occurred to me. I never thought of my *position* at all in this sense. I've always felt that I had a fine childhood. It seems, now, that I must have had a remarkable one. To begin with, I had a very strong father

figure. Surrounded by the deep and abiding love of my Grandmother Austin (whom I adored); the clear, unfaltering knowledge of my father's love and his openly expressed pride in me, and the definite disciplines set by my grandmother which provided the staunch and unchallengeable framework in which I moved, I knew absolute security. (The disciplines were unchallengeable because I never had the least desire to challenge them. I would have done anything not to disappoint Grandma or make her feel bad, and I was so very happy and secure that only an idiot would have tried to upset the situation.)

In consequence of all this, as I grew older, the inner strength which that sense of security had built in me, served always to make me feel equal to anyone, male or female, and very often superior. Feminism, as such, was of no moment to me—none at all. Privately, it has always seemed ridiculous, but that's neither here nor there. It makes no difference to me what anybody else thinks about it.

So your interpretation of the story as a female struggle for autonomy within a hostile male environment is entirely YOUR interpretation. You've read into the story what you wished to—what pleases YOU. That it was never—by any wildest stretch of the imagination—the concern of the originator of the story makes such an interpretation a definite and complete distortion, and in this respect I question its authenticity. The story is no longer MY story at all. The skeleton remains, but it has become your story. Right? How far is it permissible to go, in the name of folklore, and still be honest in respect to the original narrative?

Beatrice brings up a crucial issue in oral narrative scholarship—who controls the text? If I had not sent my grandmother a copy of my work, asking for her response, I could perhaps have avoided the question of my intrusion into the texts I collect. Discussions with our field collaborators about the products of our research are often overlooked or unreported by folklore scholars. Luckily, my grandmother is quite capable of reading, responding to, and resisting my presentation of her narrative. For my own and my grandmother's versions provide a radical example of how each of us has created a story from our own experience. While I agree that the story has indeed become *my* story in the present context, I cannot agree that my reading betrays the original narrative.

Beatrice embraces an idealist model of textual meaning that privileges authorial intentions. It makes sense for my grandmother to read the story in this way. From my own perspective, however, the story does not really become a story until it is actualized in the mind of a receptive listener/reader. As my consciousness has been formed within a different social and historical reality, I cannot restrict my reading to a recuperation of original authorial intentions. I offer instead a different reading, one that values her story as an example to feminists of one woman's strategy for combating a limiting patriarchal ideology. That Bea's performance constitutes a direct opposition to established authorities reveals for me how gender ideologies are not wholly determinative or always determinative of female identity.[10]

Nevertheless, despite my confidence in the validity of my reading as a feminist scholar, personally I continue to be concerned about the potential emotional effect alternative readings of personal narratives may have on our living subjects. The performance of a personal narrative is a fundamental means by which people comprehend their own lives and present a "self" to their audience.[11] Our scholarly representations of those performances, if not sensitively presented, may constitute an attack on our collaborators' carefully constructed sense of self. While Bea and I have discussed our differences at length and come to an amicable agreement about how to present them (i.e., the inclusion of her response to my initial reading in the final text), I might have avoided eliciting such a violent initial response from her if I had proceeded differently from the outset.[12]

I could have tried to elicit my grandmother's comments on the story's meaning before I began the process of interpretation. During the taping session itself, however, this would have proved problematic. As I stated earlier, oral personal narratives occur naturally within a conversational context, and often the performance of one narrative leads to other related performances. These displays of verbal art provide an important context for understanding how the narrative in question is to be viewed, and from my perspective it would not be productive to break the narrative flow in order to move to the very different rhetorical task of interpretation and analysis.

Furthermore, during a narrative performance of this type, both narrator and listener are caught up in the storytelling event. Although associative commentary about the stories is common, at this stage in the fieldwork exchange neither narrator nor listener is prepared to reflect analytically on the material being presented. Indeed, the conscious division of a storytelling session into discreet story units or thematic constellations of stories occurs at the later stage of review and study.

Nevertheless, the narrator's commentary on and interpretation of a story can contribute greatly to the researcher's understanding of it. I now feel I ought to have arranged a second session with my grandmother in which I played her the taped version and asked her for her view of its function and meaning. Time constraints prevented me from doing so. I did solicit an interpretation from Bea with not much success after I had written and she had read my initial version of this article. At that time Beatrice insisted that the story was simply an amusing anecdote with no deep or hidden meanings. Although it may be that some narrators are not prepared to interpret their own stories analytically, Bea's reaction may have been due to her sharply felt loss of authorial control.

With the benefit of hindsight, let me review two points that proved especially sensitive for my grandmother. First, Bea reacted very strongly to the feminist identity my interpretation implied she had. Though some might quibble that this problem is simply a matter of labels, the word "feminist" often has negative, threatening connotations for women who have not participated in the feminist movement. More important, Bea's objection points to an important oversight in my own research process.

When I began the task of interpretation, I assumed a likeness of mind where there was in fact difference: I was confident that my grandmother would accept my view of the story's meaning. After all, she had been very excited about working with me when I told her I wanted to study older women's life experience narratives. She sent me a great deal of material and commentary on the difficult conditions of women's lives in nineteenth- and early twentieth-century Maine, material and commentary that seemed on the surface to convey a feminist perspective. Moreover, she offered her own accounts and stories, some of which dealt with very sensitive matters, assuring me that I should feel perfectly free to use whatever proved helpful to me in my research. How, then, did we, who had a close, confidential, long-standing relationship, manage to misunderstand each other so completely?

The fieldwork exchange fosters a tendency to downplay differences, as both investigator and source seek to establish a footing with one another and find a common ground from which to proceed to the work of collecting and recording oral materials. Additionally, as we are forever constructing our own identities through social interactions, we similarly construct our notion of others. My grandmother has always appeared to me a remarkably strong, independent woman, and thus, even though she had never called herself a feminist, it was an easy step for me to cast her in that role. Although she knew that I considered myself an activist feminist, to her I have always been, first and foremost, a granddaughter. She was, therefore, unprepared for the kind of analysis I performed on her narrative. The feminist movement has been criticized before for overgeneralizing about women's experience in its initial enthusiasm of sisterly identification. Yet it bears repeating that important commonalities among women often mask equally important differences.[13]

For Beatrice, another troubling feature of my interpretation is the portrait it presents of her father. Here the problem arises from our different understandings of what the narrative actually is. I approach the story as a symbolic construction and the people within it are, for me, dramatic characters. Thus, Beatrice's father, the antagonistic figure of the story, becomes a symbol of repressive male authority in my interpretation. For Beatrice, however, the story remains an account of a real experience, embedded in the larger context of her life. She brings to her reading of the "characters" a complex of associations built up over a shared lifetime. From this perspective my interpretation of her father is absolutely false. Whether or not it "works" for the father figure in the story, it does not define the man. In fact, Beatrice's father was one of the few people who encouraged and supported her during the difficult period after her disastrous first marriage. She remembers her father with a great deal of love and admiration and speaks often of the special relationship they had with one another. Indeed, if anyone was the villain of Beatrice's youth, it would have been her mother, a cold, judgmental woman. Nevertheless, in a written account of the racetrack story composed shortly after the event took place, Beatrice herself remarks that at the track, "Father and the Buzzels were acting very male," quarreling over the results of the races.[14]

When I sent Beatrice a copy of my essay in which *her* narrative had suffered a sea change, she naturally felt misrepresented. To complicate matters, my original essay contained a great deal of theory that was unfamiliar and at times incomprehensible to her. Embedded in the context of my own scholarly environment, I had not bothered to provide any accompanying explanation of that theory. Thus, if I had "misread" her text, I also gave her every opportunity to misread mine. I now feel that had I talked to Bea about my ideas *before* I committed them to writing, presented her with drafts, or even arranged to have her read the paper with me so that we might discuss misunderstandings and differences as they arose, her sense of having been robbed of textual authority might not have been as strong as it was.

I am not suggesting that all differences of perspective between folklorist and narrator, feminist scholar and speaking woman, should or can be worked out before the final research product is composed. Nor am I suggesting that our interpretations must be validated by our research collaborators. For when we do interpretations, we bring our own knowledge, experience, and concerns to our material, and the result, we hope, is a richer, more textured understanding of its meaning.

I am suggesting that we might open up the exchange of ideas so that we do not simply gather data on others to fit into our own paradigms once we are safely ensconced in our university libraries ready to do interpretation. By extending the conversation we initiate while collecting oral narratives to the later stage of interpretation, we might more sensitively negotiate issues of interpretive authority in our research.

Quite possibly, this modification of standard practice would reveal new ways of understanding our materials to both research partners. At the very least, it would allow us to discern more clearly when we speak in unison and when we disagree. Finally, it would restructure the traditionally unidirectional flow of information out from source to scholar to academic audience by identifying our field collaborators as an important first audience for our work. Lest we, as feminist scholars, unreflectively appropriate the words of our mothers for our own uses, we must attend to the multiple and sometimes conflicting meanings generated by our framing or contextualizing of their oral narratives in new ways.

Postscript

On July 8, 1989, after a ten-month absence, I visited Beatrice and gave her a copy of the present version of this paper for her final comments. She took it to her study, read it, and then the two of us went through it together, paragraph by paragraph. At this juncture she allowed that much of what I had said was "very true," though she had not thought about the events of her life in this way before. After a long and fruitful discussion, we approached the central issue of feminism. She explained, once again, that feminism was not a movement that she had identified with or even heard of in her youth. Nevertheless, she declared that if I meant by feminist a person who believed that a woman has the right to live her life the way she wants to regardless of what society has to say about it, then she guessed she was a feminist.

Thus, the fieldwork exchange had become, in the end, a true exchange. I had learned a great deal from Beatrice, and she had also learned something from me. Yet I would emphasize that Bea's understanding and acceptance of feminism was not something that I could bestow upon her, as I had initially and somewhat naively attempted to do. It was achieved through the process of interpretive conflict and discussion, emerging as each of us granted the other interpretive space and stretched to understand the other's perspective. While Bea's identification with feminism is not crucial to my argument, it stands as a testament to the new possibilities for understanding that arise when we re-envision the fieldwork exchange.

Notes

The material upon which this essay is based was originally presented in a paper entitled "Horsing Around with the Frame: Narrative, Memory, and Performance," presented at the *Fifth Annual Graduate Women's Studies Conference* at Rutgers University, New Brunswick, New Jersey, in March 1988.

1. Richard Bauman, *Verbal Art as Performance* (Prospect Heights, Ill.: Waveland, 1977), p. 11. For a discussion of the differences between narrated and narrative events, see Richard Bauman's introduction in his *Story, Performance, and Event* (New York: Cambridge University Press, 1986).

2. The present "crisis of interpretation" is due to a number of historical factors. Most broadly, the political challenge to Western imperialism has weakened Western claims to authority in many other areas of cultural exchange. Members of groups that have traditionally formed the subject of ethnographic research have recently appeared in university departments and offered penetrating critiques of the biases in previous research. "Native" peoples at home have gained new access to recording equipment and are now constructing self-representations without the intervention of the "foreign" scholar. For a discussion of new experiments in ethnographic texts, see James Clifford and George E. Marcus, eds., *Writing Culture: The Poetics and Politics of Ethnography* (Berkeley, Calif.: University of California Press, 1986), and George E. Marcus and Michael M.J. Fischer, *Anthropology as Cultural Critique: An Experimental Moment in the Human Sciences* (Chicago: University of Chicago Press, 1986).

3. For a discussion of the sexist bias in folklore scholarship generally, see Marta Weigle, "Women as Verbal Artists: Reclaiming the Daughters of Enheduanna," *Frontiers* 3, no. 3 (1978): 1–9.

4. The racetrack narrative I present here forms part of an extended taping session I conducted with my grandmother during a three-day visit to her home in December 1986. A transcription of the full version of Beatrice's narrative appears in my article "Horsing Around with the Frame: The Negotiation of Meaning in Women's Verbal Performance," *Praxis* (Spring 1990): 83–107.

5. This remark occurred in a narrative that immediately preceded the racetrack narrative in our taped conversation.

6. In the conversation following the narrative, Bea mentions another race at Topsham that she attended years later where "none of the horses looked like much of anything" to her. Significantly, Topsham does *not* provide the material for a narrative, but is mentioned in passing as a contrast to the race we are considering here.

7. If one considers the conversation surrounding the narrative, it is interesting that this story forms one of a series of humorous anecdotes about Maine characters, mostly older men, known for their intransigence and willful refusal to modify idiosyncratic (my grandparents would add, idiotic) behaviors despite appeals to their reason or better selves by the victimized dependent family or community members. However, in most of my grandparents' stories of this type, the suffering younger characters must resort to clever subterfuge in order to induce their elders to change. *This* story, in contrast, represents a youthful victory in an open and publicly declared contest, the tactics of subterfuge being relegated to minor characters, helper figures, both on the course and in the stand.

8. This and the following information was related to me during the same three-day period of taping, but it does not form the immediate context of conversation for the racetrack narrative.

9. In her later letter to me, Beatrice explained that Hod Buzzel "didn't represent me as he should have; he didn't do a damn thing for me, except try to sell me out to the Besses." (The Besses were the wealthy farming family of Beatrice's first husband.)

10. One of my original purposes in presenting this narrative was to challenge the notion that women are passive victims of patriarchal oppression. Without denying the constraints of socially reified gender ideologies on women's expressiveness, it seems important to recognize women's active role in constructing their own identities and, in the process, transforming social ideals. Beverly Stoeltje discusses the dialectic between individual behavior, changing environments, and ideals of womanhood in " 'A Helpmate for Man Indeed': The Image of the Frontier Woman," in *Women and Folklore: Images and Genres,* ed. Claire R. Farrer (Prospect Heights, Ill.: Waveland Press, 1975), pp. 25–41.

11. Victor Turner views performances as reflexive occasions set aside for the collective or individual presentation of the self to the self in "Images and Reflections: Ritual Drama, Carnival, Film and Spectacle in Cultural Performance," in his *The Anthropology of Performance* (New York: The Performing Arts Journal Publications, 1987), pp. 121–32. For a discussion of how personal narratives are tools for making sense of our lives, see Barbara Myerhoff, "Life History among the Elderly: Performance, Visibility and Remembering" in *A Crack in the Mirror: Reflexive Perspectives in Anthropology,* ed. Jay Ruby (Philadelphia: University of Pennsylvania Press, 1982), pp. 99–117.

12. In several lengthy postessay discussions, Beatrice, my grandfather Frank, and I discussed both the story and what happened to it during the process of transmission. After hearing the revised version (in which my grandmother's comments were included), Frank stated that he had learned to see features of the society in which he grew up that he had never really been aware of before. Beatrice was less enthusiastic about my alternative reading, but agreed that my perspective was thought-provoking. For her, the more general issue of how stories are transformed with each new telling was the most interesting point of the essay, and she expressed a desire to continue working on projects of the same type.

13. Equally serious is the tendency to discount as vestiges of false consciousness attitudes or behaviors that do not fit into our own vision of feminist practice. In a cogent critique of this tendency in feminist research, Rachelle Saltzman demonstrates how women who use sexist-male jokes within their own gender group see this activity as an expropriation for use rather than an acceptance of a belittled female identity, in "Folklore, Feminism and the Folk: Whose Lore is it?" *Journal of American Folklore* 100 (1987): 548–67.

14. Quotation from a letter written to Beatrice's second husband, Frank Hanson, 6 August 1944.

5

Narrative Structures, Social Models, and Symbolic Representation in the Life Story

Marie-Françoise Chanfrault-Duchet

To the memory of Marie G., who died in December 1988

The life-story approach has, in recent years, come to be seen as a successful medium for collecting women's words, that is, for reaching a social "group" that does not often speak on the social stage, or, more precisely, whose discourse has not, until recently, been perceived as legitimate. But the women's words collected by way of the life story are neither mere gossip nor words that can be treated as a set of information providing direct access to women's mentality. In this essay, women's words are viewed as embedded in a narrative—that is, in a specific scheme that makes sense.

On the basis of a narrow definition of the life story, I shall propose an interpretive model focusing, on the one hand, on the analysis of narrative and textual structures and, on the other, on the socio-symbolic contents these structures bring into play. After a brief comparative study of two life stories that I personally collected, with two women who had similar life courses but produced very different narratives, I shall argue for the importance of such an analysis in understanding women's oral history as a feminist methodology.

The Narrative of a Social Self

Since some confusion exists in oral history among the different products of an interview, it is important at the outset to define the life story accurately as both an object and a genre. Drawing on my past work, I define the life story through two features: (1) the specifically narrative and "literary" nature of the object produced in a dialogue; and (2) the social nature of the self dramatized in the narrative.[1]

The narrative dimension refers to the fact that the life story aims, by means of a coherent and global process, to account for the whole of the informant's life experience until the moment of the interview. This means that the narrative encompasses not only the temporal and causal organization of facts and events considered significant, but also the value judgments that make sense of this particular life experience. In turn, such a view implies that the most crucial information resides not in the answers given to specific questions, but rather in the narrative organization itself. The life story represents a meaning system complete unto itself, i.e., it is a text. Such a definition, moreover, excludes interviews based on questionnaires, even if only "semi-structured" ones, as well as reports on specific events or stages of life, even when told in the first person.

The second feature of my definition deals with the social nature of the self dramatized in the narrative. This dimension is directly dependent on the institutional framework of the interaction. In most cases, the historian who asks for an autobiographical narrative has been, in effect, commissioned by an institution, as occurs with academic research. In this respect the university world represents an arm of a society that wants to collect information about its components, its different processes, and its past. As a result, when oral historians first formulate their requests, they do not establish a genuine inter-subjective relation. As commissioned by society, they do not ask for a narrative focused upon the inner self, but rather for an accurate narrative focused upon the social self viewed in relation to its past.

From the perspective of a feminist methodology, this situation draws partic-ular attention to the fact that, in women's life stories, the social self does not merely occupy a place within the social order; rather, its place is overdeter-mined by the status of woman. This means that women's life stories, unlike men's, deal not only with the relation between the self and the social sphere, but also, and above all, with woman's condition and with the collective repre-sentations of woman as they have been shaped by the society with which the woman being interviewed must deal.

Toward an Interpretive Model

The definition given above implies that if we are not to miss the richness of the collected material, we must construct a specific interpretive model able to take into account the narrative and textual dimension, the social context, the symbolic representations brought into play, and, finally, the relations among these diverse elements. I have outlined in an earlier essay[2] the problems of analyzing life stories from the point of view of sociology, and shall now simply take up the main lines of my general argument in order to emphasize the specific questions raised by the processing of narrative data in the field of oral history. Some years ago, R. J. Grele[3] pointed out the interdisciplinary paths that could be utilized in the analysis of material collected in oral history. Few practitioners, however, have followed his lead; most have preferred, instead, to borrow their methodological tools from only one discipline, sociology, and have concentrated on content analysis. In fact, the two techniques most frequently utilized aim at overcoming and reducing the excess of information with which the oral historian has to cope. On the basis of a confusion with the curriculum vitae—an object that becomes the focus of T. Abel's theory, through the notion of the "biogram"[4]—the life story is reduced to a summary, which makes it possible to compare the life courses of members of a particular social group. This technique, however, misses essential information provided by the narrative. The second technique attempts to deconstruct the narrative, to restore information that, however significant for historians, has lost the meaning it originally had within the narrative context.[5] As the discussion of my two examples will show, facts and events take their meaning from the narrative structure in which they are embedded.

Techniques such as those discussed above ultimately miss what F. Ferrarotti calls the "heuristic potential"[6] of the life-story approach and reduce the collected material to the function of mere illustration of the thesis defended by the historian. Given that life stories, as N. K. Denzin has argued,[7] demand a hermeneutic approach rather than the use of techniques borrowed from the "positive" sciences, my work emphasizes the narrative and textual analysis of the material as a means of approaching the socio-symbolic contents brought into play in the narrative. I shall therefore argue that in order to utilize the life story fully, oral historians must have recourse to an interdisciplinary approach that borrows its concepts and methods initially from narratology and textual analysis.

From Narrative Structures to Socio-Symbolic Information

When the collected material is sufficiently elaborated to be considered a real narrative (i.e., when it does not consist only of answers to the historian's questions),[8] it reveals the existence of a form that can be identified through specific features and that corresponds to a particular discursive and literary genre: the life story.

In fact, when one makes the effort to examine the form and not only the content of the collected material, refrains can be heard on the tape, and recurrences—relations among facts, events, and comments—can be discerned in the transcript. These elements come to shape the meaning system that governs and informs the life story. I shall attempt to demonstrate how this works, while highlighting the relations between formal features and socio-symbolic information.

Key Phrases

Refrains most often appear by way of an assertion such as: "It was natural," or "We were obliged to," "I did not want to, but what could I do?," "We had to," "I refused," etc. The phrase catches the attention of the listener-reader by the regularity of its recurrence. Far from being a manifestation of rambling talk, these refrains arise on the surface of the text as formal markers that accent the narrative. I shall refer to them as "key phrases." They aim to define a type of relation between the self and the social sphere, that is, the community (which contributed to the formation of the self), and, more broadly, the society as a whole. The key phrase, then, expresses the harmony, the indifference, the ambiguity, the conflict, and so on, existing between self and society.

Within the framework of the female life story, such phrases aim to express the image of the self the interviewee intends to provide, as viewed through the distance between, or conformity to, the image of woman that is in current use in her family circle or social group, on the one hand, and the hegemonic social model, on the other.

Key Patterns

The surface recurrences are articulated with formal recurrences that, on the deeper level of narrative, appear in the narrator's anecdotes. I shall refer to these formal recurrences as the "key pattern" of the narrative structure. Aiming to dramatize the self, this pattern reproduces throughout the narrative a recognizable matrix of behavior that imposes a coherence on the speaker's life experience, the coherence of the self. This pattern most often deals with the reproduction or transgression of the hegemonic social model, i.e., the dominant model that finds its way into social groups beyond the specific social model available to each group. Speakers, in fact, attempt to express—in narrative terms—their relation to social models. In their anecdotes, they picture themselves confronted with a dominant model and always actualizing the same pattern of behavior: identification, acceptance or at least compromise, and so on, on the one hand; defiance, refusal, exclusion, and so on, on the other.

The Narrative Model

A careful analysis of the narrative, based on this key pattern, allows the historian to identify one or, as is usually the case, several narrative models. These are borrowed from literary forms disseminated in social discourse through oral tradition, written literature, and television series. I call these the epic, the romanesque (from the French *roman,* novel), and the picaresque models.[9] The epic model reveals an identification with the values of the community; the romanesque model expresses "the quest for authentic values in a degraded world,"[10] and the picaresque model reflects an ironic and satirical position in relation to hegemonic values. All three models, then, are manifestations of a particular quest for values, a quest that contributes to the dynamics of the narrative and gives an axis of meaning and coherence to the life experience and to the self.

Since the female life story, as mentioned earlier, is overdetermined by woman's status, the romanesque model (as dramatized, for example, in Balzac's character Rastignac) tends to impose itself on women who, for the most part, wish to escape the female condition in the form in which it is at the moment socially dictated. But it must be emphasized that this model rarely occurs alone: it is almost always linked to features associated with other models.

The importance of these narrative models for the historian lies in the fact that they convey a particular vision of history. Although there is a risk here of excessive simplification, it could be said that the epic model refers to a vision in which the subject melds with the community, which, in its values, is beyond change; the romanesque model dramatizes a vision in which the subject views the possibilities of change through the notions of "progress" and individual challenge; and the picaresque model elaborates a vision in which change is confronted through a questioning of the dominant social values.

The Use of Myths

On a deeper level, the level at which the narrative exists as a closed meaning system, the life story brings myths into play. I am here referring not to mythical tales from the oral tradition, which may find their way into the narrative as "inlays" inasmuch as the speaker fades as a subject in the narrative and instead tells solely the history of the community through events and heroes held as significant by the collective memory. Rather, I am now referring to those features that may be identified through markers such as stereotyped images, gestures, attitudes, behaviors, or simply the connotations of particular words. The organization of these markers relates to myths that refer to the collective memory, the imaginary and unconscious, and thus to symbolic universes—for every society, every culture, builds its particular semiological systems for mapping and deciphering the world.

Thus the myths at play in a given narrative, which express systems of representation, can be viewed as particular mediations (for they correspond to shared knowledge) allowing speakers to communicate—in social terms— the meaning they want to give to their experience. Inasmuch as these myths refer to symbolic systems, to ideological and axiological frameworks, they reveal speakers' value-judgments of their life experience.

These myths are organized around two axes: one refers to collective history, the other to the individual's history. The collective myths might, for example, concern the Golden Age, the Lost Paradise, the Ideal City, the Exemplary Strike, the Revolution, and so on. Within the female life story, which is over-determined, these myths incorporate socio-symbolic images of Mother and of Woman: the generatrix Mater, the foster Mother, the bad Mother, the exemplary Spouse, the Girl who went astray, the Prostitute, etc. As for the individual myths, which I shall refer to as the "foundation myths of the self," these are dramatized by one or several anecdotes related by the subject as central to the process of individuation; in this sense they portray "primal scenes." But since they represent the core of the narrative's singularity, it is difficult to take them out of context and turn them into a list. Instead, they will be discussed below in the context of my two examples.

These two axes of myth do not work in isolation. The articulation between them contributes to producing the tension in the narrative between self and society, making it possible for the speaker to present herself or himself as a social actor, that is, as a subject involved in history.

The Task of the Historian

The different formal features of the narrative shape a system of meaning determining the particular worldview that the interviewees claim as their own in its singularity, but that the historian must analyze and place back in its larger context.

The text produced in the interaction is in fact nothing other than the narrative answer given by the speaker to the demand formulated by the oral historian and overdetermined by the field of research. The task of the historian is, then, on the basis of a precise description of the structural features at work in the narrative, to outline and analyze the complex social problematic that the interviewee has developed in the life story. In other words, narrative data is converted into information of a sort relevant for the discipline of history, and this is achieved by focusing on the vision of history, the social models, and the symbolic representations at play in the narrative.

Within the framework of women's oral history, this means that the historian has to bring out the link, as presented in the narrative, between the speaker's ego and women's status and image. This concerns women's history (or its possibility, as viewed by the interviewee) and the individual's history, on the one hand, and, on the other, the relations (presented as the basis of the self) of the assumed self-image to the different images of woman made available by social models and symbolic representations. On this level, the theoretical framework could be Althusser's notion of ideology as a system constituting the individual as subject, and his discussion of "ideological state apparatuses" as the medium of this process.[11] These notions could be reconsidered so as to help highlight the different ways in which women receive and interpret the social models of femaleness produced and controlled by institutions such as the family, the church, etc.

Marie and Germaine: A Similar Life Course, Two Different Narratives

The comparative analysis of two life stories I collected between 1984 and 1987 provides a demonstration of the interpretive model I am proposing. Given the limits of this essay, only the main lines of the analysis can be drawn here.

These two life stories belong to a larger corpus of interviews dealing with women's perceptions of the changes in woman's condition since World War I. But the biographies of my two informants reshaped this problematic, so that it came to focus on two main features: (1) the status of wife of a seasonal migrant worker (which implied the woman's responsibility, as she acted in her husband's absence as both father and mother, for the home and family that were left behind), and (2) the migration to town (my two informants left the countryside for good after World War II). The research specifically concerned the evaluation of the role played by these women's aspirations in the couple's eventual decision to emigrate to the city.

Marie G. (born in 1902) and Germaine F. (born in 1910) present life courses that are similar in many respects. Natives of Creuse, an economically poor region in the center of France, they both faced difficult childhoods; Marie had seven brothers and sisters, Germaine was the daughter of an unmarried mother. Both had to leave school prematurely to work as maids until they got married. Marie married a neighbor; Germaine, pregnant at the age of seventeen, was obliged, against her will, to marry the child's father. Marie and Germaine both became the spouses of Creusois bricklayers and had children (Marie had three; Germaine, two). They suffered the age-old fate of women such as themselves: to provide for the family's needs, Creusois men have pursued work as bricklayers throughout France all year long, leaving their women behind and returning only for the harvest. Unlike Marie, Germaine once tried to follow her husband, but, pregnant for the second time, she returned to her village.

The Second World War increased their difficulties: with their husbands mobilized, the women now had to provide for the family's needs. Germaine did the washing for the women of her village for five years, until her husband came back from captivity. As for Marie, she hired herself out as a dayworker on a farm. When her husband, now demobilized, joined the Resistance, Marie, in addition to her own work, took charge of arranging for provisions for the refugees who had settled in her village.

After the war, Marie and Germaine left the countryside and "emigrated" to Orléans, where they rejoined their husbands—Germaine in 1946, Marie in 1948. Although from different villages, they were both integrated into the émigré Creusois community and settled in miserable housing in converted brothels on the Rue des Juifs, in a district that was once the Jewish ghetto. Since their husbands' wages were too low to provide for the family's needs, they worked as maids and as seasonal workers in a chocolate factory. Retired and widowed, each lived alone, at the time of the interview, in a district they did not want to leave. They saw each other frequently. They both refused to go back to Creuse, although they wished to be buried there. Marie died in 1988, at the age of 86.

If content analysis highlights the analogy between the two life courses (an analogy dependent on social overdetermination), the narrative approach and its elaboration make it possible to demonstrate that the meaning given to this life experience is different in each narrative. In fact, these two life stories convey two different visions of history and two different modes of relating to female identity.

Two Modes of Relating to Society

Identifying and analyzing the key phrase makes it possible for the historian to sketch the type of relation each subject has to her or his society.

In Marie's narrative, the key phrase is, in French, *c'était obligé,* a colloquial expression that has to be translated into English as "one was obliged to." Literal French versions of the turns of phrase "one was obliged to" (French: *on était obligé*) or "we were obliged to" (French: *nous étions obligés*) are indeed very often found in narratives, but Marie does not use these expressions, which include personal pronouns. Instead, she uses an impersonal subject (the demonstrative pronoun: it), so as not to appear in this statement as a grammatical subject, i.e., as a social actor identifying with or accepting an order that she acknowledges but rejects; thus, in the narrative, she establishes a distance between the self and social models, models that she presents as *external* constraints. The key phrase *c'était obligé,* which punctuates her narrative, thus aims to express the conflictual nature of Marie's relationship with her society.

In Germaine's narrative, the key phrase that often opens or concludes anecdotes and descriptions is "I did not want to . . . but what could I do?" To explain this expression, we must go back to the tape and to the performance of the interview. Between the two parts of this sentence, a silence or sometimes a sigh can be heard on the tape. And during the interview, whenever she pronounced this phrase, Germaine made a gesture with her hand that expressed something like the idea of fate. Germaine's first movement is to refuse the social order and especially the female role as dictated by tradition in Creuse, but in a second movement she states that she accepted it nonetheless. This key phrase thus conveys the ambiguity of her relation to society, as she searches for a compromise between self and social constraints.

Two Patterns of Behavior

The individual's relation to society is apparent in the narrative through the key pattern, which aims to present a specific pattern of behavior as central for the self. On the basis of an interpretation of this pattern, it is then possible for the historian to determine the perspective that organizes the narrator's life experience, giving it its characteristic coherence and meaning.

In Marie's narrative, according to the axis pointed to by the key phrase, the pattern that makes it possible to map and decipher her life experience has to do with defiance. This pattern aims to dramatize, in narrative terms, the conflict between self and society. In her anecdotes, Marie always depicts herself obeying social constraints and the social order, but simultaneously shows—through attitudes, gestures, or even words—her deep refusal. The abhorred mistress (employer)—who in Marie's narrative embodies this social order—is most of the time the addressee of this defiance, as is apparent in these two passages:

> When my mistress saw my sons going to Mass, on Sunday, she looked at them in such a way. . . . I said to myself: "It bothers you, Madam, but that's how it is!" She felt that they were too smart for a domestic's sons. . . . Poor kids, they got only one suit of clothes a year!

> One evening, I was coming back with the cows. We had fifteen cows! It was something! I had a stick, for keeping them on the path. [The mistress] was there on the edge of the path. And then she said to me: "Don't beat the cows! Don't frighten them!" I answered her . . . I had my stick in my hand, like this . . . "One must not beat the wrong beast, of course!" I don't know if she understood. She was the cow! She was an old cow!

In Germaine's story, on the other hand, a double pattern, of transgression compensated for by expiation, is at play; this makes it possible for her to view her life experience in terms of a painful compromise inducing Germaine to withdraw into herself. By this pattern she tends to explain how she transgressed both the social rules dictating sexual behavior (which condemned her to marry her child's father) and the Creusois tradition, as apparent initially when she refused to let her husband leave, thus relegating the family to a lower economic and social position:

> My husband was always away. He was in the north when we married, then in Paris, then . . . But I didn't like it. I didn't want such a life. Once he was about to leave, but I would not let him go. I cried, I yelled . . . so that he stayed in the village. He worked in the street, cleaning gutters.

A second occasion on which she transgressed the Creusois tradition was when she left the countryside to follow her husband to Orléans, a decision she expiated by settling in a converted brothel, a location that in her view constituted a form of exclusion from society (we shall return to this point later).

Two Visions of History

Analysis of the narrative models at play—as evidenced by the key pattern—makes it possible to account for the vision of history that governs and informs each life story.

In Marie's narrative, the quest for values takes the shape of the quest of the romanesque hero, ready to face the world alone. But it is overdetermined by two other models. Through the picaresque model, Marie, with a hint of sarcasm, initially mocks herself, thereby expressing the fact that she has been unable to master the world, to change it on her own, or even to achieve her own desires. But the most important model here is the epic one, reflecting the values of the Revolution of 1789 and of human rights (which, in Marie's view, were ignored in the social life of Creuse).[12]

Marie presents herself as an epic hero—a hero, not a heroine, because she goes beyond the female dimension. Indeed, when viewing her life as a struggle, she means not a gender struggle but rather a class struggle. Thus, she depicts herself in her anecdotes as "Madame G.":

> Then the mayor came to my house and said to me, "Madame G., I've brought you some refugees. Do your best to provide for them."

Here, Marie claims not merely her status as a woman, but also and above all a social status that she wants to have acknowledged. She is not "Marie, the maid," but "Madame G.," Citizen of the Republic as defined by its values: Liberty, Equality, Fraternity. Identifying herself with these values, Marie dramatizes them in the evocation of her everyday life during the war: defying her Pétainist employers and the authorities' interdiction, she secretly collects food to share among the inhabitants of the village and the refugees, thus becoming foster mother of the community.

The vision of history that informs Marie's narrative presents change as the result of a collective revolt to conquer rights; this point will be confirmed by the analysis of myths, below.

In Germaine's narrative, the quest for values likewise takes the shape of the quest of the romanesque hero. The narrative model is embedded in a compensatory dynamics: the heroine's yearnings aim to fill the lacks experienced in childhood in the arenas of social, material, and emotional security. Germaine intends to defy the Creusois female model by conforming to an urban one: that of the unified family. She achieved her goal a first time when working for employers who played the role of a family, a second time when she followed her husband to the north, and, finally, when the whole family settled in Orléans. But the romanesque model is here subverted by an inverted epic model: that of the curse incurred through personal failings or what Germaine views as "sins." Thus, whenever she evokes the achievement of her aspirations, she mentions that it results from a transgression that she must forever expiate (on the model of her mother's "sin").

She is expelled from "paradise" a first time by her pregnancy out of wedlock:

> I felt at home with these people. Really. Well-nourished, first of all, and they had central heating. . . . And they were so nice! I was the maid, sure, but in a certain sense I was their daughter, too. And then, unfortunately, I met . . . I

mean . . . I went astray, as people say. And then I had to marry the father and leave them.

The second expulsion results from a new pregnancy, one she did not want, that compels her to go back to her mother. Finally, she experiences moving into a converted brothel in Orléans as the expiation of all her transgressions.

The vision of history that informs Germaine's narrative presents change as the result of individual conquests for which a heavy price must be paid. Since she does not take complete responsibility for what she views as transgressions, the social model of woman hovers over her as a constraint and functions as a superego. In her view, the female condition remains a status ever burdened by a curse.

Two Views of the World

The vision of history conveyed in the life story is overdetermined by the worldview expressed through myths that refer to symbolic universes.

The collective myths at play in Marie's narrative refer to the stereotyped images of rural riots, of "jacqueries," but also of the Revolution of 1789. By means of metaphors and connotations, the anecdotes dramatize situations in which Marie, for example, threatens her mistress with her stick or evokes, through the slaughtering of cattle, her mistress's beheading. Marie dramatizes revolutionary violence: in her narrative, as in *The Marseillaise,* she sheds an impure blood that waters the furrows reconquered by the peasants.[13]

These collective myths are directly articulated with the "foundation myths of the self" through which Marie, by means of symbolic references, depicts herself as socially oppressed. For example, she brings up the fact that once her mistress stole bread from her:

> One evening, my mistress came into my house to steal my bread. It was dark. I was in the garden with the children and I saw her coming out with something in her hand. I used to store the bread in a box in the kitchen, so that I always had bread left for the children. She had taken my bread! The box was empty. We had to eat the soup without any bread! The next day she said to me: "I borrowed some bread from your kitchen." She never gave it back! She had stolen my bread, the bread for my children!

And, on another occasion, Marie's mistress stole firebrands:

> One day my mistress had gone to Mass and on her way back she entered my house while I was away. We had open fires in fireplaces at that time. . . . So, she had taken a shovel full of brands to light her own fire and she had put out my fire. A neighbor came over and told me: "Madame G, you should shout 'Stop thief!' She came into your house when nobody was there! She has no right to come in!"

Marie is not merely mentioning objects here. Implicitly presenting bread and fire as symbolic elements—in this case, as life principles—Marie conveys through narrative means the idea that her mistress hinders her from living.

Thus, the worldview that organizes Marie's narrative corresponds, on the social level, to the class struggle. And, using Althusser's definitions, it is possible to highlight the ideological dimension of the narrative and demonstrate that this view does not refer to an ideology conveyed by adherence to a political party (Marie was never a militant of the French Communist Party, for example), but to the Creusois oral tradition, on the one hand, and to the history lessons heard at school, on the other—an analysis I have elaborated elsewhere.[14]

As for Germaine's narrative, although it evokes a similar life course and numerous identical features, it articulates a pacific quest: for abundance, comfort, and human warmth. These elements crystallize in a foundation myth: that of the "Palais de Dame Tartine" (the title of a French nursery rhyme that depicts the Land of Milk and Honey). Through this myth, Germaine rejects the image of the Creusois farm woman alone with her children in a cold house, and identifies herself instead with the image of a contented woman who gives and receives food in a comfortable and warm setting. This image, which tends to coincide with the idealized one of the urban woman in her modern kitchen, more or less consciously motivated Germaine's emigration.

The myth of the "Palais de Dame Tartine" functions to define Germaine's first position as maid to her "foster-parent/employers" and then her work in the chocolate factory. Moreover, whereas Marie briefly depicts the factory as a place where she was oppressed by forewomen, and where she stole chocolate in order to resell it and thus restore social justice, Germaine, by contrast, describes the factory, through the symbolism of food and human warmth, as the place where she was able to achieve her aspirations. She depicts herself there as satisfied, socially acknowledged, and happy to manufacture sweets that she could eat in the warmth of the ovens with her new family: the women with whom she worked.

But, unlike Marie's narrative, the foundation myth is here threatened by collective myths that are borrowed not from national history but from the Judeo-Christian cultural stock. Thus, whereas Marie does not evoke the episode of the converted brothel as significant, Germaine makes it the key sequence in her narrative, in which selected collective myths emerge that refer to the socio-symbolic image of woman in its predominant occidental form.

Since she lives on the Rue des Juifs (and even there is excluded and pointed to), in a red house with big nails on the door (the stigmata of her "sins"), Germaine portrays herself as condemned to be locked up in the (former) brothel (in French, *maison close*):

> When we arrived and I saw all those red houses there, with nails and wickets on the doors, I asked my husband, "Where have you brought us? Tell me !"

He said: "You wanted to follow, so follow!" Because he would have liked to leave me behind in the country with the children! But I was fed up with that life. . . . So it was the Rue des Juifs or nothing!

The worldview given to us through these symbolic patterns is a feminine one referring to the historical and cultural image of woman. Unlike Marie, Germaine does not succeed in going beyond this image. She reveals herself, in the narrative, as imprisoned by an image of woman that compels her to redeem through expiation her own, and her mother's, original "sin." This dimension is conveyed through another myth: that of the purifying water. In fact, although Germaine, as a maid, has done mostly housecleaning, she persists in her narrative to speak of "washing," as if she could symbolically wash away her "sins."

Although Germaine is not a practicing Catholic, what is presented here is indeed a religious worldview, one that she attempts to offer up to us in a pathetic way as the view with which she is compelled to identify herself yet which, deep in her heart, she rejects.

Implications of This Analysis

The life story approach in oral history makes it possible to go beyond the preconstructed discourses and "surface assertions" collected through survey research. It highlights the complexity, the ambiguities, and even the contradictions of the relations between the subject and the world, the past, and the social and ideological image of woman—i.e., how women live, internalize, and more or less consciously interpret their status. Thus, the life story approach has to be considered as a methodological tool providing access to a body of information that is more detailed, more discerning, but also far more complex to analyze than that collected through other approaches. The "narrative data" of the life story demand a type of analysis that, as I hope I have demonstrated, is of great relevance for the study of history.

What does this mean for women's oral history? In terms of a feminist methodology, the principal aim is not merely to report on or testify to women's lives past and present, although this has its own legitimacy and utility,[15] nor to collect women's words, record female voices, or induce women to speak in a performance that often resembles a celebration. The aim, furthermore, is not to lead the speaker, by means of her narrative, to a clear consciousness of her relationship to the social image of woman, past and present. Notwithstanding R. J Grele's suggestion,[16] the construction of narrative is here not a conscious process but a preconscious one,[17] which means that any such consciousness-raising, if attempted, must take place *after* the analysis. But it would be illusory and ethically questionable to use the narrative as a means to transform the conceptions held by the interviewed woman. This would be to practice a kind of savage social therapy.

The aim of the life story as a feminist methodology lies elsewhere. It has to do with the attempt to understand and analyze, in the present and for the future, that which women, as social actors involved in history, have held as significant in the past, and how they have perceived and interpreted this through the ideological blueprints that they have internalized. The life-story approach has to be viewed as a scientific one using precise notions, theories, and processes whose results have to be returned to the society that commissioned the research and, indirectly, to women themselves, *to be utilized*. This means that to realize the full potential of this methodology, we must acknowledge not only that the life story conveys information about facts and events (which, however, could be obtained by other means), but also that these facts and events are inscribed in patterns that relate to their socio-symbolic contents and that reflect, through complex processes, women's mentalities. These patterns, as I have argued, can be mapped and deciphered.

Careful analysis of life stories, emphasizing the socio-symbolic contents, should, then, enable us to create a typology. This process could be carried out by comparing the results of analyses in the fields of history, sociology, ethnography, and so on. In this way a kind of "meta-analysis" could be done, based on the work of practitioners in different fields, and with it we could think through the modes of female identification, these being understood as the different ways in which women confront the institutions that reproduce and dictate social models of and for women.

But this process must not remain within the narrow confines of academic research and academic knowledge. It must have social repercussions as well. The interpretive model I have proposed can help women, as social actors, to bypass the traditional networks of identification and forge new models of femaleness. Thus the social image of woman—and therefore her condition—can evolve and ultimately be transformed.

Notes

1. See, for example, Marie-Françoise Chanfrault-Duchet, "Le pouvoir de la parole dans le récit de vie," in *Pouvoir et Société,* Proceedings of the Fifth International Oral History Conference, Barcelona, Spain, 1985, pp. 119–26; idem, "Dire les relations sociales en milieu rural: la mémoire collective comme medium," contribution to the Sixth International Oral History Conference: Myth and History, Oxford, England, 1987, to be published in M. Villanova, ed., *Historia y Fuente Oral* 4 (Barcelona, Spain, 1990); and idem, "Le système interactionnel du récit de vie oral," *Sociétés* 18: *Histoires de vie, Récits de vie* (May 1988): 26–31.
2. See M.-F. Chanfrault-Duchet, "Le récit de vie: données ou texte?" *Cahiers de recherche sociologique* 5, no. 2 (Autumn 1987): 10–28.
3. Ronald J. Grele, *Envelopes of Sound: The Art of Oral History* (Chicago: Precedent Publishing, 1975). See especially the essay entitled "A Surmisable Variety: Interdisciplinarity and Oral Testimony," pp. 157–95.
4. Theodore Abel, "The Nature and Use of Biograms," *American Journal of Sociology* 53 (1947): 111–18.

5. This approach is frequently referred to in the *Oral History Review,* and in *Life Stories— Récits de vie,* an English-French journal edited by Paul Thompson and Daniel Bertaux (Colchester, G.B.: University of Essex).

6. Franco Ferrarotti, *Histoire et histoires de vie: La méthode biographique dans les sciences sociales.* (Paris: Méridiens-Klincksieck, 1983), p. 56.

7. Norman K. Denzin, "Alternative Theories of Biographical Analysis," article published in the I.S.A.-R.C. 38 *Biography and Society Newsletter* 4 (May 1985): 5–13, and "Interpreting the Life of Ordinary People," article published in *Life Stories—Récits de vie* 2 (1986): 6–20.

8. The production of a *real narrative* implies that the interviewee has been able to organize the information conveyed by her (his) memory in such a way as to give it coherence and significance. In other words, the interaction scheme governing the exchange has succeeded in overdetermining the communication frame of the interview, so that a narrative relationship has been established in which the set of questions and answers refers not to the questionnaire prepared by the historian but to the narrative itself. It must, however, be acknowledged that this situation remains rather rare in material collected by oral historians. When the interview does not reach the narrative and textual level, the failure may be viewed as the result of (1) the interviewer's attitude: s/he remains imprisoned in the framework of the positive sciences and refuses, more or less consciously, to become a real narratee in the interaction; (2) the interviewee's inability to present herself (himself) as the subject and hero of a narrative aiming to communicate an experience laden with signification; and/or (3) the attitude of both members of the interaction. On these issues, see my articles cited above and Grele, *Envelopes of Sound.*

9. In a different context, Kevin Murray points out the importance of narrative models such as romance, comedy, and tragedy for the field of biography. See Kevin Murray, "Drama and Narrative in the Construction of Identities," in *Texts of Identity,* ed. John Shotter and Kenneth J. Gergen (London: Sage Publications, 1989), pp. 176–205.

10. Definition proposed by Lucien Goldmann, *Pour une sociologie du roman* (Paris: Gallimard, 1964), p. 23.

11. Louis Althusser, "Ideology and Ideological State Apparatuses," in *Lenin and Philosophy and Other Essays,* trans. Ben Brewster (New York: Monthly Review Press, 1971).

12. See Chanfrault-Duchet, "Dire les relations sociales en milieu rural."

13. See the refrain of the French national anthem, *La Marseillaise:*
    Take up arms, citizens!
    Form your battalions!
    Let's march! Let's march!
    Let an impure blood
    Water our furrows!

14. See Chanfrault-Duchet, "Dire les relations sociales en milieu rural."

15. See, for example, Adeline Geaudrolet, *Amours paysannes: Travaux et déboires sexuels d'une femme de la campagne,* ed. Isabelle Laurent and Michel Valière (Paris: Stock, 1980), a life story reporting on moral constraints and sexual behavior in Poitou in the first half of this century. See also two French bestsellers: Emilie Carles, *Une soupe aux herbes sauvages* (Paris: J.-Cl. Simoën, 1977), the life story of a schoolmistress in Savoy; and Serge Grafteaux, *La Mère Denis: L'histoire de la lavandière la plus célèbre de France* (Paris: Delarge, 1976), the life story of an old washerwoman from Normandy who became a celebrity advertising washing machines and a sort of myth embodying, in the France of the 1970s, the exemplary rural woman of the past. Adeline Geaudrolet's life story was published with a commentary stressing facts, traditions, and morals in the past in Poitou but without a real analysis of the narrative, thereby missing the socio-symbolic content. As for the two other narratives cited above, they are presented without any commentary and seem to exploit a new literary field: the story of the "ordinary woman" as a contemporary romanesque heroine.

16. Grele, *Envelopes of Sound,* p. 215.
17. See Chanfrault-Duchet, "Orality, Chorality of the Life Story," a contribution to the Twelfth World Congress of Sociology, Research Committee 38: Madrid, July 1990, to be published in Régine Robin, ed., *Orality and Narrativity of the Life Story* (1992).

6

A Third World Woman's Text: Between the Politics of Criticism and Cultural Politics

Claudia Salazar

> Those anthropologists,
> sociologists and historians who
> poke at our bones,
> our social systems
> and past events
> try to tell us
> who we are.
>
> When we don't read
> their book
> they think we are
> rejecting
> our heritage.
>
> So, they feel
> sorry for us
> and write
> more books
> for themselves.
> —Lenore Keeshig-Tobias, "Those Anthropologists"

In the "Third World," women's autobiographical texts have become an integral part of the intellectual, ideological, political, and even armed struggle waged by oppressed and silenced people against the powers of repressive states and hegemonic groups. However, the attempt to place some of these testimonies and autobiographies into larger contexts (both material and textual) of relations of power is not without problems. In Western intellectual circles, for instance, there is a tendency to romanticize these voices and to conceive of the subjects of the testimonials unproblematically—as always resisting their oppression through various strategies of textual subversion. While there is undoubtedly a certain truth to the quality of textual "play" in such readings of testimonial narratives, we must be careful not to overlook the "worldliness" of the struggles waged through and in discursive spaces.

My purpose in this essay is to address this tension. I will begin by doing a close reading of one of one of the best-known oral histories of a Latin American woman, attempting to analyze the ways in which this oral history directly and indirectly addresses and transgresses socially coded binary oppositions such as text/context, personal/political, public/private, knower/known, orality/literacy, and high culture/low culture. In the second part of this paper I shall attend to some of the complexities of production and translation of "cultural otherness" by discussing important criticisms of ethnographic writing practices that have emerged in recent political/theoretical debates in anthropology. Finally, I will conclude by bringing the text to its larger material context through some reflections on the politics of women's oral histories.

Reading *Rigoberta:* Textual Transgressions

I . . . Rigoberta Menchú can be broadly characterized as the testimony of a Guatemalan Indian organizer fighting for her people's civil rights. Defying the literary conventions of this genre, Rigoberta's testimony is not, however, the recounting of the personal itinerary of an illiterate woman living in a particular historical context. Rather, as the opening lines of the text reveal, this woman's story *is* her people's history of oppression:

> My name is Rigoberta Menchú. I am twenty three years old. This is my testimony. I didn't learn it from a book and I didn't learn it alone. I'd like to stress that it's not *my* life, it's also the testimony of my people. It's hard for me to remember everything that's happened to me in my life since there have been many very bad times but, yes, moments of joy as well. The important thing is that what has happened to me has happened to many other people too: My story is the story of all poor Guatemalans. My personal experience is the reality of a whole people [emphasis in the original].[1]

As pointed out by Barbara Harlow,[2] Third World women's autobiographies or oral histories of resistance tend to allocate the private and domestic experiences of the narrator to the historical and public context of their social-political struggles. Rigoberta's way of introducing herself can be read as a rhetorical attempt to restructure the relationship between the personal and political through a subversion of Western individualism. The "I" that initially positions Rigoberta as the author of the text or the subject of meaning is soon undermined by her own recognition that her life story contains the life histories of all poor, oppressed Guatemalans. According to Doris Sommer, however, it would be a mistake to see Rigoberta's "I" as a metaphor for a plural subject. Rather, Rigoberta's first voice expresses "a metonymic relationship of shared experience and consciousness."[3] Acknowledging the differences between individuals in the community, she sees herself simply as *part* of that community. This effacement of Rigoberta's self, together with her denial that her experiences are somehow unique or extraordinary, remains, throughout the text, her strongest political statement:

> I'd like to say here that I wasn't the only important one. I was part of a family, just like all my brothers and sisters. The whole community was important. (p. 117)

The private/public dichotomy becomes blurred in a textual move that is politically motivated. For Antonio Gramsci, experience (conceptualized as a complex set of habits, dispositions, cultural inventories) is perhaps the most crucial site of political struggle over meaning.[4] As Rigoberta says:

> Well, I started thinking about my childhood, and I came to the conclusion that I hadn't had a childhood at all. I was never a child. . . . I hadn't had enough food to grow properly, I had nothing. I asked myself: "How is this possible?" I compared it to the life of the children of rich people I'd seen. How they ate. Even their dogs. They even taught their dogs only to recognize their masters and reject the maids. All these things were jumbled up in my mind, I couldn't separate my ideas. That's when I began making friends from other villages in Uspantán. I asked them: "What do you eat? How do you make your breakfast? What do you have for lunch? What do you eat for supper?" And yes, they said the same: "Well, in the morning we eat *tortillas* with salt and a little *pinol*. At midday, our mother brings *tortillas* and any plants she finds in the fields." "At night we eat *tortillas* with chile," they said, "chile with *tortillas,* and then we go to sleep." So everything was the same. It gave me a lot to think about. *I have to tell you that I didn't learn my politics at school. I just tried to turn my own experience into something which was common to a whole people.* I was also very happy when I realized that it wasn't just my problem; that I wasn't the only little girl to have worried about not wanting to grow up. We were all worried about the harsh life awaiting us. (pp. 117–18, my emphasis)

By reconstructing and re-articulating her own and other women's experience of hunger, exploitation, humiliation, and pain as a political discourse, and by placing it "within the minutiae of everyday life,"[5] Rigoberta connects the personal—i.e., "the cultural, the material-historical, the linguistic-conceptual network which forms a person"[6] or social identity—to the larger context of social relations. Shared oppression is thus apprehended as the result of a particular and systematic unequal distribution of economic, political, and cultural power. Moreover, in an attempt to recover and politicize the materiality and historicity of the everyday (the personal), Rigoberta also reframes the relationship between theory and practice. As she tells us, remembering her mother:

> [She] couldn't express her views about political things; but she was very politicized through her work and thought that we should learn to be women, but women who were useful to the community. (p. 218) . . .
>
> [She], of course, didn't know all these ideas, all these theories about the position of women. But she knew all these things in practice. (p. 221)

Feminist claims that the political is also personal find its expression in this Quiché Indian woman's "discovery" that her self cannot be defined in individual terms but rather only as a collective self engaged in a common struggle. In this way, Rigoberta's symbolic re-appropriation of the private as public enables her to construct a new social identity for the Indians, an identity that, in turn, becomes a ground for political struggle. In fact, according to Barbara Harlow, as the Spanish title to Rigoberta's testimony suggests (*My name is Rigoberta Menchú and this is how my consciousness was born*), the story documents the awakening in her of a political consciousness followed by redefinitions of her gender, ethnic, and linguistic identities.[7] However, and as I will elaborate later in this essay, it is important to stress that Rigoberta is not simply doing away with the private/public opposition. On the contrary, she is recoding it in such a way that the private becomes public and vice versa. What is public for Rigoberta is her private life—thus she tells about *her* story. What is private, on the other hand, are the ways of her community, which she keeps hidden from us.

In *Conditions and Limits of Autobiography,* George Gusdorf argues that one of the "metaphysical preconditions" of autobiographies is consciousness of self (one's agency) in shaping the historical field.[8] According to the Popular Memory Group, the attempt to recover an agent's (conceptualized here as a collective) intervention in history—its forms of consciousness as it "struggle[s] for a better world"—is what characterizes the project of popular historiography.[9] Rigoberta's testimony can be seen as one example of such struggles over forms of consciousness (memory): an understanding of her people's oppressive material conditions becomes the means by which to transform popular consciousness, or, in a more Gramscian language, commonsense beliefs. Because these beliefs are always ideological—the result of hegemonic articulations to win the support of subordinate groups—to act upon this terrain is Rigoberta's first revolutionary tactic:

> I remember that it was my job to explain to the children of the community that our situation had nothing to do with fate but was something which had been imposed on us. I taught them that they had to defend themselves against it, to defend our parents' rights. I'd have a sort of political chat with the children, although I wasn't very clear about our situation politically. But my experiences told me what I needed. I didn't need speeches or courses or anything like that. I didn't have to read books because my experiences were born of suffering. I, who'd hardly had a pair of shoes by the time I was fifteen. Shoes: they protected feet against the heat and the stones. But, all the same, I didn't really know what to do with them. (p. 120)

Together with the shaping of her political consciousness, Rigoberta also realizes that language and cultural representations are important weapons in fighting oppression at both the ideological and the material levels. As Barbara Harlow points out, a recognition that ethnic and linguistic barriers contribute to keep the various Indian groups divided and politically ineffective in terms of confrontational action and grassroots resistance added more force to this woman's determination to learn the language of the oppressor[10]: "They've always said, poor Indians they can't speak, so many speak for them. That's why I decided to learn Spanish" (p. 157).

To speak Spanish meant for Rigoberta to be able to represent her people and to undermine the authoritative discursive constructions of the Indians made by others (by intellectuals, those who "only sign paper"). It also forced her to cross a cultural terrain mapped by several and often antagonistic codes. As Doris Sommer explains, because oppressed groups occupy a marginal position vis-à-vis existing discourses, they must be able to speak in many codes, for no single discourse will be sufficient to their revolutionary situation. The best strategy, then, is to decenter language, to make the discursive field unstable and flexible. As Sommer states:

> The trick is not to identify the correct discourse and to defend it with dogmatic heroism but to combine, recombine, and continue to adjust the constellation of discourses in ways that will respond to a changeable reality.[11]

The question of representation, then, is seen as a crucial moment in the Indian's quest for political and cultural empowerment.

As a response to specific material, intellectual, and social circumstances in many Third World countries—circumstances such as brutal repression and censorship—Rigoberta's and other women's personal narratives (as shown by Barbara Harlow) are playing an important role in intervening and inscribing in the historical record the political-cultural trajectories and collective memories of raped/silenced/erased ethnic "minorities."[12] Their struggles also become symbolic struggles in their attempt to forge a new social identity for themselves vis-à-vis their representation in dominant Western discourses. However, due to the unequal distribution of cultural capital, the Indians gain access to Western discursive spaces primarily via an investigator who collects their voices and studies their ways of life.

In the next section, I want to examine the distribution of power and knowledge between the ethnographer (an anthropologist, oral historian, traveler, etc.) and the "native" by analyzing Rigoberta's text in terms of the complexities of production and translation of "cultural otherness." In doing so, I will be alluding to some themes that have emerged in recent political/theoretical critiques of ethnography. More specifically, I will argue that Rigoberta's text in fact represents the intersection of many and contradictory discourses/voices, including that of the ethnographer.

Rereading *Rigoberta:* Poststructuralist Considerations

The Making and Unmaking of Texts

Recent debates in poststructuralism and ethnography, appearing, for example, in the collection of essays *Writing Culture,* have begun both to problematize, in a radical way, traditional interpretive practices of cultural representation and to challenge the authoritative, transparent voice of its texts.[13] Insofar as cultural descriptions are always textually mediated, it is argued, literary processes such as metaphor, figuration, and narrative "affect the ways cultural phenomena are registered, from the first jotted 'observations,' to the completed book, to the ways these configurations 'make sense' in determined acts of reading."[14] A focus on textual practices will reveal that cultural representation cannot offer more than a "constructed understanding of the constructed native's constructed point of view."[15] Moreover, "post-ethnographers" contend that to the extent that culture is not a static object of analysis but a multiplicity of negotiated realities within historically contextualized (and contested) communicative processes, their object of representation is not a world or a people, but fleeting "instances of discourse."[16] Thus, in trying to give a new orientation to the ethnographic field, such critics, first of all, openly acknowledge that its truths are "inherently partial, committed and incomplete,"[17] and, second, attempt to create a text within a context of collaborative story-making that celebrates discourse over text, dialogue over monologue, polyphony over monophonic authority.

In light of these debates, I would like to argue, following Clifford, that to analyze thoroughly a life-history text, the critic should engage not only in the act of interpretation but in a deconstruction of the text's relations of production as well.[18]

Crapanzano, in a review essay on life histories, notes a number of problems that ethnographers face when collecting and transcribing testimonial accounts. Given that the life history consists of a transformation from an oral production to a written product, the other is always speaking through the world of the text.[19] As Ricoeur has pointed out, once discourse becomes text, its openness as dialogue, together with its evocative and performative elements, are lost: the punctuation and silences of speech are gone; the events in the life of the narrator often follow a chronological pattern, partly induced by the questions the ethnographer poses; it is edited, translated, and, finally, given a title.[20] In sum, living becomes easily organized into a continuous narrative, and "events are embalmed in the structure of the text."[21] In what follows, I will use Rigoberta's testimony to illustrate how the voice of the "natives" is placed/displaced by a number of problematic editorial interventions.

Struggle over Voice: Rigoberta *as a Specific Case*

As an example of the interventionist practices carried out by editors of testimonies, we need only turn to Elisabeth Burgos-Debray's introduction to *I . . . Rigoberta Menchú.* There, Burgos-Debray briefly discusses her work in textualizing Rigoberta's story while making concessions to both the requirements of autobiography and the demands of the book market. As she tells us, after the transcription of the tapes,

I established a thematic card index, first identifying the major themes (father, mother, childhood, education) and then those which occurred most frequently (work, relations with *ladinos,* linguistic problems). This was to provide the basis of the division of the material into chapters. I soon reached the decision to give the manuscript the form of a monologue. . . . By doing so I became what I really was: Rigoberta's listener. I allowed her to speak and then became her instrument, her double by allowing her to make the transition from the spoken to the written word. I have to admit that this decision made my task more difficult, as I had to insert linking passages if the manuscript was to read like a monologue, like one continuous narrative. I then divided it into chapters organized around the themes I had already identified. I followed my original chronological outline, even though our conversations had not done so, so as to make the text more accessible to the reader. . . . Once the manuscript was in its final form, I was able to cut a number of points that are repeated in more than one chapter. Some of the repetitions have been left as they stand as they lead in to other themes. That's simply Rigoberta's way of talking.[22]

What is revealing in the above passage is how deeply transformed Rigoberta's way of talking becomes, despite the editor's naive beliefs to the contrary. One could argue that Burgos-Debray's editorial orchestration in the highly problematic role of Rigoberta's transparent "double" produces a text that is more informative of her and her readers' own interpretive agendas than of Rigoberta's, hence transforming the latter's testimony into a Western logocentric mirror that reflects our own assumptions about what a narrative by someone like Rigoberta *should* look like. The demands of the market with respect to books on women's oral histories further overdetermine the shape and content of Rigoberta's narrative. These demands, in turn, force the editor into real struggles regarding whether to comply with them or to resist them, and the decisions made are often followed by doubts. Burgos-Debray confesses this ethical dilemma when doing the editing:

It was pointed out to me that placing the chapter dealing with birth ceremonies at the beginning of the book might bore the reader. I was also advised simply to cut it or include it in an appendix. I ignored all these suggestions. *Perhaps I was wrong,* in that the reader might find it somewhat off-putting. But I could not leave it out, simply out of respect for Rigoberta [my emphasis].[23]

I . . . Rigoberta Menchú also brings to the foreground important elements of interventionist strategy that work to facilitate consumption of otherness. The autobiographical individualistic "I" followed by a pregnant pause (conveyed by the ellipsis) that introduces Rigoberta's name conjures up an image of an exotic, mystified Other (source of fascination and fear) at the same time that it situates the reader at a comfortable, safe distance. Such textual violence becomes apparent when a close reading of the structure of address in Rigoberta's testimony reveals her insistent and continuous subversions of the Western notion of a coherent self. Hence, through multiple layers of editorial orchestrations a second, and even third, voice is brought to bear upon Rigoberta's muted speech.[24] Rigoberta's story is insured a place in bookstore shelves for the "facile consumption of cultural Otherness."[25]

A recurring problem undergirding the project of collecting oral histories, one identified by Crapanzano, refers to the power difference between the ethnographer and the Other that structures the interview context in the form of an interplay between demand and desire.[26] The demand that the Other expose itself (vulnerability) and the desire to know (power/knowledge) that guides the ethnographic project inevitably create a hierarchical field of forces that opens up different discursive positions for its participants to take up. Analyzing the social relations of research, the Popular Memory Group writes:

> The practice of research actually conforms to (and may in practice deepen) social divisions which are also relations of power and of inequality. It is cultural power that is at stake here, of course, rather than economic power or political coercion . . . It is . . . *he* [the oral historian] . . . that produces the final account, *he* . . . that provides the dominant interpretation, *he* that judges what is true and not true, reliable or inauthentic. It is his name that appears on the publication. It is he who receives a portion of the royalties and almost all the "cultural capital" involved in authorship. It is his *amour propre* as "creator" that is served here. It is his professional standing among his peers that is enhanced in the case of "success." In all this, at best, the first constructors of historical accounts—the "sources" themselves—are left untouched, unchanged by the whole process except in what they have given up—the telling. They do not participate, or only indirectly, in the educational work which produces the final account.[27]

When we finally glimpse the backstage production of oral histories, another play unfolds before our eyes: monologues are unveiled beneath the semblance of dialogues, and authorial control is found lurking underneath promises of a free interplay of voices. In the place of a feminist vision of an emancipatory project, we confront a text that is incomplete, insufficient, and lacking. It is in this context that Rigoberta's (contained) resistance to, and suspicion of, scriptural authority acquires profound meaning ("they live in nice houses and sign papers" [p. 138]). In fact, her awareness of the power relationship between intellectuals and lay people and her indictment of the former's oppressive theoretical discourses form just one instance of the many transgressions that her narrative enacts:

> There is something else we are discovering in Guatemala to do with intellectuals and illiterate people. We've learned that we haven't all got the ability of an intellectual: an intellectual is perhaps quicker and able to make finer syn-

theses. But nevertheless, others of us have perhaps the same ability for other things. Before, everyone used to think that a leader had to be someone who knew how to read, write and prepare documents. And our leaders fell into that trap for a time, and said: "I am a leader, it's my job to lead and yours to fight." Well, in every process there are certain exchanges which have to be made. That is not unusual. I think that every movement has gone through the process whereby an opportunist arrives, feels that he is worth more than the others and abuses their confidence. At one time, many of our leaders would come from the capital to see us in the *finca* [plantation] and say: "You peasants are stupid, you don't read or study." And the peasants told them: "You can go to Hell with your books. We know you don't make a revolution with books, you make it through struggle." (pp. 222–23)

In a world of persisting inequalities, when knowledge can no longer be conceptualized in neutral terms but rather as inherently enmeshed in power relations, Rigoberta, in ways similar to those of others occupying the margins, counterposes the secrets of the Indians to the quest for truth of the ethnographer. Thus, in the beginning of her testimony, she politely forewarns us that "Indians have been very careful not to disclose any details of their communities, and the community does not allow them to talk about Indian things. I too must abide by this" (p. 9). Like Zora Hurston's negroes, who offer to the white a featherbed resistance ("I'll put this play toy in his hand, and he will seize it and go away. Then I'll say my say and sing my song"),[28] Rigoberta offers truths punctuated by silences. In the closing lines of her story, she reminds us again:

. . . I'm still keeping my Indian identity a secret. I'm still keeping secret what I think no-one should know. Not even anthropologists or of intellectuals, no matter how many books they have, can find out all our secrets. (p. 247)

Rigoberta's silence here is not just a matter of keeping secrets; rather, it is in itself a tactic of resistance:

When we began to organise ourselves, we started using all the things we'd kept hidden. Our traps—nobody knew about them because they'd been kept hidden. Our opinions—whenever a priest came to our village we all kept our mouths shut. We women covered ourselves with our shawls and the men kept their heads bowed. We pretend we're not thinking of anything. But when we're all together, amongst ourselves, we discuss, we think, we give our views. What happens is that, since we've never been given the opportunity to speak, express our opinions, or have our views considered, we haven't bothered to make ourselves heard just for the fun of it. . . . This is why Indians are thought to be stupid. They can't think, they don't know anything, they say. (p. 170)

After 247 pages of testimony, the inside/outside opposition has not been dismantled but reaffirmed. Rigoberta's story may misinform as well as inform, with strategic silences confronting the violence that foregrounds the ethnographic encounter. Perhaps we can say, with Barbara Johnson, that

> there is no Universalized Other, no homogeneous us for the self to reveal itself to. Inside the chemise is the other side of the chemise: the side on which the observer can read the nature of his or her own desire to see.[29]

Amongst veiled promises of featherbed resistances by the blacks and silences by the Indians, it seems appropriate to ask ourselves, then, what is the politics of Third World women's testimonies? In the final part of this essay I will return Rigoberta's text to its material context and argue that her understanding of the discursive construction of the Indians and ladinos in terms of symbolic polarities of high and low, and her determination to transgress them at least in the cultural terrain, constitute her most subversive, as well as her most politically promising, move.

The Politics of Women's Life Histories

To debate matters of politics inevitably forces us to look back from the text to the world—to the historical field of postmodern capitalism, neocolonialism, and the international division of labor. This move is fundamental if we want to avoid the entrapments of a purely discursivist stance regarding our readings of life historical texts. For, as Lawrence Grossberg puts it, to limit our analysis to discussions of how the other is "interpellated into . . . a system of textual signifying differences" is to elide the "worldliness" quality of such texts.[30] Life-history texts are, after all, the product of an encounter between the ethnographer (a real Self) and real "others"—who cannot and must not be reduced to a discursive construction of our language. Although some of the recent critiques of ethnographic textual practices are illuminating in many aspects—as I tried to show in my reading of Rigoberta's testimony—they tend, as Paul Roth argues, to offer subversion of ethnographic authority/voice as an antidote against colonialism.[31]

To articulate a more politically effective counter-hegemonic critique of colonialism in our intellectual practices we need, *in addition to textual analysis,* to involve ourselves in the struggles of those on the other side of the international division of labor. As pointed out by Abdul JanMohamed, to acknowledge the material reality of the Other and to avoid deliberate deafness to its voice, the critic (and, in my case, the "Third World" academic) must confront the political task of making the marginal central in the development of an alternative critique coming from outside the hegemonic cultural centers. This critique would "articulate and help to bring to consciousness those elements of minority literature that oppose, subvert, or negate the power of the hegemonic culture."[32] Such a project, in turn, would undoubtedly involve both locating those sites within which the "subaltern" has been speaking (e.g., listening and collecting personal narratives) and articulating conditions of possibility (material, institutional, cultural) that open up for her speech a contestatory place in the Western discursive economy.

One of the ways of effecting political transformation, Stallybrass and White argue, is for the "low/debased" to control domains of discourse by challenging the hierarchy of sites of discourses.[33] By recounting history from "below" and revaluing her people's experiences as a legitimate source of knowledge, Rigoberta's text may be interpreted as an attempt to invert the polarities, among others, between orality/literacy, theory/practice, and expert knowledge/common knowledge. The role of the sympathetic anthropologist who listens, in turn, may be conceptualized as attempting to make visible the interconnections of the reciprocal productions between high and low culture. However, her work must not cease here, for the unequal distribution of practices and skills will, at best, remain intact; the larger relations of subordination are not changed by such minority criticism. At worst, it may just reproduce the conditions of impossibility that silence the "other." To play a more transformative role in the formation of a sense of history that takes into account the larger context of collective struggles, the ethnographer/critic must work on democratizing the social relations of research. One suggestion, posited by the Popular Memory Group, is to develop forms of community-based writing and publishing that challenge the unequal distribution of cultural capital and skills. Another alternative is to develop connections between socialist and feminist theory and popular movements, so as to make cultural power accessible to all those involved in different struggles.[34]

Controlling sites of discourse, inverting the hierarchy of discourses, and negating/subverting the hierarchy itself are what Jonathan Dollimore identifies as "stages in a *process* of resistance."[35] For its success this process also requires what Benita Parry calls "a cartography of imperialist ideology" as well as "a conception of the native as historical subject and agent of an oppositional discourse."[36] For, after all, Rigoberta speaks, and speaks loudly. Against the backdrop of capitalist relations of exploitation and internal colonialism, Rigoberta's testimony, despite its constructed character, its many voices, its mystifying editorial elements, stands as an important part of a counter-hegemonic strategy of intervention in the political Imaginary of dominant cultures. Her text is radically altering the cultural model that governs the practices of domination and subordination. It also uses the symbolic resources of Western liberal-democratic discourse to construct a new political identity—that of citizen—for the Indians:

> In our community we are all equal. We all have to help one another and share the little we have between us. There is no superior and inferior. But we realized that in Guatemala there was something superior and something inferior and that *we* were the inferior. The *ladinos* behave like a superior race.

> Apparently there was a time when the *ladinos* used to think we weren't people at all, but a sort of animal. All this became clear to me (p. 123, emphasis in the original)

In fact, by demanding democratic rights for the Indians, Rigoberta's text, together with other similar social movements by other ethnic groups in Latin America, are beginning to articulate an emancipatory vision of political community that has hitherto been located by theorists such as Ernesto Laclau and Chantal Mouffe exclusively in the liberal-democratic tradition of Western societies.[37]

Finally, we can say that resistance narratives such as Rigoberta's are emerging as a way of opening a discursive space for "subjected knowledges" to (re)write the historical record. These autobiographies, as de Certeau would put it, are the most vivid testimonies of a peasant and Indian revolution "taking shape in fact and consciousness" and they are already "stirring the silent depths of Latin America."[38] As Rigoberta states:

> I was travelling all over the place. I went down to the coast. I had some political work to do, organising the people there, and at the same time getting them to understand me by telling them about my past, what had happened to me in my life, the reasons for the pain we suffer, and the causes of poverty. When you know there is work to do and you are responsible, you try and do it as well as you can because you have suffered so much and you don't want your people to go on suffering. I knew all the contacts, and I had many jobs to do; carrying papers, machines, leaflets, texts for teaching people. . . . And I was anxious to do my best, to learn a lot. Because I believe my life has taught me many things but human beings are also made to learn many more. (p. 162)

Notes

I am grateful to Keya Ganguly for her invaluable comments on earlier drafts of this essay. I would like also to thank Larry Grossberg and Cheris Kramarae for their important suggestions and friendly support. Lenore Keeshig-Tobias's poem originally appeared in *Fireweed: A Feminist Quarterly* 22 (Winter 1986), p. 108.

1. Elisabeth Burgos-Debray, ed., *I . . . Rigoberta Menchú: An Indian Woman in Guatemala,* trans. Ann Wright (London: Verso, 1984). All further references to this work will be to this edition and will be included in the text. As noted later, the English title is significantly different from the original Spanish. [Note: Although the title page of the book does not include ellipses, the cover does. The ellipses will be used hereafter only when their inclusion is essential for meaning.]
2. Barbara Harlow, *Resistance Literature* (New York: Methuen, 1987).
3. Doris Sommer, " 'Not Just a Personal Story': Women's *Testimonios* and the Plural Self," in *Life/Lines: Theorizing Women's Autobiography,* ed. Bella Brodzki and Celeste Schenck (Ithaca, N. Y.: Cornell University Press, 1988), pp. 107–30.

4. Antonio Gramsci, *Selections from the Prison Notebooks,* trans. Quintin Hoare and Geoffrey Nowell-Smith (New York: International Publishers, 1971).

5. Liz Stanley and Sue Wise, " 'Back into the Personal' or: Our Attempt to Construct 'Feminist Research' " in *Theories of Women's Studies,* ed. Gloria Bowles and Renate Duelli Klein (Boston: Routledge and Kegan Paul, 1983), pp. 192–209.

6. Michael Ryan, *Marxism and Deconstruction: A Critical Articulation* (Baltimore, Md.: Johns Hopkins University Press, 1982).

7. Harlow, *Resistance Literature.*

8. George Gusdorf, "Conditions and Limits of Autobiography," in *Autobiography: Essays Theoretical and Critical* ed. James Olney (Princeton, N.J.: Princeton University Press, 1980), pp. 28–48.

9. Popular Memory Group, "Popular Memory: Theory, Politics, Method," in *Making Histories: Studies in History-Writing and Politics,* ed. Richard Johnson, Gregor McLennan, Bill Schwarz, and David Sutton (Minneapolis, Minn.: University of Minnesota Press, 1982), pp. 205–52.

10. Harlow, *Resistance Literature.*

11. Sommer, " 'Not Just a Personal Story,' " p. 121.

12. Harlow, *Resistance Literature.* It should be observed that it is somewhat ironic to call the Indians in Guatemala "minorities" when they constitute approximately eighty percent of the total population. In this essay I am using "minority," as well as concepts of "margin" and "center," as political categories.

13. James Clifford and George Marcus, eds., *Writing Culture: The Poetics and Politics of Ethnography* (Berkeley, Calif.: University of California Press, 1986).

14. James Clifford, "Introduction: Partial Truths," in Clifford and Marcus, eds., *Writing Culture,* p. 4.

15. Vincent Crapanzano, "Hermes' Dilemma: The Masking of Subversion in Ethnographic Description," in Clifford and Marcus, eds., *Writing Culture,* p. 74.

16. Clifford, "Introduction: Partial Truths," p.14.

17. Ibid., p.7.

18. Ibid.

19. Vincent Crapanzano, "Life Histories," *American Anthropologist* 86, no.4 (1984): 953–60.

20. Paul Ricoeur, "The Model of the Text: Meaningful Action Considered as a Text," in *Interpretive Social Science: A Reader,* ed. Paul Rabinow and William M. Sullivan (Berkeley, Calif.: University of California Press, 1979), pp. 73–101.

21. James Clifford, "On Ethnographic Allegory," in Clifford and Marcus, eds., *Writing Culture,* p. 106.

22. Elisabeth Burgos-Debray, "Introduction," in idem, ed., *I . . . Rigoberta Menchú* p. xx.

23. Ibid.

24. Debates on the epistemological difference between oral and textual are far from settled. By redefining what is to be taken as a text (i.e., from logocentric representation to the inclusion of all systems of signification), Derrideans erase the difference between speech and writing. Insofar as writing *(écriture)* is conceived as a "broad range of marks, spatial articulations, gestures, and other inscriptions at work in human cultures" (Clifford, "On Ethnographic Allegory," p. 117), it is argued that writing precedes speech. Hence, any culture possessing an oral literature and/or ritual practices is already writing itself. See Stephan Tyler, "On Being out of Words," *Cultural Anthropology* 1, no. 2: 131–136, and Arnold Krupat, "Poststructuralism and Oral Literature," in *Recovering the Word: Essays on Native American Literature,* ed. B. Swann and A. Krupat (Berkeley, Calif.: University of California Press, 1987), pp. 113–28, for responses to, and further appraisals of, the discourses on orality and literacy.

25. John Dorst, "Rereading *Mules and Men:* Toward the Death of the Ethnographer," *Cultural Anthropology* 2, no. 3 (1987): 305–18.

26. Crapanzano, "Life Histories."

27. Popular Memory Group, "Popular Memory: Theory, Politics, Method," p. 220 (emphasis in original). Although the Popular Memory Group, by using the masculine pronoun in this passage, is referring exclusively to the male academic, I would like to suggest that having *him* replaced by a female academic would not necessarily alter the unequal relations of research. However, as the various oral histories collected by women who follow an explicit feminist agenda indicate, they do reflect a greater sensitivity to, as well as a willingness to change, such power imbalances. For examples of writings dealing with these issues, see Daphne Patai (*Brazilian Women Speak: Contemporary Life Stories* [New Brunswick, N.J.: Rutgers University Press, 1988]) and the extensive work of Margaret Randall with Latin American women.

28. Zora Neale Hurston, *Mules and Men,* (Bloomington, Ind.: Indiana University Press, 1935), pp. 4–5.

29. Barbara Johnson, "Thresholds of Difference: Structures of Address in Zora Neale Hurston," in *Race, Writing, and Difference* ed. Henry Louis Gates, Jr. (Chicago: University of Chicago Press, 1986), pp. 317–28.

30. Lawrence Grossberg, "Wandering Audiences and Nomadic Critics," *Cultural Studies* 2, no.3 (1988): 377–91.

31. Paul A. Roth, "Ethnography Without Tears," *Current Anthropology* 30, no, 5 (1989): 555–69.

32. Abdul JanMohamed, "Humanism and Minority Literature: Towards a Definition of a Counter-Hegemonic Discourse," *Boundary 2,* 13, no.1 (1984): 281–99.

33. Peter Stallybrass and Allon White, *The Politics and Poetics of Transgression* (New York: Cornell University Press, 1986).

34. Popular Memory Group, "Popular Memory: Theory, Politics, Method."

35. Jonathan Dollimore, "The Dominant and the Deviant: A Violent Dialectic," *Critical Quarterly* 28, nos. 1–2 (1986): 179–92 (emphasis in original).

36. Benita Parry, "Problems in Current Theories of Colonial Discourse," *Oxford Literary Review* 9, nos. 1–2 (1987): 27–58.

37. See, for instance, Ernesto Laclau and Chantal Mouffe, *Hegemony and Socialist Stragegy* (London: Verso, 1985).

38. Michel de Certeau, *Heterologies: Discourses on the Other* (Minneapolis, Minn.: University of Minnesota Press, 1986).

III

Dilemmas and Contradictions

In rejecting traditional practices rooted in assumptions of the researcher's separateness, neutrality, and distance from the subjects of research, feminist discourse has emphasized, instead, commonality, empathy, and sisterhood. These assumptions also often collide with the realities of actual research situations, as many of the practices and perspectives proposed by feminists generate, in their turn, new problems, ironically undermining the very principles they were designed to embody.

Judith Stacey, a sociologist, describes one version of this dilemma. Dissatisfied with the abstract character of most research in historical sociology, she turned to the ethnographic method, which, like oral history, promised to be interactive and empowering—hence nonexploitative of the research "subject." Stacey's essay, while arguing for feminists' use of critical ethnographic methods, discusses her growing awareness that delusions of alliance, far more than problems of separateness, threaten the development of appropriate feminist models.

The warning sounded by Stacey is reinforced by anthropologist Sondra Hale's self-critical account of her experience interviewing a leading Sudanese activist. It is not only narrators but also researchers who are at risk of developing inappropriate expectations that can result in feelings of having been abused by the research process. Hale describes how, in the course of discarding traditional research methodologies, she developed a set of expectations that eventually led to a sense of betrayal, disappointment, and anger. Her essay is remarkable for its frank exploration of issues rarely addressed.

Whereas Stacey's and Hale's critiques focus primarily on the relationship between individual interviewer and narrator, Daphne Patai emphasizes the material disparities that typically separate researcher and researched. These systemic inequalities determine who gets to do research on whom. Naming our research "feminist," Patai argues, in no way resolves the ethical dilemmas growing out of such structural disparities.

These three essays, by their intense focus on uncomfortable and problematic aspects of the research process, foreground matters too often ignored or downplayed even by feminist researchers. In this way they serve to dramatize the dangers of an uncritical embrace of feminist discourse.

7

Can There Be a Feminist Ethnography?

Judith Stacey

Most feminist researchers, committed, at a minimum, to redressing the sexist imbalances of masculinist scholarship, appear to select their research projects on substantive grounds. Personal interests and skills meld, often mysteriously, with collective feminist concerns to determine a particular topic of research, which, in turn, appears to guide the research methods employed in its service. Indeed, in such a fashion, I chose my dissertation project, a study of patriarchy and revolution in China designed to address major theoretical questions about Western feminism and socialism. The nature of this subject, compounded by limitations in my training, necessitated that I adopt a macro-structural, abstract approach based almost exclusively on library research. And, as a consequence, its textual product offered an analysis of socialism and patriarchy that, as several reviewers justly complained, left out stories about actual women or patriarchs.[1] My dissatisfaction with that kind of research process and outcome led me to privilege methodological considerations over substantive interests when I selected my next research project, a fieldwork study of family and gender relationships in California's Silicon Valley. I was eager for a "hands on," face-to-face research experience, which I also believed was more compatible with feminist principles.

When I began my Silicon Valley research project in 1984, the dominant conception of feminist research among feminist scholars advocated research on, by, and especially *for* women, and drew sharp distinctions between the goals and methods of mainstream and feminist scholarship.[2] Feminist scholars had begun to express widespread disenchantment with the dualisms, abstractions, and detachment of positivism, and were rejecting the separations between subject and object, thought and feeling, knower and known, and political and personal—as well as the reflections of these separations in the arbitrary boundaries of traditional academic disciplines. Instead, most feminist scholars advocated an integrative, transdisciplinary approach to knowledge, one that would ground theory contextually in the concrete realm of women's everyday lives. The "actual experience and language of women is the central agenda for feminist social science and scholarship," asserted Barbara Du Bois in 1983, in an essay advocating "Passionate Scholarship," and only a minority of feminist scholars ventured to dissent.[3] Indeed, feminists were celebrating "feeling, belief, and experientially based knowledge," which draw upon such traditionally feminine capacities as intuition, empathy, and relationship.[4] Discussions of feminist methodology generally assaulted the hierarchical, exploitative relations of conventional research, urging feminist researchers to seek instead an egalitarian research process characterized by authenticity, reciprocity, and intersubjectivity between the researcher and her "subjects."[5] "A methodology that allows for women studying women in an interactive process," Renate Duelli Klein argued, "will end the exploitation of women as research objects."[6]

Judged by such criteria, the ethnographic method, by which I mean intensive participant-observation study that yields a synthetic cultural account, appears to be ideally suited to feminist research. That is why in "The Missing Feminist Revolution in Sociology," an essay reflecting on the limitations of feminist efforts to transform sociology, Barrie Thorne and I wondered with disappointment why so few feminist sociologists had turned to the ethnographic tradition of community studies within the discipline, a tradition that seemed to us far more compatible with feminist principles than were the more widely practiced positivist methods.[7] Many other feminist scholars shared the view that ethnography was particularly appropriate to feminist research.[8] Like a good deal of feminism, ethnography emphasized the experiential. Its approach to knowledge was contextual and interpersonal—therefore attentive, like most women, to the concrete realm of everyday reality and human agency. Moreover, because in ethnographic studies the researcher herself was the primary medium, the "instrument" of research, this method drew on those resources of empathy, connection, and concern that many feminists considered to be women's special strengths and that, they argued, should be germinal in feminist research. Ethnographic method also appeared to provide much greater respect for and power to one's research "subjects" who, some feminists proposed, could and should become full collaborators in feminist research.[9]

This, at least, is how ethnography appeared to me as I found myself unintentionally but irresistibly drawn to it in a study originally intended to be based on more conventional interview methods. An ethnographic approach seemed to resolve the "contradiction in terms" involved in interviewing women, that Ann Oakley had identified in her critique of classical sociological interview methods.[10] Oakley rejected the hierarchical, objectifying, and falsely "objective" stance of the neutral, impersonal interviewer as neither possible nor desirable, arguing that meaningful and feminist research depends instead on empathy and mutuality. And I was reassured by Shulamit Reinharz's assertion that the problems of experiential fieldwork methodology "seem minor in comparison with the quality of relations that I develop with people involved in the study and the quality of the understanding that emerges from those relations."[11]

But after two-and-one-half years of fieldwork experience, I was less sanguine about and more focused on the difficult contradictions between feminist principles and ethnographic method than on their compatibility. Hence the question in my title, which is modeled (but with a twist) on the implicit question in Oakley's "Interviewing Women: A Contradiction in Terms." The twist is that I now perceive the opposite contradiction between feminist ethics and methods than the one that Oakley discusses. I find myself wondering whether the appearance of greater respect for and equality with research subjects in the ethnographic approach masks a deeper, more dangerous form of exploitation.

There are two major areas of contradiction that I will discuss. The first involves the ethnographic research process, the second its product. Precisely because ethnographic research depends upon human relationship, engagement, and attachment, it places research subjects at grave risk of manipulation and betrayal by the ethnographer, as the following vignette from my fieldwork illustrates. One of my key informants, now a married, fundamentalist Christian, was involved in a closeted lesbian relationship at the time of her conversion. I first learned of this relationship from her spurned lesbian lover, and this only six months after working in the field. Of course, this immediately placed me in an extremely awkward situation ethically, a situation of triangulation and potential betrayal in relation to these two women and of inauthenticity toward the more secretive one. Several months later (partly, I believe, in response to her perception of my inauthenticity) this informant "came out" to me about this affair, but she asked me to respect the confidentiality of this knowledge when relating to her relatives, friends, and co-workers. Moreover, she and her rejected lover began to compete for my allegiance, sympathy, and, ultimately, for my view of their shared history.

I could give numerous other examples (such as the case of a secret of paternity, of an illicit affair, and of other illicit activities). All placed me in situations of inauthenticity, dissimilitude, and potential, perhaps inevitable, betrayal, situations that I came to understand are inherent in fieldwork research. For no matter how welcome, even enjoyable, the field-worker's presence may appear to "natives," fieldwork represents an intrusion and intervention into a system of relationships, a system of relationships that the researcher is far freer than the researched to leave. The inequality and potential treacherousness of this relationship is inescapable.

So, too, does the exploitative aspect of ethnographic process seem unavoidable. The lives, loves, and tragedies that fieldwork informants share with a researcher are ultimately data—grist for the ethnographic mill, a mill that has a truly grinding power. More times than I would have liked, this study placed me in a ghoulish and structurally conflictual relationship to personal tragedy, a feature of ethnographic process that became particularly graphic during the death of another one of my key "informants." My ethnographic role consigned me to experience this death both as friend and as researcher, and it presented me with numerous delicate, confusing dilemmas, such as whether or not, and to whom, to make a gift of the precious but potentially hurtful tapes of an oral history I had once conducted with the deceased. I was confronted as well with the discomforting awareness that as researcher I stood to benefit from this tragedy. Not only did the funeral and family grieving process serve as a further research "opportunity," the death also freed me to include more of this family's "truths" in my ethnographic account than would have been possible had the man lived. This and other fieldwork experiences forced my recognition that conflicts of interest and emotion between the ethnographer as authentic, related person (i.e., participant), and as exploiting researcher (i.e., observer) are also an inescapable feature of ethnographic method.

The second major area of contradiction between feminist principles and ethnographic method involves the dissonance between fieldwork practice and ethnographic product. Despite the aspects of intervention and exploitation I have described, ethnographic method appears to (and often does) place the researcher and her informants in a collaborative, reciprocal quest for understanding; but the research product is ultimately that of the researcher, however modified or influenced by informants. With very rare exceptions it is the researcher who narrates, who "authors" the ethnography. In the last instance, an ethnography is a written document structured primarily by a researcher's purposes, offering a researcher's interpretations, registered in a researcher's voice.[12]

In this sense, too, elements of inequality, exploitation, and even betrayal are endemic to ethnography. Perhaps even more than ethnographic process, the published ethnography represents an intervention into the lives and relationships of its subjects. As author, an ethnographer cannot (and, I believe, should not) escape tasks of interpretation, evaluation, and judgment. It is possible (and most feminists might claim it is crucial) to discuss and negotiate one's final presentation of narrative with informants, but this does not eliminate the problem of authority, and it can raise a host of new contradictions for the feminist ethnographer.[13] For example, after several years involving scores of hours of mutual reflections on the meaning of the lesbian relationship mentioned above, this "research collaborator" asked me to leave this part of her history out of my ethnographic account. What feminist ethical principles could I invoke to guide me here? Principles of respect for research subjects and for a collaborative, egalitarian research relationship demand compliance, but this forced me to collude with the homophobic silencing of lesbian experience, as well as consciously to distort what I considered to be a crucial component of the ethnographic "truth" in my study. Whatever we decided, my ethnography was forced to betray a feminist principle.

Indeed, the irony I now perceive is that ethnographic method exposes subjects to far greater danger and exploitation than do more positivist, abstract, and "masculinist" research methods. And the greater the intimacy—the greater the apparent mutuality of the researcher/researched relationship—the greater is the danger.

The account I have just given of the paradoxes of feminist ethnography is falsely innocent. I have presented my methodological/ethical quandaries the way that I first conceptualized them as a feminist researcher, innocent as I then was of relevant methodological literature by ethnographers who have long grappled with related concerns. I am no longer so innocent and ignorant, but I retained this construction to help underscore a curious fact. There has been surprisingly little cross-fertilization between the discourses of feminist epistemology and methods and those of the critical traditions within anthropology and sociology.[14] Most pertinent is the dearth of dialogue between feminist scholarship and the contemporaneous developments in the literature referred to as the "new" or "postmodern" or "poststructuralist" ethnography.[15] This is curious, because the new or postmodern ethnography is concerned with issues quite similar to those that concern feminist scholars, and, at first glance, offers a potential resolution to the feminist ethnographic paradox.[16]

Postmodern ethnography is critical and self-reflexive ethnography and has created a literature of meditation on the inherent, but often unacknowledged, hierarchical and power-laden relations of ethnographic writing.[17] Like feminist scholars, critical ethnographers tear the veil from scientific pretensions of neutral observation or description. They attempt to bring to their research an awareness that ethnographic writing is not cultural reportage, but cultural construction, and always a construction of self as well as of the other. In James Clifford's words, the "historical predicament of ethnography" is "the fact that it is always caught up in the invention, not the representation of cultures."[18] And at rare moments, critical or "postmodern" ethnographers incorporate feminist insights into their reflexive critiques. Vincent Crapanzano, for example, suggests that "interpretation has been understood as a phallic, a phallic-aggressive, a cruel and violent, a destructive act, and as a fertile, a fertilizing, a fruitful, and a creative one," and he self-consciously retains the male pronoun to refer to the ethnographer "despite his or her sexual identity, for I am writing of a stance and not of the person."[19]

As I understand it, the postmodern ethnographic solution to the anthropologist's predicament is to acknowledge fully the limitations of ethnographic process and product and to reduce their claims. Like feminists, critical ethnographers eschew a detached stance of neutral observation, and they perceive their subjects as collaborators in a project the researcher can never fully control. Moreover, they acknowledge the indispensably intrusive and unequal nature of their participation in the studied culture. Even more than most feminist scholars, I believe, critical ethnographers have been excruciatingly self-conscious about the distortions and limitations of the textual products of their studies. Here they have attempted first to acknowledge fully and own up to the interpretive authorial self, and, second, to experiment with dialogic forms of ethnographic representation that place more of the voices and perspectives of the researched into the narrative and that more authentically reflect the dissonance and particularity of the ethnographic research process.

Finally, postmodern ethnographers, influenced by deconstructionist fashions, aim only for "Partial Truths"—as James Clifford titled his introduction to a major collection of this genre:

> Ethnographic truths are thus inherently *partial* —committed and incomplete. This point is now widely asserted—and resisted at strategic points by those who fear the collapse of clear standards of verification. But once accepted and built into ethnographic art, a rigorous sense of partiality can be a source of representational tact.[20]

This reflexivity and self-critique of "postmodern" ethnographic literature parallels and has much to contribute to feminist methodological reflections. It probably unwittingly exploits some of the latter as well, as feminist social scientists have published similar reflections on matters of the self, commitment, and partiality in research.[21] At the least, the critical ethnographic literature might temper feminist celebrations of ethnographic methods with a salutary note of humility about the limitations of cross-cultural and interpersonal understanding and representation. I certainly favor much more dialogue and exchange between the two than has taken place to date.

Recently, feminist anthropologist Marilyn Strathern also noted the surprising paucity of engagement between feminism and the new ethnography and, in an important contribution to such dialogue, offered an analysis of the grounds for mutual resistance that undergird what she termed the "awkward relationship" between the two.[22] Feminism and critical anthropology, Strathern claimed, are mutually "vulnerable on the ethical grounds they hold to be so important": "each has a potential for undermining the other" because they rest upon incompatible constructions of the relationship between self and "Other."[23] Feminism, Strathern argued, presumes an antagonistic relationship to the male Other, a presumption that grounds its acute sensitivity to power inequalities and has the power to undermine those anthropological pretensions of alliance and collaboration with the Other upon which new ethnographic strategies for multiple authorship reside. Anthropology, in turn, from its cross-cultural vantage point, suggests the illusory nature of feminist pretensions of actual separation from men of their own culture.

I view the resistances somewhat differently. Feminism's keen sensitivity to structural inequalities in research and to the irreconcilability of Otherness applies primarily, I believe, to its critique of research by men, particularly to research *by* men, but *about* women. The majority of feminist claims about *feminist* ethnographic and other forms of qualitative research, however, presume that such research occurs almost exclusively woman-to-woman. Thus, feminist researchers are apt to suffer the delusion of alliance more than the delusion of separateness, and to suffer it more, I believe, than do most poststructuralist ethnographers. Recall the claims about empathy and identification between feminist researchers and the women they study, and the calls by feminist scholars for an egalitarian research process, full collaboration, and even multiple authorship with which this essay began. It strikes me that a fruitful dialogue between feminism and critical ethnography might address their complementary sensitivities and naivetés about the inherent inequalities and the possibilities for relationships in the definition, study, and representation of the Other.

While I hope to further such a dialogue, in the end, I agree with Strathern that the relationship between feminism and ethnography is unavoidably ambivalent. I am less convinced than she of the virtues of this awkwardness, but I agree that while it can be mitigated, it cannot be effaced. Even an exhaustive, mutually beneficial exchange cannot resolve the feminist ethnographer's dilemma. First, the postmodern strategy is an inadequate response to the ethical issues endemic to ethnographic process and product that I have encountered and described. It acknowledges, but does little to ameliorate, the problems of intervention, triangulation, or inherently unequal reciprocity with informants; nor can it resolve the feminist reporting quandaries. For example, acknowledging partiality and taking responsibility for authorial construction could not reduce my handling of the lesbian affair to a matter of "representational tact."

My current response to the question in my title is that, while there cannot be a fully feminist ethnography, there can be (indeed there are) ethnographies that are partially feminist, accounts of culture enhanced by the application of feminist perspectives. There also can and should be feminist research that is rigorously self-aware and therefore humble about the partiality of its ethnographic vision and its capacity to represent self and other. Moreover, even after my loss of ethnographic innocence I believe the potential benefits of "partially" feminist ethnography seem worth the serious moral costs involved.

Indeed, as Carole Joffe has suggested to me, my assault on the ethical foundations of fieldwork may have been unduly harsh—a fairer measure, perhaps, of my prior illusions about ethnographic virtue than of ethnographic vice.[24] Certainly, as she and Shulamit Reinharz assert, field-workers can and do form valuable relationships with many of those whom we study, and some of our unsolicited interventions into the lives of our informants are constructive and deeply appreciated. For example, a daughter of the informant whose death I mentioned above later consoled me on the sudden death of my own father and thanked me for having allowed her to repair her hostile relationship with her father before he died by helping her to perceive his pride in and identification with her. Often fieldwork research offers to particular research subjects practical and emotional support and a form of loving attention, of comparatively nonjudgmental acceptance, that they come to value deeply.

But then again, beneficiaries of such attention may also come to depend upon it, and this suggests another ethical quandary in fieldwork, the potential for, indeed the likelihood of, desertion by the researcher.[25] Yet rigorous self-awareness of the ethical pitfalls in the method enables one to monitor and then to mitigate some of the dangers to which ethnographers expose their informants. I conclude in this Talmudic fashion to leave the dialogue open, believing that an uneasy fusion of feminist and critical ethnographic consciousness may allow us to construct cultural accounts that, however partial and idiosyncratic, can achieve the contextuality, depth, and nuance I consider to be unattainable through less dangerous but more remote research methods.

Notes

This is a slightly revised version of an essay with the same title that appeared in *Women's Studies International Forum* 11, no. 1 (1988): 21–27. I am grateful to Gloria Bowles, Mary Frank Fox, Carole Joffe, Suad Joseph, and Barrie Thorne for their challenging and constructive responses to an early draft.

1. Judith Stacey, *Patriarchy and Socialist Revolution in China* (Berkeley and Los Angeles: University of California Press, 1983).
2. Perhaps the most comprehensive summary of the characteristic distinctions between these approaches that feminists draw appears in several pages of tables detailing contrasts between the two in Shulamit Reinharz, "Experiential Analysis: A Contribution to Feminist Research," in *Theories of Women's Studies,* ed. Gloria Bowles and Renate Duelli Klein (London: Routledge and Kegan Paul, 1983), pp. 168–72.
3. Barbara Du Bois, "Passionate Scholarship: Notes on Values, Knowing and Method in Feminist Social Science," in Bowles and Duelli Klein, eds., *Theories of Women's Studies,* p. 108.
4. Liz Stanley and Sue Wise, " 'Back into the Personal' or: Our Attempt to Construct 'Feminist Research,' " in Bowles and Duelli Klein, eds., *Theories of Women's Studies.*
5. Renate Duelli Klein, "How to Do What We Want to Do: Thoughts about Feminist Methodology"; Maria Mies, "Towards a Methodology for Feminist Research"; Du Bois, "Passionate Scholarship"; Reinharz, "Experiential Analysis"; and Stanley and Wise, " 'Back into the Personal,' " all in Bowles and Duelli Klein, eds., *Theories of Women's Studies.* Also see Stanley and Wise, *Breaking Out: Feminist Consciousness and Feminist Research* (London: Routledge and Kegan Paul, 1983).
6. Duelli Klein, "How to Do What We Want to Do," p. 95.
7. Judith Stacey and Barrie Thorne, "The Missing Feminist Revolution in Sociology," *Social Problems* 32, no. 4 (1985): 301–16.
8. Duelli Klein, "How to Do What We Want to Do"; Mies, "Towards a Methodology for Feminist Research"; Reinharz, "Experiential Analysis"; and Stanley and Wise, *Breaking Out* and " 'Back into the Personal.' "
9. Duelli Klein, "How to Do What We Want to Do"; Mies, "Towards a Methodology for Feminist Research"; Reinharz, "Experiental Analysis"; and Stanley and Wise, " 'Back into the Personal.' "
10. Ann Oakley, "Interviewing Women: A Contradiction in Terms," in *Doing Feminist Research,* ed. Helen Roberts (London: Routledge and Kegan Paul, 1981), pp. 30–61.
11. Reinharz, "Experiential Analysis," p. 185.
12. For just this reason, Duelli Klein, Mies, and, to a lesser extent, Stanley and Wise argue against this approach and for fuller collaboration between researcher and subjects, particularly for activist research in the tradition of Paulo Freire, research generated by and accountable to grassroots women's movement projects. But, as Carol Smart and Stanley and Wise recognize, such an approach places severe restraints on who and what can be studied and on what can be written, restraints that could seriously harm feminist interests. Carol Smart, "Researching Prostitution: Some Problems for Feminist Research" (unpublished paper, Institute of Psychiatry, London, n.d.).
13. In "Researching Prostitution," Carol Smart offers important reflections on the adverse implications of this ethical principle when feminists study, as she believes we should, the powerful, the agents of social control rather than their targets.
14. Critical reflections on the ethics and politics of fieldwork have a long history in both disciplines, and by now the literature is vast. For important examples from the past two

decades, see Talal Asad, *Anthropology and the Colonial Encounter* (London: Ithaca Press, 1973); Robert Emerson, *Contemporary Field Research: A Collection of Readings* (Boston: Little, Brown, 1983); Norma Haan, Robert N. Bellah, Paul Rabinow, and William M. Sullivan, eds., *Social Science as Moral Inquiry* (New York: Columbia University Press, 1983); Dell Hymes, ed., *Reinventing Anthropology* (New York: Vintage, 1974); Barrie Thorne, "Political Activist as Participant Observer: Conflicts of Commitment in a Study of the Draft Resistance Movement of the 1960s," *Symbolic Interaction* 2, no. 1 (1978): 73–88; and Barrie Thorne, "You Still Takin' Notes? Fieldwork and Problems of Informed Consent," *Social Problems* 27 (1980): 284–97.

15. James Clifford and George Marcus, eds., *Writing Culture: The Poetics and Politics of Ethnography* (Berkeley and Los Angeles: University of California Press, 1985). Howard Becker makes a similar point about the unfortunate paucity of exchange between critical traditions in sociology and those in poststructuralist anthropology in a review of a major text on new ethnography. Howard Becker, "The Writing of Science," *Contemporary Sociology* 16, no. 1 (1987): 25–27.

16. A few recent feminist essays published after I first wrote and published this paper indicate that feminists, at least, have begun to engage the postmodernist ethnographic literature. I cite these in note 21 below. Thus far there is less evidence of engagement with feminist literature by male anthropologists within the postmodernist discourse.

17. A good sampler and bibliography of postmodern ethnographic criticism appears in Clifford and Marcus, eds., *Writing Culture*. Other important texts include James Clifford, "On Ethnographic Authority," *Representations* 1, no. 2 (1983): 118–46; Vincent Crapanzano, "The Writing of Ethnography," *Dialectical Anthropology* 2 (1977): 69–73; George Marcus and Dick Cushman, "Ethnographies As Texts," *Annual Reviews of Anthropology* 11 (1982): 25–69; and George Marcus and Michael Fischer, *Anthropology as Cultural Critique* (Chicago: University of Chicago Press, 1986).

18. James Clifford, "Introduction: Partial Truths," in Clifford and Marcus, eds., *Writing Culture,* p. 2.

19. Crapanzano, "The Writing of Ethnography," p. 52.

20. Clifford, "Introduction," p. 7.

21. For examples of parallel feminist works, see Susan Krieger, "Beyond 'Subjectivity': The Use of the Self in Social Science," *Qualitative Sociology* 8, no. 4 (1985): 309–24; Mies, "Towards a Methodology for Feminist Research"; and Michelle Rosaldo, "Moral/Analytic Dilemmas Posed by the Intersection of Feminism and Social Science," in Haan, Bellah, Rabinow, and Sullivan, eds., *Social Science as Moral Inquiry;* and Stanley and Wise, *Breaking Out*. Recently, feminist anthropologists have begun to criticize the appropriation and exclusion of experimental feminist ethnographic literature by male critical ethnographers. See Deborah Gordon, "Writing Culture, Writing Feminism: The Poetics and Politics of Experimental Ethnography," *Inscriptions,* nos. 3/4 (1988): 7–24; and Frances E. Mascia-Lees, Patricia Sharpe, and Colleen Ballerino Cohen, "The Postmodernist Turn in Anthropology: Cautions from a Feminist Perspective," *Signs* 15, no. 1 (Autumn 1989): 7–33.

22. Marilyn Strathern, "An Awkward Relationship: The Case of Feminism and Anthropology," *Signs* 12, no. 2 (1987): 276–92.

23. Ibid., p. 289.

24. Carole Joffe, personal communication to author, 1986.

25. In her inimitable witty style, Arlene Kaplan Daniels discusses the etiquette of abandoning one's research subjects as well as other ethical questions in fieldwork. See her "Self-Deception and Self-Discovery in Fieldwork," *Qualitative Sociology* 6, no. 3 (1983): 195–214. I believe that the problem of desertion is more serious in long-term ethnographic studies than in those based on the more limited contact that is characteristic of other forms of qualitative research.

8

Feminist Method, Process, and Self-Criticism: Interviewing Sudanese Women

Sondra Hale

In this essay I analyze a specific methodological and ideological situation, one that is more complex than suggested by Ann Oakley's formulation that interviewing women is "a contradiction in terms."[1] This complexity is the product of layers of paradigmatic and ideological shifts. It is not feminist thought alone that has shaped my struggle as a white, Western woman dealing with such issues as cultural imperialism, ethnocentrism, loyalty, betrayal, abandonment, respect, and truth in anthropological research for and about women. The process has been a long one, the outgrowth of years of personal/ political change, and the result of many years of "fieldwork" in northern Sudan. After briefly describing this process, I analyze one recent interview/ oral history that exemplifies with particular force the contradictions, ironies, dilemmas, and problems I have encountered. I conclude this essay with some questions about the applicability of "feminist" methodology when we cross race, class, and cultural boundaries. I hope that the essay will be read, above all, both as a criticism of a monolithic approach to "feminist process" and as a criticism of my own process.

My stays in Sudan span some twenty-nine years and involve seven trips for a total of six years of residence. In my last two field-trips (1981, to investigate women's urban workforce participation; 1988, to examine the impact on women of the "Islamic Trend" government), I have been using oral history methods, which we anthropologists usually refer to as field interviews.[2] The interview process has given me considerable pause, as has anthropological fieldwork in general. The "paradoxes and expectations" of anthropological field-workers have been well-documented in the last two decades, and it is is not my goal to to critique the method of "participant observation" and the ethnocentrism inherent in the concept of "doing fieldwork among 'the other.' "[3]

In exploring these ideas, I hope to emphasize that my long-standing dilemmas have been as much ethical and personal as academic and political, just as my long contact with Sudan has been as much personal as professional.

Paradigm Shifts and the Interview Process

A number of epistemological changes have been relevant to my experience conducting interviews in Sudan. In the early 1960s, when I first went to Sudan and began to do research on social and political changes among Sudanese women, I was, unconsciously and un–self-consciously, imbued with Freudianism and inspired by liberalism and some vague egalitarianism learned from my mother. "Interviews," all of which were very informal on that first visit, took the form of conversations with hundreds of women and girls over a period of three years.[4] These were often intense friendship interactions in which I felt and was made to feel an "insider." At the time, to have suggested otherwise to me would have incurred my incredulity. Sudanese people would continuously gratify me by saying that I did not seem like an American; newspaper articles extolled my character and proclaimed me an honorary Sudanese. This seemed like a supreme validation. As an American (i.e., not British), I was spared being classified as a colonial or even an ex-colonial; and the concept "neocolonialist" was not yet commonly used. I led a charmed life in still-colonial Khartoum, embraced so completely by a women's community and given special treatment. At the time I did not fully comprehend my special and elite status, but being accorded high status was an unusual experience for someone from a working-class background, and, in my innocence at the time, I relished it. All I could think about was that I wanted to stay there forever. And a part of me wanted to *be* Sudanese.

Sudan had been independent for only five years when I arrived, and the headiness of the nationalist period was in the air. Furthermore, the Algerian revolution ended in those years, and the international left, and nationalists and leftists of the Third World, were expressing ideas about socialism, Arab socialism, the Third World, colonialism and imperialism, the Bandung Conference, and so on. Such ideas were being played out against a backdrop of one of the world's poorest countries.

By the third and fourth trips (1971–72 and 1973–75), I had completed several years of graduate work in African studies and anthropology. I was a campus activist profoundly influenced by the student and civil rights movements, and by the ideas of the old and new left. For the first time I was forced to question my right to carry out research in Sudan, to objectify people through the interview method for my own career ends, even to *be* in Sudan, and forced also to question the worth of the academic enterprise itself.

All academic fields were being scrutinized and reevaluated at the time, and African studies and anthropology were no exception. Anthropology was being referred to as "the child of imperialism" and the anthropologist as a "reluctant imperialist."[5] We were compelled to rethink the history of the field and its highly suspect raison d'être.[6] In this critique, Sudan was a "featured area," as evidenced by a major work, *Anthropology and the Colonial Encounter,* edited by Sudanist anthropologist Talal Asad.[7] Such works caused many of us to question whom we were serving. The romance of the anthropologist in the role of "marginal native" began to be replaced by charges of racism and exploitation.[8] These developments meant that I had to face the subtle racism of my romantic attachment to Sudan.

It was time to *reinvent* anthropology.[9] That reinvention took many forms: rewriting our history; emphasizing the necessity of serving the people who are the subjects of our research; challenging the elitism of the academic enterprise; "studying up" instead of constantly objectifying the poor and powerless[10]; studying our own culture (i.e., doing fieldwork in the United States); and writing more truthful accounts of the fieldwork experience. Perhaps most relevant to the issues of this essay were the awareness of the importance of subjectivity and the realization that the researcher/interviewer should not be abstracted away—two main points that grew out of the critique of positivism. In short, there was a significant call for a more reflexive and critical anthropology, greater social responsibility, and an insistence that all knowledge is political.[11]

All of these ideas had a considerable impact on my thoughts about the ethics of social science methods, thoughts that preceded and presaged the appearance of "feminist process" and feminist methodology as part of my intellectual and activist vocabulary. In the early 1960s the egalitarianism and cultural relativism that I had carried with me through life demanded that I respect my "informants," which included protecting their anonymity.[12] By the 1970s, while doing research on the Nubian response to relocation, I was intent on informing the people I interviewed of exactly what I was doing. I had also stopped (1) "tricking" people into exposing themselves; (2) intentionally luring them into contradictions; (3) using one "informant" to expose or contradict another; and, in general, (4) manipulating people to obtain the "truth" and the "facts." Although I had had to obtain my research permit from a government at that time suspicious of Nubians, I still tried to be honest with everyone about my research and assumed that my first responsibility was to serve the Nubian community.[13] However, a problem emerged as I realized that there were competing segments of "the Nubian community." Ultimately, one of my first major ethical dilemmas in research resulted from my "discovery" that the accentuated Nubian ethnicity under threat, which I was analyzing, was partially a result of the manipulation of Nubian ethnic identity by upper-class Nubians and the assertion of this identity for this elite's political/economic gain. Most of my interviewees were "working-class" or former small farmers and merchants; most of my Nubian hosts, one of whom was my sponsor and hence responsible to the government for my conduct, were upper-class.

Questions of "insider" and "outsider" were constantly with me in the 1970s research sojourns. Perhaps the most profound effect of the critique of positivism of the 1960s and 1970s, however, was my recognition that *I* was part of the problem. The research "outcome" was affected by the very presence of the researcher; it was not possible to be objective.

It goes without saying that the social and historical location I have had vis-à-vis classes, institutions, and the Sudanese nation-state profoundly affected my approach to Sudanese studies. Consequently, my claims to objectivity, if ever I had them, have been tempered. I knew I could not be a totally "objective observer" because each interview, each episode of observation, and each form and content of participant observation were affected by what I had already experienced, by the ways in which people already viewed me, and by the fact that most of my knowledge came from living there and unconsciously acting out my roles within an intricate social network (teacher, tennis celebrity, confidante, actor in local repertory, researcher, socialite). I was not only very visible, but sometimes, also, a very suspicious character. Many Sudanese queried why I seemed to like Sudan so much and how I could be so "well-integrated" into Sudanese society.[14]

It is by now commonplace to speak of one's pessimistic moments in the field, those feelings of inadequacy that are exacerbated by the constant self-questioning and doubts about the worth of one's contribution, the validity of the data, and the morality of it all.[15] Nonetheless, with all of the newly acquired sensitivity to the ethical and political issues of research that affected the new, progressive anthropologists (and others) of the late 1960s, there remained notions that some degree of distance was desirable, that we students of the social sciences were the authorities, and that there was a truth—or at least some universals—"out there." Although we might speak of integrating theory and practice, the stress was on theory, which was thought of as distinct from experience, ideology, opinion, rhetoric, and emotion.

Feminist Process

In some cases, feminist theory, method, and ideology presented me with very different ways of looking at research; in other cases, feminist scholarship stood on the shoulders of the research strategies discussed above.

Among methods/strategies new to me in the late 1960s and revived for me through feminism were consciousness-raising, criticism/self-criticism and small-group process, commonly referred to as "feminist process." In fact, the stress on consciousness-raising was a highly influential method of the left that had been carried over into feminism.

Several challenges to well-developed modes of thinking either antedate or emerge with the rise of feminist theory and methodology. Skeptics questioned binary oppositions and dichotomous thinking, e.g., subject/object; insider/outsider; observer/observed; oppressor/oppressed; and in-group/out-group. Challenged as well was the linear process by which the out-group was depicted as trying to assimilate to the in-group, for example; the "Oriental" as becoming Western. A later development significant to feminist theorists and methodologists was the process of the "outsider" "writing back," a response to the fact that Westerners had for centuries studied and spoken for the rest of the world. Now Orientalism was being subverted; the Western gaze was being met, just as the male gaze would soon be met.[16] The question was raised about who has the authority to speak for any group's identity and authenticity. How have the articulated self-identifications of groups set apart as "different" affected research formulation and analysis? The acknowledgement of multidimensional identities and ideologies was accompanied by the recognition that we all have different socially mediated constructions of reality.[17]

A significant number of feminist researchers has rejected positivism and empiricism, railing against method as centerpiece, at the same time that we have validated *how* something is done and valorize the means over the ends, process over product. Renate Duelli Klein has identified the importance of *conscious subjectivity,* the validating of each woman's subjective experience, to which Marcia Westkott has added *intersubjectivity,* in which the researcher compares her work with her own experiences as a woman and a scientist, and shares the resulting reflections with the researched, who in turn, might change the research by adding her opinion.[18]

Duelli Klein also lays considerable stress on the importance of "faking," a process that conventional research attempts to avoid and researchers devise tricks to eliminate. "Faking" is giving socially desirable responses and, I would add, "politically correct" responses (what the narrator thinks the listener wants to hear), rather than "honest" ones. Duelli Klein reminds us that, for women, faking may always have been necessary for survival and needs to be taken seriously and incorporated as a phenomenon into our research.

So much of what feminist methodology entails is dynamic: the unmeasurable *process.* A woman ("interviewee," "narrator," oral historian of her own life, autobiographer) should always be encouraged to be herself in the sense not only of being honest but also of not remaining anonymous; to be the subject of her own life; to express her feelings; to relate her personal experiences; to reinvent herself; to reinvent history (especially: to interject herself into history); and to act. Her answers will not always fit his questions, nor "ours" either.

The above layers of paradigmatic and, thus, methodological shifts formed a "model," an amalgam, in my mind. It was with this ideal that I approached the interviewing process in Khartoum, Sudan, in 1988. This experience subsequently provoked thoughts about another kind of cultural imperialism: the imposition of "feminist process" in a cross-cultural interview.

Contrasting Feminisms: An Interview with Fatma Ahmed Ibrahim[19]

In the remainder of this essay I discuss one of my struggles with ethnocentrism, cultural imperialism, and "feminist" scholarship. The protagonist/narrator of this situation is Fatma Ahmed Ibrahim. She is a folk hero in Sudan and has been referred to as "the Sudanese Pasionaria" for her role in the 1985 overthrow of the military dictatorship.[20] As the leading activist in the main women's organization, the Women's Union (WU), for over thirty years, she has been Sudan's most visible woman politician. As a member of the Sudanese Communist Party (SCP), she has been in the vanguard of nearly every collective action carried out against the various repressive governments. She has been jailed many times and has spent years under house arrest. Her husband, al-Shaafi, the vice president of the World Federation of Trade Unions, was executed in 1971 by the Sudanese military government for his supposed role in an attempted coup d'état that year against the dictatorship of Jaafar Nimieri.

The Women's Union was banned for most of the Nimieri regime, which spanned the period 1969–85. This resulted in limited underground activity for a number of years. After Nimieri's military regime was overthrown in 1985, political parties and associations were once again legal, and Fatma emerged to reactivate the Women's Union.[21]

One of my goals in going to Sudan in 1988 was to interview Fatma Ahmed Ibrahim and, so I dreamed, to obtain permission to become her biographer. There are few, if any, published oral histories of African or Middle Eastern women political figures in English. Very little has been written about this famous woman, even in Arabic. I hoped to make a contribution to Sudanese studies and to feminist studies by illuminating the career of one of the most courageous and famous of contemporary Middle Eastern women. She was also an important source for a study I was embarking on: the relationship of women to *sharia* (Islamic law) and the effects of rising Islamism. I also felt she could contribute enormously to my ongoing assessment of gender and the socialist/communist movement in Sudan.

After many years of self-imposed silence (because of not wanting either to be seen as betraying or inadvertently actually to betray the Sudanese left), I had finally published a rather critical account of the relationship of the Sudanese Communist Party to the Women's Union. I argued that the former had dominated the ideological content of the latter, allowing little latitude and thwarting many feminist demands.[22]

Although my article on the SCP and WU was based on years of conversations with left Sudanese, I had never interviewed Fatma. I needed to hear her point of view, especially with regard to the relationship of the WU and SCP. I probably wanted to be "proven" wrong about the dominance of the SCP over the WU and the resulting stagnation on women's issues, hoping, I suppose, to hear Fatma describe how the WU is self-critical, open to new ideas, and independent from the SCP.

My interview appointment with Fatma was therefore shaped by my expectation that she would not only offer me valuable information for my various research agendas but also enlighten me about the role of women in Sudanese society. I hoped that she would stimulate my thinking about a number of intellectual and political contradictions and, by reassuring me of the leadership of Third World women in the general emancipation of women, help to redefine feminism for me. In short, I expected that Fatma would reveal to me not only her role as an innovative theorist within the Sudanese women's movement, but also the infallibility of the Women's Union—although, of course, I anticipated that these revelations would be tempered by her own self-criticism and critical assessment of the organization. As might be expected, Fatma revealed to me only what she saw as strategic to reveal. It was, instead, the technique for unfolding her story that gave me pause.

The encounter with Fatma brought to the fore a number of issues about using a single approach in feminist oral history. For example, what do we do when the narrator of the oral history is not a "feminist" in the ways that many Western feminists understand that word? What problems emerge when the narrator uses what the listener interprets as "masculinist" techniques of communication and presentation? That is, as in the case of Fatma, what problems arise when the narrator is "feminist" in ideology and goals, but uses a methodology or process nearly antithetical to that of the interviewer's feminism? This is an especially troublesome problem when one considers how *process,* in Western feminist pedagogy, research methodology, and theory, has tended to dominate over *product.*

I had been told some time earlier that Fatma would not agree to an interview with an American, especially since her anti-Americanism increased after having been refused a visa to the United States in 1985. I was therefore surprised and pleased that she agreed to the interview. Our first encounter was an informal conversation in which Fatma gave me permission to be her biographer. We decided that I would ask her a few initial background questions and that the real biographical material would be collected on my next trip to Sudan. As she had also agreed to be interviewed about my current research topic on women and rising Islamism, I gave her a list of questions and set up an appointment for another time.

When we met for the more formal interview, I began by trying to tell her a bit about myself, wanting to be as honest as possible about my experiences in Sudan, my politics, and my feminist views. I also wanted to tell her about the weaknesses and gaps in my research project. She, however, was not interested. Probably she had investigated me through our mutual friends, and learned enough to be willing to talk with me; perhaps this also gave her as much information about me as she felt she needed.

We then began the session. I was able to ask only one question regarding the timing of ex-military dictator Nimieri's imposition of *sharia* in 1983. Rather dismissively she offered me the unsurprising response that it was his last chance to remain in power. Then she took that opportunity to move directly into her own agenda by giving me other reasons: "the general opposition was strong, the Muslim Brothers (*Ikhwan*), in particular. . . . The Muslim Brotherhood had failed to stop progressive women under the umbrella of Islam. And this is why they failed. . . ." With that response and without taking a breath, she began discussing the accomplishments of the Women's Union, a topic that dominated the rest of the interview.

At the level of content, it could have been an enlightening experience to have the embodiment of the Women's Union tell me about the organization for nearly three hours. Nonetheless, there were some areas where I found

Fatma's methods difficult in terms of my own preparation and the process to which I was accustomed. She did not respond directly to my questions, followed only her own agenda, perhaps intentionally misinformed me, either consciously or unconsciously manipulated my emotions, and seemed nondemocratic or patronizing toward many people she mentioned—competitors, sisters in the organization, and working-class or peasant women. Furthermore, even though I had tried earlier to set a tone of self-criticism in my discussion of some left and feminist groups in the United States, no self-criticism was ever offered by her. Her responses tended to aggrandize the accomplishments of the WU or the SCP and were reminiscent of the rhetoric found in the literature of the two organizations.

The Women's Union has made claims in print that it is the voice of ordinary women, that it speaks for them. Fatma constantly used "we" and "they" in reference to the educated women of the Union and "backward" women, respectively: "Although we [the educated women of the Front] know what women need, it is always better hearing it from them—even though they are ignorant." In fact, as this quotation indicates, she often set herself apart from most other Sudanese women. Also, when we were discussing the women's rights movement in 1965, she mentioned that she and the Union supported equal pay for equal work even though it applied only to graduates of the university and to teachers. When I interjected a statement that assumed "we" (she and I and any other feminist) are self-critical of the failure to extend that right to peasant and working-class women and that we, of course, view such a stance as an unfortunate expediency, she ignored what I said. Fatma's primary credo was: "The first thing is to educate them [ordinary women]. If they are not convinced, I cannot do it for them." She made reference to tricking women into doing things, e.g., getting them to sewing classes so that they could be taught literacy.

Although Fatma frequently mentioned "women's issues," these were never spelled out, even when she discussed the splits within the organization around "women's issues" versus "national politics"—nor did she ever question that dichotomy. Some women in the Union, according to Fatma, did not think it was appropriate for women to work on national politics. She was part of the faction that urged women's participation in the national political movement. When I asked her to define "women's issues," she ignored the question.

At least in the context of the interview, Fatma took an uncritical stance toward the SCP, even in its relationship to the WU. She stated that there were no contradictions between the Party and the Union, no differences on women's issues, that the Union was totally independent, and that the women of the Party never mixed Party business with Union business. She alluded to a split in the Party in which some women left, but would not explain the split. While some of her evasiveness about the SCP was understandable, the questions I was asking were carefully selected not to trespass on strategic elements of Party organization.

Although the Union was not banned at the time of the interview, and the leadership has always been well known, Fatma neglected to mention her colleagues, even when I prodded her a bit with names that I knew as a means of understanding the dynamics within the Union. She used "we" in describing a demonstration, an election, or a delegation, but these were anonymous "we's." By taking for herself most of the credit for leadership of all the crucial events, even when she was describing periods in which she had been imprisoned or under house arrest, she relegated other very famous and important figures to the background. When I asked if there were any new cadre coming up the ranks, her negative reply as well as her body language did not permit my protest. She ignored my comment that I had seen many young faces at a recent left event. Finally, when I asked if there was a new segment of the WU, particularly younger members, who might be arguing new ideas and taking the organization in a different direction, she responded by describing the careful nurturing of new people, for example, by taking young members with her to other towns where she would make speeches and would give them the freedom to say what they think.

With regard to her "competitors" and to splits within the organization, she gave no credence to legitimate differences and made what I thought were personal attacks on her competitors by name, or dismissed or maligned those who had different approaches to women's issues. For example, she spoke bitterly about the funds the Sudanese government and outside agencies have given the Bedri family (who operate Ahfad College for Women and are liberal advocates of women's rights) to work on women's issues, accusing them of working on the wrong issues with the wrong strategies and pocketing the money.

Or, along the same lines, she described how, in 1965, when the Union was working out a women's rights platform, two members of the WU opposed giving four months' maternity leave and wanted only seven days to be given instead. When I probed for an elaboration of the arguments of these known feminists, Fatma responded in a vein that she often repeated: that the women were dupes of President Nimieri.

She often dealt with her political foes with such name-calling—for example, referring to particular liberal women as "Muslim Sisters" (member of the *Ikhwan,* Muslim Brotherhood), meaning Muslim fundamentalist or political reactionary. I expressed surprise that she referred to a known democratic woman in this way. Fatma was evasive, saying, "She was not so organized then." Deconstructing this phrase, I understood Fatma to be insinuating that the woman was a Muslim Sister at heart even in those earlier years, but that it was only in later years that she joined the fundamentalist organization. Neither is likely.

These examples were not the only seemingly intentional pieces of misinformation Fatma gave me. She also tried to obscure the positive attributes of the 1973 Constitution (developed under Nimieri), and attempted to justify the

Union's opting to fight for political rights over economic rights (if these can be divided), because "the majority of the women were housewives." I did not expect the foremost Sudanese feminist to make such a statement about the economic role of women in Sudan. Every Sudanese feminist and every Sudanist knows the high percentage of women who work in agriculture, who are employed in cottage industries, who are are self-employed near their homes, or who perform personal services not enumerated in the census.

Possibly because Fatma assumed that, as a Westerner, I had certain views about female circumcision, she brought it up a number of times, usually in a defensive manner, though it is my policy not to discuss the topic at all in the United States, and not in Sudan unless invited. "Circumcision is the symptom, not the disease," she said. Again she offered education as a solution to long-range eradication, and was very critical of all the women and women's groups working to eradicate the custom (such as the Bedri family, mentioned above). She argued that the problem was exaggerated by "outside forces" (i.e., Western feminists), to which I partially agreed, advocating myself that this is an issue for Sudanese to address and no one else. Then she presented an argument that established her priorities: "When you look at the percentage of women who are dying from circumcision or in childbirth, it is a very small percentage. But when you look at the percentage of women dying of hunger, it is very great. Which is more important?" Although I was indicating agreement, she did not acknowledge it, and continued as if I were protesting.

In general, Fatma's attitude toward "traditional culture," both in her writings and in this interview, seemed contradictory. She devoted much time and energy to denouncing the *zaar*, a seemingly harmless spirit possession "cult." When I introduced my ideas about *zaar*, and mentioned that some feminists see the ritual as a form of resistance and a statement of women's solidarity, she was not interested.[23] Whereas in the interview and in her writings she has referred to the need for the WU to work against such traditional customs as the *zaar*, her attitude about the role of Islam, which some might also consider "traditional culture," is very different. Fatma judges the decision of the SCP and the WU in the 1950s to coexist with Islam to be a highly effective strategy, "a stroke of genius," which saved these organizations. Because she sees Islam as private, she maintains that "there is no contradiction between our [women's] struggle and the real aims of Islam." But this has meant that family status laws, which, as Fatma readily admits, constrain women, are not targeted for change by the WU because "they are too closely tied to religion."

Absent from the exchange over Islamic culture was any discussion about the elements in Islam that can be used to emancipate women and those that can be used to oppress, such as some of the personal status laws in *sharia*. I am not suggesting that Fatma Ahmed Ibrahim is unaware of the complexities of the role of women in Islam, only that she apparently deems it strategically sound to argue an uncritical position *in public*. And, apparently, I qualified as "the public."

One of my dilemmas—whether appropriate or not—was that I felt relegated to the category of mere listener. It seemed inconsequential that I am a sister feminist from a country that has a vigorous women's movement, a leftist, and someone knowledgeable about Sudan and sympathetic to the Party and Union.

Conclusion

The experience of interviewing Fatma required a twofold deconstruction: personal/experiential and analytical. On the personal/experiential level, I began to fear that I would censor myself in writing about Fatma Ahmed Ibrahim. Otherwise, I reasoned, my critical account of the interview would necessarily be a betrayal. How could I be critical toward someone for whom I have always had enormous respect and who is such an important figure in Sudanese history? Besides, Fatma had been warm, polite, and generous, giving me hours of her time for what might have seemed to her an abstract (armchair) enterprise, while she herself was engaged in the real work of women's survival in the context of Third World poverty.

The few Sudanese feminists with whom I discussed the interview did not see why I was agonizing over it and urged me to use the material to stimulate a discussion on the direction of the Women's Union. But I had already had this experience with Sudanese feminists, of being encouraged to publish something critical, partially based on information given me by them, only to have them "abandon" me when I did. I began to understand that one can be used as a vehicle for making public certain criticisms, but that the urging to be critical is not insurance against abandonment. And abandonment can leave one with the feeling not only of being politically incorrect, but of betraying Sudanese. Nonetheless, following solely one's own agenda seems amoral at best.

Following one's own agenda is, of course, a potential negation of the empowerment and validation process of the feminist biographer/interpreter/facilitator. A possible resolution, in addition to acknowledging the different agendas and forms of feminism Fatma and I each had, is to temper the criticism of the content of the interview through self-criticism, both direct and implied. I hope, in fact, that this entire essay will be read as implied self-criticism as well as a critique of some aspects of Western feminism, namely the dominance of process. Among the serious problems with such self-reflexivity, however, especially for those of us engaged in dialogue about de-centering the West, is that the white, Western researcher once again puts herself at the center; the Third World narrator is marginalized.

An important sphere of self-criticism relates to my expectations and "feminist" assumptions. Because Fatma and I are two feminists from the same general backgrounds (i.e., middle-class teachers and left activists), with the same general agenda—to emancipate women and facilitate the Sudanese socialist revolution—I had incorrectly presumed more unity on major issues.

Whether Fatma's offering me only socially desirable—or what she saw as "politically correct"—responses was an attempt to use me to forward positive propaganda, or whether this was a version of history to which she truly subscribed, the result was an interview in which she described only the glorious moments of the Women's Union and only her positive acts. The effect is that I was given a portrait of a lifetime of work in which there were no contradictions, no mistakes, and no moments of human frailty: a heroic narrative.[24]

Her agenda, then, was to convince me of the nobility of her cause and her crucial and effective role in it so that I would write it in just that way. Mine, of course, was to carry out research for which she was one of the vehicles. Although such a cynical interpretation flies in the face of the feminist credo of research *for* women, any other claim seems disingenuous. I also wanted information that would help me understand the vanguard role I believe Third World women can play in the emancipation of women everywhere. As a feminist activist, I, too, think of myself as having a cause. But it was presumptuous of me to act as if she and I shared the *same* cause, which then led me to expect her to acknowledge that and to affirm my role in that cause.

Furthermore, I had assumed we had the same basic "constituency," leftists and feminists. But the situation was more complicated than that in terms of who our listeners are. During the course of the exchange, Fatma had to take into consideration her professional/political reputation, as I did mine. She was carrying the load of what the Party expects from her and needed to think about who would be hearing the interview. Both of us had to be aware of what others might expect from the interview: the Union and Party would want to come out of the situation "whole"; readers of my research would want a critical appraisal. She and I were both protecting the political reputations of others: she, the heads of the Party and members of the Union; and I, certain Sudanese feminists of the left with whom I have been associated for years.

In the case of this interview, the interactional and intersubjective were mediated by different concepts of modesty; authority; self-disclosure; what it means to be "honest"; the role of "faking"; and when it is acceptable to "use" someone. Furthermore, when the oppressed is in dialogue with a representative of the oppressor, even though they are both feminists, "national" goals may, at least momentarily, outweigh "feminist" goals. And, certainly, the product may outweigh the process. Fatma may have been justified in using me, deeming me invisible, objectifying me as a conduit to forward a cause for which she has worked all of her life. And I, despite my white guilt and my perhaps inevitable role as the colonizer, may be justified in feeling that both my egalitarian sentiments and my particular brand of feminist process had, somehow, been violated.

The disappointment I experienced obviously stemmed from my overdrawn expectations and from my particular understanding of "feminist process." The disappointment may also have come from my lingering arrogance about being considered an "insider." Fatma was a stranger to me and I to her. Still, I wanted the same validation from her that I had received in the past. I was not just *any* interviewer or researcher; I had been given honorary membership and had carried out nearly three decades of research on Sudan.

More perplexing and somewhat convoluted is the issue of class location. Fatma is from a privileged class, if not economically, at least in traditional status. And, although she may have seen me as privileged—an American professor, as white, as the neocolonizer, the exploiter—my origins are working-class. My location in the American left also had relevance. Along strictly political lines, one of the persistent problems I have had with Sudanese leftists is their disdain toward the American left.

On an analytical level, my experience of interviewing one of Sudan's outstanding figures can be seen as instructive of the flaws in certain Western feminist ideas about methodology. The privileging of the process over the product can have a profound effect on our scholarship: on our ability to create any distance, to evaluate the narrator's life as separate from our own, and to assume a critical attitude without personalizing. Relying on interactional female identification and the power of shared experience may work in certain situations. But there may very well be a contradiction between facilitating a situation where a woman is the narrator of her own life—holding center stage—and the interactional process. To put it in the Sudanese context, when there are class differences and/or racial differences, or when the interviewer represents the colonizer and the narrator the colonized, it is not appropriate for the interviewer/biographer to want "equal time," or expect to be equally affirmed. Is it logical for me, a white Western feminist interviewing a Sudanese, to expect to be addressed as I see myself, when I may represent so many other categories to her?

Yet, to return to the questions raised in the introduction, can any biographer avoid imposing what we have become? If we are committed to a particular theory and methodology, and are engaged in praxis, is it authentic to be or do otherwise? If, however, in a situation such as the one described above, we try to act as more than conduits of the narrator's story, e.g., as interpreters, dialogists, or even collaborators, do we become cultural imperialists?

So much of what anthropologists do "in the field" is, to a large extent, contrived, even that intense centerpiece method referred to as "participant-observation." Yet some feminists have redefined the interview as something more akin to participant-observation. The interviewer sets up the situation and then participates in it. Being and doing are important both to the narrator and to her feminist interpreter. It is possible, however, that the small but significant degree of distance demanded in conventional participant-observation shields the interactional and intersubjective interpreter of another woman's life from false assumptions of mutuality. At the same time, in the "feminist interview," for the most part, the closeness and intersubjectivity remain artificial and temporary, frustrating expectations and potentially creating tensions between different feminisms.

My "dream of a common language"[25] had been dashed by the interview, but perhaps that was because, although I had remembered a form of "feminism," I had forgotten some anthropology, politics, and history.

Notes

The interviews referred to were carried out for projects supported by the American Centre for Research in Egypt, Inc. (1971); Fulbright-Hays (1971–72); African Studies Center, University of California at Los Angeles (1971–72); American Association of University Women (1973–74); National Endowment for the Humanities (1981); and University of California at Los Angeles Center for the Study of Women (1988). I would like to thank Nilda Rimonte and Linda Vogel for their sophisticated and challenging commentaries.

1. Ann Oakley, "Interviewing Women: A Contradiction in Terms," in *Doing Feminist Research,* ed. Helen Roberts (London: Routledge and Kegan Paul, 1981), pp. 30–61.
2. The term "Islamic Trend" was used by Sudanese in 1988 to describe the movement toward Islamicizing the Sudanese state, including the imposition of *sharia* (Islamic law).
3. The Phrase "paradoxes and expectations" is borrowed from John Middleton, *The Study of the Lugbara: Expectation and Paradox in Anthropological Research* (New York: Holt, Rinehart, and Winston, 1970).
4. Sondra Hale, "The Nature of the Social, Political, and Religious Changes among Urban Women: Northern Sudan," *Proceedings of the Third Graduate Academy of the University of California, UCLA, April 11–12, 1965* (Los Angeles: The UCLA Graduate Student Association, 1966), pp. 127–40. Although for many years it was the only study of northern urban Sudanese women and, as a consequence, was much cited, I have often used this study as an object lesson in ethnocentrism.
5. Kathleen Gough, "Anthropology: Child of Imperialism," *Monthly Review* 19, no. 11 (1967): 12–27; Wendy James, "The Anthropologist as Reluctant Imperialist," in *Anthropology and the Colonial Encounter,* ed. Talal Asad (London: Ithaca Press, 1973), pp. 41–69.
6. For a good bibliography of these critiques, see Peter Forster, "A Review of the New Left Critique of Social Anthropology," in Asad, ed., *Anthropology and the Colonial Encounter,* pp. 23–38.
7. Ibid. Also included in Asad's volume is Abdel Ghaffar M. Ahmed, "Some Remarks from the Third World on Anthropology and Colonialism: The Sudan," pp. 259–70.
8. "The anthropologist has been a marginal man for most of anthropology's history. . . . [H]e almost invariably 'came on' as marginal to society. To members of his family he was 'the strange one' who was more interested in primitive rituals . . . than modern rituals." Morris Freilich, ed., *Marginal Natives: Anthropologists at Work* (New York: Harper and Row, 1970), p. vii. For some of the same themes, see Hortense Powdermaker, *Stranger and Friend* (New York: W. W. Norton, 1966).
9. Term borrowed from Dell Hymes, ed., *Reinventing Anthropology* (New York: Vintage, 1972).
10. For example, Laura Nader, "Up the Anthropologist—Perspectives Gained from Studying Up," in Hymes, ed., *Reinventing Anthropology,* pp. 284–311.
11. For example, Bob Scholte, "Toward a Reflexive and Critical Anthropology," in Hymes, ed., *Reinventing Anthropology,* pp. 430–57. In 1968 a Social Responsibilities Symposium was published in a special section of *Current Anthropology* 9, no. 5 (1968): 391–436. See especially Gerald Berreman, "Is Anthropology Still Alive?" pp. 391–96 in this section, as well

as his " 'Bringing It All Back Home': Malaise in Anthropology," in Hymes, ed., *Reinventing Anthropology,* pp. 83–98.

12. By the 1970s I was cognizant of the left critique of cultural relativism (e.g., Hymes, ed., *Reinventing Anthropology*), but that criticism was later made more succinct by feminist theory and ideology.

13. This ethical choice was dramatized after I returned to the United States in 1972 and found a letter from the Sudanese Ministry of Interior demanding my recorded interviews and/or the transcriptions of interviews with sixty-seven Nubian men and women. I ignored the request, risking not being allowed to do research in Sudan again.

14. I deal with these processes at some length in my doctoral dissertation, *The Changing Ethnic Identity of Nubians in an Urban Milieu: Khartoum, Sudan* (Anthropology Department, University of California, Los Angeles, 1979), pp. 35–40.

15. It may have been "commonplace" by the 1970s to write in a personal way about one's field experiences or to talk personally about the field, e.g., Paul Rabinow, *Reflections on Fieldwork in Morocco* (Berkeley, Calif.: University of California Press, 1977); Rosalie Wax, *Doing Fieldwork: Warnings and Advice* (Chicago: University of Chicago Press, 1971); Jean Briggs, *Never in Anger* (Cambridge, Mass.: Harvard University Press, 1970); Peggy Golde, ed., *Women in the Field: Anthropological Experiences* (Berkeley, Calif.: University of California Press, 1970); Middleton, *The Study of the Lugbara;* Powdermaker, *Stranger and Friend;* David Maybury-Lewis, *The Savage and the Innocent* (Cleveland, Ohio: World Publishing Company, 1965); and, as discussed in a review article by Dennison Nash and Ronald Wintrob, "The Emergence of Self-Consciousness in Ethnography," *Current Anthropology* 13 (1972): 527–42. But when anthropologist Laura Bohannan wrote so personally in 1954, she not only felt that she had to write under a pseudonym, she also fictionalized her account. Her experience of totally submerging her identity as an American and immersing herself in Tiv (Nigerian) culture to the point of nearly "losing herself" read like a horror story to me, an entering anthropology graduate student in the 1960s. Elenore Smith Bowen, pseud., *Return to Laughter* (New York: Harper & Row, 1954).

16. In 1950 Michel Leiris introduced the concept of "writing back" in "L'Ethnographe devant le Colonialisme," *Les Temps Modernes* 58 (reprinted in idem, *Brisées,* [Paris: Mercure de France, 1966]). This tradition has recently been most eloquently revived by Edward Said in *Orientalism* (New York: Pantheon, 1978). Also see James Clifford, *The Predicament of Culture: Twentieth Century Ethnography, Literature, and Art* (Cambridge, Mass.: Harvard University Press, 1988), p. 256. More recently, the theme of "writing back" has been explored, by, among others, Gayatri Spivak, *In Other Worlds: Essays in Cultural Politics* (London: Methuen, 1987); Bill Ashcroft et al., *The Empire Writes Back: Theory and Practice in Post-Colonial Literatures* (London: Routledge, 1989); and Homi K. Bhabha, ed., *Nation and Narration* (London: Routledge, 1990).

17. Soheir Morsy has written powerfully on this subject in "Toward the Demise of Anthropology's Distinctive-Other Hegemonic Tradition," in *Arab Women in the Field: Studying Your Own Society,* ed. Soraya Altorki and Camillia El-Solh (Syracuse, N.Y.: Syracuse University Press, 1988), pp. 69–90.

18. Renate Duelli Klein, "How To Do What We Want To Do: Thoughts about Feminist Methodology," in *Theories of Women's Studies,* ed. Gloria Bowles and Renate Duelli Klein (London: Routledge and Kegan Paul, 1983), pp. 94–95 and 98; Marcia Westkott "Feminist Criticism in the Social Sciences," *Harvard Educational Review* 49 (1979): 422–30. This is not dissimilar to Paulo Freire, *Pedagogy of the Oppressed* (New York: Seabury Press, 1970).

19. The interview, conducted in English, took place on 12 July 1988 in Omdurman, Sudan. All quotations are from this interview.

20. Eric Rouleau, "Sudan's Revolutionary Spring," *Middle East Report* 15 (1985): 4. Dolores Ibarruri Gómez (1895–1981), known as "La Pasionaria," was a famous revolutionary in the Spanish Civil War who symbolized courage and spirit.

21. In June 1989, there was another military coup d'état that overthrew the democratically

elected government and installed a military junta. All political groups and professional associations were banned, and all political meetings were proclaimed illegal. See Alan Cowell, "Sudan's New Rulers to Press for End to Civil War," *The New York Times,* 2 July 1989, p. 1; and Andrew Buckoke, "The Military Seizes Power in Troubled Sudan," *The London Times,* 1 July 1989, p. 7. The left was especially decimated—meaning, of course, that the WU and the SCP are banned again.

22. Sondra Hale, "The Wing of the Patriarch: Sudanese Women and Revolutionary Parties," *Middle East Report* 16 (1986): 25–30. Sudanese women leftists had argued with me, not so much along theoretical/ideological lines but to keep the criticism of the left "in-house" until the SCP and WU were strong again. In this last decade, in particular, Western left feminists have become impatient with the relationship between Marxism and feminism and with the responses of left organizations to feminist ideas. For example, see S. Rowbotham, L. Segal, and H. Wainwright, *Beyond the Fragments: Feminism and the Making of Socialism* (London: Merlin, 1979). Most recently this theme has been ably explored in *Promissory Notes: Women and the Transition to Socialism,* ed. S. Kruks, R. Rapp, and M. Young (New York: Monthly Review Press, 1989). My critique is in this tradition, but I feel a necessity here to comment that, for many years, I have been a strong supporter of both the WU and the SCP.

23. Sondra Hale, "Women's Culture/Men's Culture: Gender, Separation, and Space in Africa and North America," *American Behavioral Scientist* 31 (1987): 115–34.

24. Such an approach, a heroic narrative, although very legitimate for her purposes, may not be so for mine. With that realization, not to mention other "process" differences, I will have to reassess whether or not I still want to be Fatma's biographer. After she reads this essay, she may have second thoughts as well.

25. This expression is borrowed from Adrienne Rich, *The Dream of a Common Language: Poems, 1974–1977* (New York: W. W. Norton, 1978).

9

U.S. Academics and Third World Women: Is Ethical Research Possible?

Daphne Patai

The short answer to the question posed by my subtitle is, in my view, "No." But much more than that needs to be said. To which "U.S. academics" am I referring? What is meant by "Third World women?" What is "ethical" research? Before addressing these questions, I must make explicit a term that, though not named in my title, frames the comments that follow: my concern is above all with feminist academics and with the meaning of feminism in research situations governed by inequalities and hierarchies—situations, in other words, that routinely unfold in the real world. These inequalities, which may also occur in many other settings, are readily apparent when one considers the average U.S. female academic—white and middle-class—in contrast to her average "Third World" object of research: nonwhite and/or poor. Although exploitation and unethical behavior are always a possibility when research is conducted with living persons, this danger is increased when the researcher is interviewing "down," that is, among groups less powerful (economically, politically, socially) than the researcher herself.[1]

In the discussion that follows, I use the image of the North American academic researcher interviewing women from the so-called Third World to epitomize an interaction typically characterized by systemic inequality. In such situations, it is the very existence of privilege that allows the research to be undertaken.

Academics who are not feminists also experience moral dilemmas as they conduct research with living persons, which is why ethical guidelines delineating proper procedures exist in many disciplines. These guidelines generally follow the medical injunction: do no harm. Yet even such a minimal directive, if taken seriously, would paralyze researchers, for we are usually unable to gauge, let alone control, the potential consequences of our procedures and of the research products in which they result. But I would go beyond this minimal directive and set instead a maximalist feminist ethic, for while questions about ethics occur in many contexts, they take on special urgency in the case of women—feminists—doing research with women. In practice, at this particular historical moment, such questions seem to demand special attention from feminists. As I see it, the goals and procedures of feminism ought to be the generally human ones. But they are not; at least not yet. Hence feminists—because we are among the few who articulate commitments and political priorities—must invoke that better human model of behavior that is as yet nowhere to be found. In an ideal world there would be no feminist ethics, because "feminism" arises precisely due to the fact of patriarchy and oppression in the real world. In this sense our concerns are indeed uniquely feminist—with the proviso that "feminism" ought to be viewed not as an absolute but as a time-bound concept and movement, appearing in many guises and variations.

Some scholars, however, may take amiss any suggestion that we need to be concerned about the ethical implications of our research. Mere discussion of this issue threatens to raise the specter of norms imposed on all researchers, which would necessarily interfere with the autonomy of the individual researcher, an autonomy that is perhaps the prime value in contemporary western culture. Gail Webber encountered such views in a small minority of those replying to a questionnaire in which she asked respondents to choose from among fourteen items the kind of statement on ethics they considered most important for feminists. The majority selected as their first choice the statement: "Feminists seek social, political, and economic equality for all women." But the very word "ethics" had negative connotations for some. Webber cites a few such comments: "I think the whole idea [of ethical guidelines] is bizarre and even dangerous. When do we get the feminist mind police uniforms? It's bad enough as it is." "One person's dogma is another's repression. When will we schedule the inquisition? I object to the whole idea of ethical behavior guidelines?" "Sounds like the '14 commandments.' "[2] It is instructive that, in these reactions, "guidelines" have been construed to suggest "dogma" and institutionally imposed control.

My own starting point is somewhat different. I assume that we are doing something other than merely pursuing our own careers and adding knowledge to the world, and that we must raise questions about the ethics of our behavior in relation to those on and with whom we do our research. I also take it as a given that most women doing research on women are moved by commitments to women. Such research is *for* women, as the popular formula has it, not merely by or about them. But because "women," gender notwithstanding, are not a monolithic block, ethical questions about our actions and the implications of those actions are especially appropriate.

Whether we adopt a broad or a narrow definition of feminism, if the term is to have any meaning it must involve a critique of traditional concepts and structures that have marginalized women materially and psychologically, in the world and even in their own souls. It must also ultimately aim at social transformation. Because feminism has challenged the pose of neutrality and objectivity that for so long governed positivist social science, it has forced us to scrutinize, as well, our own practice as scholars. One result is that the ethical problems of using other women as the subjects of our research become an immediate source of tension. For it is a fact that we are confronted by dual allegiances. On the one hand, we are obligated to our academic disciplines and institutions, within which we must succeed if we are to have any impact on the academy (and this in itself involves us in numerous contradictions, as part of our project entails transforming those very disciplines and institutions). On the other hand, if we take feminism seriously, it commits us to a transformative politics. In other words, most of us do not want to bite the hand that feeds us; but neither do we want to caress it too lovingly.

As I see it, the problem for us academics, who are already leading privileged existences, resides in the obvious fact that our enjoyment of research and its rewards constantly compromises the ardor with which we promote social transformation. At the very least, it dilutes our energy; at the most, it negates our ability to work for change. I do not think the current emphasis on "empowering" or "dialogic" research designs, as promising as these are, has done much to mitigate this fundamental contradiction.[3] E. B. White expressed the conflict I am alluding to in a pointed phrase: "I arise in the morning," he wrote, "torn between a desire to improve (or save) the world and a desire to enjoy (or savor) the world. This makes it hard to plan the day."[4] White's subversive humor should be taken to heart by feminist scholars who often claim the moral, even as they occupy the material, high ground.

The dilemma of feminist researchers working on groups less privileged than themselves can be succinctly stated as follows: is it possible—not in theory, but in the actual conditions of the real world today—to write about the oppressed without becoming one of the oppressors? In an absolute sense, I think not, and that is the meaning of the "No" with which I began this essay. In addition to the characteristic privileges of race and class, the existential or psychological dilemmas of the split between subject and object on which all research depends (even that of the most intense "participant observer") imply that objectification, the utilization of others for one's own purposes (which may or may not coincide with their own ends), and the possibility of exploitation, are built into almost all research projects with living human beings. Some distance may well be inevitable, perhaps even biologically ordained by our enclosure within our individual nervous systems, but it is not at this level that feminist research practices can seem self-serving. This occurs, instead, when feminists imagine that merely engaging in the discourse of feminism protects them from the possibility of exploiting other women, while their routine research practices are and continue to be embedded in a situation of material inequality.

Responding to an apparent sense of the inadequacy of conventional research practices, feminist scholars whose work depends on personal interviews—who invite personal disclosures—have attempted to focus on the research process as an occasion for intervention and advocacy. To be sure, there are many occasions for such activism, ranging from consideration of how a research project is initially formulated and who sponsors it, to questions regarding the uses the research will or might eventually serve, the forms in which its results will be disseminated, and the material benefits (such as career-building, status, and royalties) that derive from it. To these problems as well, which emerge in many research situations, feminism has brought its special sensibility—

without, however, making as much progress in actuality as in the realm of discourse.

Before going into detail concerning the nature of these dilemmas, let me describe how I became concerned with the ethics of research. My own experience of inequalities between researcher and researched did not occur as a result of theorizing about such encounters. In the early 1980s, as part of a project that eventually became a book, I conducted sixty lengthy personal interviews in Brazil.[5] I interviewed ordinary, "invisible" women: domestic servants, factory workers, nuns, housewives, secretaries, prostitutes, entrepreneurs, schoolgirls, landowners, and women from many other walks of life. The women were of diverse ages and races, and many more of them—as is true of all Brazilians—were poor than rich. Perhaps because I was not trained in the social sciences, I had not internalized a conventional research persona. Thus, when I began conducting interviews in Brazil, I was keenly aware of being cast into a special role. I discovered the legitimizing function of "having a project," of appearing with a tape recorder and the magic word "research," which turned what might have seemed to be mere personal curiosity into something else—something official, perhaps imposing. The nearly automatic respect I was granted made me feel enveloped by a kind of protective aura; this was an experience unlike anything I had encountered in my past work as a literary critic.

In this general frame of mind, I was slowly made aware of the questionable nature of the interactions on which my research depended. It was the summer of 1981—that is, it was summer in North American terms, but winter in Brazilian terms. In the city of Recife, in the northeast of Brazil, I met Teresa, a black woman who did laundry and ironing for some white acquaintances of mine. She agreed to talk with me and suggested that we go to her house after her morning's work. From the bus stop at the bottom of a hill, we trudged up a muddy road through the slum where she lived. Teresa was not yet forty-five years old, but appeared to be much older. Only four feet ten inches tall and weighing perhaps eighty pounds, she looked very thin and frail, and had almost no teeth. As we approached her dwelling, I saw that a piece of metal wire held shut a low and rickety wooden gate in the make-shift fence that surrounded the shack. Teresa untwisted the wire and invited me in. Paintings and statues of Christ decorated the front room, along with pictures of naked women and soccer stars put up, she explained, by her grown-up son, who also lived there. As in many poor neighborhoods in Brazil, there was no indoor toilet, no sewer facilities, but there was running water (which Teresa shared with a few neighbors who had none, and then also shared the bill) and electricity. Despite my repeated attempts to refuse her offer of food, which perhaps offended her, Teresa insisted on giving me something to eat and drink. She went to the refrigerator and got me a bottle of soda and then brought over a piece of cake—the one remaining piece that was sitting on a plate on top of an otherwise bare counter. I accepted the food, and Teresa sat next to me at the table that occupied most of the front room and watched me eat.

I do not really know how much food there was in Teresa's house on that particular day, but the refrigerator was bare when she opened it, and she herself looked worn out and undernourished. On my return to Brazil two summers later, I learned that she had died suddenly of a heart attack a few months after our meeting.

Thus, long before I began to think about the larger issues of how we use other people in our research, and how inadequate are our usual questions about our purposes or procedures, I was made aware, by that scene in Teresa's house, of the unease of being a well-fed woman briefly crossing paths with an ill-fed and generous poor woman whose life I was doing nothing to improve. Teresa, I should explain, was not by Brazilian standards especially exploited: the people she worked for, whom I knew, were decent employers. On the days that she worked at their house, she at least ate adequately. And she was paid the going rate, about $5 a week for her two days of washing and ironing. In addition to that income, she had a widow's pension of $40 a month. On a total of about $60 a month, then, she supported herself and contributed to the support of her twenty-three-year-old son and occasionally of another relative as well. It was all a very ordinary Brazilian story, the kind that well-fed people usually respond to in terms of individual charity, before turning their attention to other things.

When, some years later, I sat down to write about Teresa, other questions intruded. Did she, on that day, imagine that I would describe her appearance and the poverty of the house? Did she have an inkling that the food she served me might become part of her story, that everything about the episode might in turn be served up to readers far away? How would she have felt about it had she known these things? Would she have recognized herself in my sketch of her? Might she have thought that I had portrayed her weaknesses more than her strengths? Would she have felt betrayed? Used? And do these things matter? She never asked me any questions about what I was planning to do with her words (although I explained my project in a general way), let alone with the other impressions I was taking away from our meeting.

If I had to guess what she felt about my interest in her life, I would say that she was somewhat frightened but also pleased at the attention. I suppose that the prospect of being part of a foreigner's book—a book that she, being illiterate, could never have read even if it had been published in Portuguese—meant something to her. When we left her house, as she accompanied me back to the bus stop at the bottom of the hill, we passed one of her neighbors leaning out her front window. As soon as we were slightly out of hearing range, Teresa commented that she had asked this neighbor if she, too, would like to talk with me, but the woman had said no. Teresa then smiled at me complicitously and said "gente sem cultura"—people with no breeding. That comment is one of my few clues to what our conversation meant to Teresa and it, of course, is problematic. Did I provide Teresa with a fleeting opportunity to escape her situation by allying herself with a white foreigner? What does such an encounter have to do with the claims of feminism? Does one even have the right to interfere in people's lives in this small way? Is the formal permission—the agreement people lend to the interview situation and the use of their words—an exoneration?

It was difficult to stay within the usual rules of the interviewing game in the face of the very real material inequalities that divided me from many of the women I interviewed. All researchers who work with living persons face problems of this sort, but the researcher who utilizes oral history, especially when foregoing questionnaires and the narrow definitions that are common in topical and thematic oral history, faces particularly intense versions of these more general ethical problems. The reasons for this can be readily understood: when lengthy personal narratives, in particular, are gathered, an intimacy (or the appearance of intimacy) is generated that blurs any neat distinction between "research" and "personal relations."[6] We ask of the people we interview the kind of revelation of their inner life that normally occurs in situations of great familiarity and within the private realm. Yet we invite these revelations to be made in the context of the public sphere, which is where in an obvious sense we situate ourselves when we appear with tape recorders and note pads eager to promote our "projects," projects for which other people are to provide the living matter. The asymmetries of the interaction are marked, as well, by the different kinds of disclosure that our interviewees make (or that we hope they will make) and that we are willing or expected to make. While often shyly curious, interviewees never, in my experience, make a reciprocal exchange a condition of the interview. And researchers are almost always much less frank than they hope their subjects will be. As Arlene Kaplan Daniels has written, "deception is an ever present part of fieldwork."[7]

The interview situation, furthermore, is often an extremely charged one emotionally. Part of what those interviewed "get" from the process is precisely the undivided attention directed at them by another individual. I was surprised, in Brazil, that virtually everyone I approached was willing, even eager, to talk to me, and by the time I had completed several dozen long interviews I became convinced that not enough people are listening, and that the opportunity to talk about one's life, to reflect on its shapes and patterns, to make sense of it to oneself and to another human being, was an intrinsically valuable experience. But unlike those researchers who believe that this makes the interview a "fair exchange," where each partner receives and gives in equal measure, I continued to be struck by the inequalities inherent in the situation, both materially and psychologically.

To take the latter issue first: without wanting to exaggerate my role in the lives of people I interviewed, I can say that I was troubled by the sense of intense emotional involvement that, in my experience, always occurs at the time of the interview. Does this not make all the more problematic the researcher's inevitable retreat to a separate life in a far-off place? Is ostensibly feminist research still so deeply embedded in the imperialist/anthropological model that this dimension of the interview situation is to be buried while researchers present fascinating portraits of exotic "Others?" Does "contributing to knowledge" justify the utilization of another person for one's own (academic, feminist) purposes? Is the relationship terminated along with the research?

Other feminist scholars, too, have been concerned with these and similar issues. In a frequently cited essay, "Interviewing Women: A Contradiction in Terms," Ann Oakley, the British sociologist, outlined her experience conducting interviews for a project on childbirth.[8] She found that the social science methods she had been taught (which she describes in some detail in her essay) simply did not work. The women Oakley interviewed regularly asked her for advice and information, and traditional social science interview guidelines turned out to be impracticable and often ridiculous in these circumstances. The prevailing methodological models typically urged the researcher to deflect questions, to keep the focus on the informant, and to avoid getting drawn into personal exchanges. But, says Oakley, when less educated pregnant women asked her questions about the mechanics of childbirth, how could she possibly answer with the recommended evasions? When people sought much-needed help by asking Oakley about her own experiences, should she cleverly deflect their questions? Such dilemmas led Oakley to reject the old models, which were dependent upon a clear and hierarchical division that definitively separated researcher and researched.

Accepting instead the insight that the personal is political, feminist researchers such as Oakley have turned their attention above all to their interactions with the subjects of their research. The model of a distanced, controlled, and ostensibly neutral interviewer has, as a result, been replaced with that of sisterhood—an engaged and sympathetic interaction between two individuals united by the fact of gender oppression. Like other researchers making this argument, Oakley believes that the outcome is not merely a better research *process* but also better research *results*.

But it is quite possible that in breaking free of the androcentric research model, feminist scholars have risked cutting the ground from under their own work. For in the 1980s a deep questioning unfolded regarding how feminist research is to be conducted. Judith Stacey, for example, in her essay "Can There Be a Feminist Ethnography?" has questioned what has perhaps become the new orthodoxy among feminist scholars engaged in ethnographic research.[9] Stacey's work points to the dangers that arise when feminist researchers are unconsciously seductive toward their research subjects, raising their expectations and inducing dependency. These problems, however, are less likely to occur when an interviewer follows the traditional distanced model. When academics do research with women of races, classes, and cultures different from their own, a common experience is that they are perceived as more powerful than the people they are researching. This no doubt proceeds from the quite accurate appraisal on the part of people interviewed that the researcher has greater access to all sorts of resources—from material goods to local officials. The expectation of positive intervention is thus set up—all the more so when the feminist researcher consciously attempts to erase distance— and too often this expectation is disappointed, leading, as Stacey points out, to feelings of betrayal and injury. This danger has always existed in research situations involving hierarchy as well as personal interaction, but feminists may be more likely to generate this particular problem, for, quite understandably, our research styles have been developing, often in an ad hoc way, in reaction to the discarded positivist model that is seen as impersonal, "masculinist."

The "feminist" research model, in other words, may in its own ways be just as ill-advised. For in a world divided by race, ethnicity, and class, the purported solidarity of female identity is in many ways a fraud—in this case perhaps a fraud perpetrated by feminists with good intentions. Having rejected the objectification of research subjects construed as "Others," the new, ostensibly feminist scenario substitutes the claim of identity, our identity as women, while often straining to disregard ethnic, racial, class, and other distinctions that, in societies built on inequality, unavoidably divide people from one another.

Such a desire to affirm oneness is exemplified in Carole J. Spitzack's essay "Body Talk: The Politics of Weight Loss and Female Identity." Influenced by Oakley's work on the importance of nonhierarchical interaction as the proper model for women interviewing women. Spitzack spent considerable time talking with each woman in her research sample prior to the actual interview: "I wanted each woman to understand that she was not simply an exploitable information source, but someone I wished to talk *with* about body experience, a person with whom I would choose to spend time outside the context of academic research" (Spitzack's italics).[10] The problem with this honorable intent is its disingenuousness. The appeal to "sisterhood," the failure to recognize difference—even when the research is conducted close to home—leads too easily to mystification. It also raises a further problem: can, and should, we do research only when we would choose to make friends with the people we are interviewing? Is it even honest to suggest that all research subjects are or need to be potential intimates? Is this an improvement on the old model? Or is it a particularly egregious form of manipulation? Spitzack's comment, in its odd parodying of women's traditional nurturing role, reveals the misuse of sentiment as a research tool—a very real danger as feminists attempt to devise alternative practices as if in a vacuum.

In the by now commonplace emphasis on the interview process and the human qualities brought by the feminist researcher to the encounter, we seem to be merely creating a bracketed moment, a moment taken out of the broader context of unequal relations in which our research is typically done. Simply enjoying this moment, and using it to revive our flagging spirits, is not enough. By abstracting the interview from the larger social context of the real world, we are in effect returning to the discarded research models that situate our research practices outside of reality. But now we have, for a short time, transported our narrators with us.

Facile assumptions about our commonality as women, and celebrations of the intimacy generated by "feminist" research methods, are inadequate responses. Instead, I believe we must question the entire system that seems to allow for no other approach than manipulative distance, on the one hand, and spurious identification, on the other. At the very least, this will keep us from mistakenly assuming that the discourse of feminism itself constitutes a solution to the fact of women's oppression.

I do not, however, think that generic solutions can be found to the dilemmas feminists face in conducting research, nor do I for an instant hold out the hope of devising exact "rules" that will resolve these issues for us. In my view, this is impossible because ethical problems do not arise as absolutes requiring "blind justice." When Anatole France observed that the law in its majestic impartiality forbids both the rich and the poor to sleep under bridges, to beg in the streets, and to steal bread, he reminded us, with bitter humor, that ethical problems emerge in concrete human contexts, contexts that are always specific and always material.[11] And I believe these problems surface with special intensity in research with living persons because many of us sense that ethics is a matter not of abstractly correct behavior, but of relations between people. The personal interview is, therefore, a particularly precise locus for ethical issues to surface—unless, that is, we are busy (as indeed we often are) suppressing our awareness of these issues.

It is in this context that I want to argue for the importance of recognizing the material inequalities that create the conditions for much feminist research. Such a focus points to the fissures between our theory and our practice. The difficulty many of us face in drawing attention to the issue of material inequalities as a key factor in research—even in feminist research—suggests, to my mind, that the desire to transform the world is often weaker than the wish to enjoy it as it is. Less caustically, one might say that perhaps we tend to avoid these problems because they could lead to despair, which makes action impossible. Like the experience of guilt, these are personal emotions, which may deflect attention from the nonpersonal, institutional, and political contours of the problem of material inequality. However powerfully we may experience these problems on an individual basis in concrete research situations, we must not lose sight of the fact that these are not, in fact, personal problems of overly sensitive individuals. They are, rather, genuine ethical dilemmas that the broader society, built on inequalities, strategically induces us to disregard.

When the inequalities between researcher and researched are extreme, all the ethical dilemmas inherent in research with living persons are intensified.

Let me outline one model I have developed for thinking about what conventionally goes on when U.S. academics interview Third World people. Collecting personal narratives, when done with professional and publishing goals in mind, is invariably in part an economic matter. The difficulty we have in establishing appropriate practices for such research situations may lie precisely in the odd transformation of familiar economic roles that the process brings about. An individual telling her own story can be construed to be in possession of raw material, material without which the entrepreneurial researcher could not perform the labor of producing a text. In this situation, it is the researcher who owns or has access to the means of production that will transform the spoken words into commodities. This may not be the main function of oral histories, life history studies, or other research projects using "native informants," but it is certainly one of the functions of such texts. Function is, after all, determined in part by one's particular vantage point. To a commercial publisher, the existence of a book as a commodity may be its main function. To a professor, the book could be a step toward promotion and salary increases.

This model of provider and extractor is, however, muddied by the fact that the researcher typically plays the role not only of capitalist but also of laborer, which may be one reason for the complacency of many of those who use personal narratives in their work. The constant shifting of roles prevents us from developing a suitable model for understanding, analyzing, and assigning rights and duties in the personal interview situation. From the point of view of the researcher's labor, the life story appears as a mere potentiality waiting to be actualized. What occurs in the preparation of a text utilizing a personal narrative does involve the transformation of "raw material," a transformation accomplished through the researcher's labor of turning spoken words into written ones, editing, translating if necessary, or studying and analyzing the stories or data.[12] One sort of discourse becomes another, and it is the transformer who derives the greatest benefit from the enterprise. Whether construed as capitalist entrepreneur or as laborer, then, the researcher is the person whose time and investment is acknowledged and rewarded. And, as in any asymmetrical exchange, exploitation is always a possibility.

In another essay I have discussed the different moments of oral history work in which ethical problems emerge, moments ranging from the interview itself, through the uses made of personal narratives and the rewards accruing to the interviewer, to postinterview obligations.[13] But it is not enough to address these specifics, for however subtle the guidelines we might develop for appropriate ethical behavior at these different stages, we must not disregard the very facts—and these are material ones—that determine who gets to do research on whom; who has access to research grants, travel funds, the press; whose words, at the most basic level, are granted authority in representing others.

The feminist precept of "returning the research"—presumably to those communities who made it possible—is one attempt to deal with the inequality of the typical exchange between researcher and researched. But even this raises many problems. How is the research returned? To whom, in what form, and to what avail? Again: of the frequent claim that the interview process, as conducted by feminists, is empowering in that it "gives a voice" to those who might otherwise remain silent, one may well ask: is it empowerment or is it appropriation?[14] When is the purported empowerment or affirmation just another psychological surrogate, a "feel good" measure, a means by which researchers console themselves for the real imbalances in power that they know—despite all the talk of sisterhood—exists? What does it mean, furthermore, for researchers to claim the right to validate the experiences of others? And even where empowerment does occur, as indeed it may, is it a justification for the appropriation that occurs along with it? The only projects that avoid these problems are those that are at all stages genuinely in the control of a community, with the community assuming the role of both researched and researcher.[15] But such projects are only a small fraction of the feminist research being conducted in many fields—all of it urgently needed to redress the distortions of generations of androcentric work that constitutes "knowledge."

The researcher's desire to act out feminist commitments, relinquish control, and involve the researched in all stages of the project runs the risk, however, of subtly translating into the researcher's own demand for affirmation and validation. Liz Kennedy, in describing her experiences with an oral history project in the lesbian community in Buffalo, New York, came to question her expectation of other people's intense involvement with the project. She found that often her subjects were not interested in her follow-up communications and failed to respond to them.[16] This reminds us that even in the best of circumstances, we must guard against foisting onto others a demand or a wish for reinforcement in our work and our concerns.[17] Otherwise, researchers may find themselves abdicating their intellectual responsibilities and training, in perpetual pursuit of their subjects' approval. It is in fact exceedingly difficult to strike a balance that neither exploits the researched nor imposes on them our own psychological demands. Which brings us once again to the simple recognition that some measure of "objectification," or separation and distance, is not only inevitable but, indeed, desirable in most research situations.

When I undertook a small survey to determine how other researchers who work with living persons dealt with the ethical problems generated by their work, I discovered that many of them were comfortable with the usual rationales: informants were becoming "part of history"; their stories were being transmitted; they were affirmed and validated in the process; the researcher perhaps (this occurred more rarely) shared royalties, or donated them to a cause reflecting the interests of the researched. It did not take feminist scholars, with our language of "empowerment," to come up with such rationales; these have been around for a long time, and are often quite correct as far as they go. Interestingly, my brief ethical survey also failed to turn up significant gender differences, with the exception that far fewer women replied to my letter than men (fourteen percent as compared to forty-three percent). The replies did, however, suggest that not gender, or feminist commitments, but what I would call more general political commitments or concerns seemed to divide those who were troubled by the ethical problems of their research from those who were not.[18]

The complexity of raising ethical questions about research with living persons can be further illustrated by looking at two types of problems. One of them is intricate and subtle, the other apparently simple and clear. The first has to do with the currently popular notion, mentioned earlier, that telling one's story constitutes "empowerment." In many respects this is of course true. Agnes Hankiss, in an intriguing article called "Ontologies of the Self: On the Mythological Rearranging of One's Life-History," discusses how, as speakers narrate their life story, they endow certain episodes with a symbolic meaning that in effect turns these episodes into myths. This is a never-ending process, she points out, for an adult must constantly select new models or strategies for life.[19] A similar idea is expressed more simply in an essay by Maria Lugones and Elizabeth Spelman: "Having the opportunity to talk about one's life, to give an account of it, to interpret it, is integral to leading that life rather than being led through it."[20]

Some researchers, however, are not content to let this process work by itself; or, rather, because they are very much aware of the subtle ways in which the researcher invariably shapes even the content of an interview, they argue that researchers ought deliberately to attempt to raise the narrator's consciousness. Marjorie Mbilinyi, for example, describes her oral history work in Tanzania in terms that reveal that "consciousness raising"—or political propaganda, as it might seem to others—was an explicit goal of the project. She considers this legitimate and desirable, an articulation of an agenda that is always present but not usually thought through by researchers.[21]

Marie-Françoise Chanfrault-Duchet, on the other hand, rejects the notion that feminist methodology should involve an attempt to transform the speaker's ideas. She refers to this practice as a form of "savage social therapy."[22] I agree. It seems to me, as well, that to turn interviews with other women into opportunities for imposing our own politically correct analyses requires an arrogance incompatible with genuine respect for others. And respect is a minimum condition if we are not to treat others as mere means to our own ends—if we are not, in other words, to reproduce the very practices of domination that we seek to challenge. In addition, to utilize the interview as an occasion for forcing on others our ideas of a proper political awareness, however we understand that, is to betray an implicit trust. Is it likely, after all, that anyone would agree to an interview if we announced beforehand that while we were getting their life story we would be steering the conversation so as to demonstrate to them what, in our view, their political situation was and how their lives should be understood accordingly? But, if this is indeed our agenda, not to set it forth at the outset is certainly to disguise our true intentions and to manipulate the person interviewed in a way that should be considered incompatible with feminism. This would be "savage social therapy," indeed.

Consider now another, apparently very minor, type of ethical breach, frequently present in even the simplest research situations utilizing personal interviews. Whether the interaction is brief and one-time or involves long-term participant-observation, a common experience of researchers is that they make promises to the people they have interviewed—to send them this or that item, to stay in touch, and so on. But with how many dozens of people can a researcher, however feminist, however sincere, consistently communicate? For how long? I found myself overwhelmed by the prospect of maintaining contact with the sixty women I interviewed in Brazil. On the other hand, on what basis should I have chosen among them? Thus, even with simple matters such as keeping one's word, not to mention the larger issues arising from structural inequalities that the feminist researcher can in no way lessen, problems of power and betrayal expose the fragility of easy assumptions of sisterhood and reciprocity.

In the end, even "feminist" research too easily tends to reproduce the very inequalities and hierarchies it seeks to reveal and to transform. The researcher departs with the data, and the researched stay behind, no better off than before.[23] The common observations that "they" got something out of it too— the opportunity to tell their stories, the entry into history, the recuperation of their own memories, perhaps the chance to exercise some editorial control over the project or even its products, etc.—even when perfectly accurate, do not challenge the inequalities on which the entire process rests. Neither does a sisterly posture of mutual learning and genuine dialogue. For we continue to function in an overdetermined universe in which our respective roles ensure that *other* people are always the subject of *our* research, almost never the reverse.

Is there no alternative, then, to insuperable distance on the one hand, and mystifying chumminess on the other? Are there no choices other than exploitation or patronage? Difference or identification? Faced with this very real dilemma, feminist researchers in today's culture of self-reflexivity often engage in merely rhetorical maneuvers that are rapidly acquiring the status of incantations. A currently popular strategy is that of "situating" onself by prior announcement: "As a white working-class heterosexual . . . ," or "As a black feminist activist. . . ." Sometimes these tropes sound like apologies, more often they are deployed as badges. Either way, they give off their own aroma of fraud, for the underlying assumption seems to be that by such identification one has paid one's respects to "difference"—owned up to bias, acknowledged privilege, or taken possession of oppression—and is now home free.[24] But this posture ignores the fact that "difference" in today's world comes packaged in socially constructed disparities. Much more than a verbal acknowledgment of personal or group identification is required. Indeed, such rhetoric once again deflects attention from the systemic nature of inequality. Identity politics, with its characteristic focus on oppression rather than exploitation, engages in a subtle maneuver by which, as Jenny Bourne notes in an incisive essay, the question of "What is to be done has been replaced by who am I."²⁵

The self-righteous tone that at times characterizes feminist work may be merely a capitulation to feminist discourse, which, like any other discourse, draws boundaries that define what we see and fail to see, what we accept and contest. Feminism, however, should not be turned into a cudgel used against ourselves or others; nor should it be a bromide allowing researchers to proceed behind the screen of an uncritical notion of sisterhood. But having raised these issues—a far easier thing to do than resolving them—I do not want to imply that the appropriate response is to abandon the complex research situations in which oral narratives are typically gathered and utilized. It is a mistake to let ourselves be overwhelmed by these problems. The fact that doing research across race, class, and culture is a messy business is no reason to contemplate only our difficulties and ourselves struggling with them. As Jenny Bourne says, "*What we do is who we are*" (emphasis in the original).²⁶ The world will not get better because we have sensitively apologized for privilege; nor if, from the comfortable heights of the academy, we advertise our identification with the oppressed or compete for distinction as members of this or that oppressed group.

Neither purity nor safety resides in calling one's research "feminist." But no controversy attends the fact that too much ignorance exists in the world to allow us to await perfect research methods before proceeding. Ultimately we have to make up our minds whether our research is worth doing or not, and then determine how to go about it in ways that let it best serve our stated goals.

There is much to be gained from the ongoing discussion of appropriate research methods. But in an unethical world, we cannot do truly ethical research. The problems I have been discussing, in other words, are political and require not only transformations in consciousness, but also, and above all, political action for their solution. Our individual research efforts thus return us to the world, which can be counted on to puncture any illusions that a "correct" feminism will resolve these matters for us.²⁷

Notes

1. Micaela Di Leonardo, *The Varieties of Ethnic Experience: Kinship, Class, and Gender among California Italian-Americans* (Ithaca, N.Y.: Cornell University Press, 1984), p. 41, has noted that it is more difficult to interview "up" than "across" or "down," for wealthy and powerful people are likely to be less receptive to scholarly interest in their personal lives. Marcia Greenlee, in a roundtable discussion on "Appropriation or Empowerment: Oral History, Feminist Process, and Ethics" (Oral History Association Meeting, Baltimore, Maryland, 16 October 1988), spoke of the consequences of such class distinctions for the interviewer: "You do not have to brief someone of high social status in what their rights

are. [They know that] they don't need to talk about certain subjects." With less powerful people, not to mention disempowered ones, however, the researcher's desire to get certain information is often in conflict with ethical behavior that would protect the subject's interests. Greenlee believes that it is crucial to explain to those we interview that they can at any point say "I don't care to comment on that for the record." She also protests against the constraints imposed by sponsoring institutions or government agencies which often set the researcher's interests in opposition to those of the researched.

2. Gail Webber, "Sisterly Conduct: Do Feminists Need Guidelines for Ethical Behavior with One Another?" *Women's Studies International Forum* 8, no. 1 (1985): 57.

3. See, for example, Patti Lather, "Feminist Perspectives on Empowering Research Methodologies," *Women's Studies International Forum* 11, no. 6 (1988): 569–81. Lather's empowering methodologies are greatly undermined by her selection of a homogeneous research environment: a university classroom in the United States.

4. Cited in Israel Shenker, "E. B. White: Notes and Comment by Author," *New York Times,* 11 July 1969, p. 43.

5. Daphne Patai, *Brazilian Women Speak: Contemporary Life Stories* (New Brunswick, N.J.: Rutgers University Press, 1988).

6. A different, perhaps traditional, view of this issue is expressed by Jack D. Douglas, in his essay "Living Morality versus Bureaucratic Fiat," in *Deviance and Decency: The Ethics of Research with Human Subjects,* ed. C. B. Klockars and F. W. O'Connor (Beverly Hills, Calif.: Sage Publications, 1979), pp. 13–33. Douglas writes that the relationships we develop in friendship and in research situations differ only in degree, and that we have fewer social obligations to our research subjects since we tend to be less intimate with them Carrying on about moral problems in social research, in his view, "may be very satisfying to our feelings of pride," but "it is a great distortion of social realities. The fact is that all human beings are social researchers" (pp. 27–29). Cited by Karol R. Ortiz, "Mental Health Consequences of Life History Method," *Ethos* 13, no. 2 (Summer 1985): 99–120. Such a perspective of course does away with any discussion of "ethical" dilemmas, while quietly affirming the inevitability of a particular social "reality."

7. Arlene Kaplan Daniels, "Self-Deception and Self-Discovery in Fieldwork," *Qualitative Sociology* 6, no. 3 (Fall 1983): 196.

8. Ann Oakley, "Interviewing Women: A Contradiction in Terms," in *Doing Feminist Research,* ed. Helen Roberts (Boston: Routledge and Kegan Paul, 1981), pp. 30–61.

9. Judith Stacey, "Can There Be a Feminist Ethnography?" *Women's Studies International Forum* 11, no. 1 (1988): 21–27, and, in a slightly revised version, in this volume.

10. Carole J. Spitzack, "Body Talk: The Politics of Weight Loss and Female Identity," in *Women Communicating: Studies of Women's Talk,* ed. Barbara Bate and Anita Taylor (Norwood, N.J.: Ablex Publishing Corp., 1988), pp. 54–55. At times, the disclosures made in the course of a lengthy life-history interview exceed the bounds of intimate conversation and resemble instead a confession. For a discussion of the moral aspects of confession that is suggestive for those who elicit life histories, see Sissela Bok, "Confession and Moral Choice," in *Foundations of Ethics,* ed. Leroy S. Rouner (Notre Dame, Ind.: University of Notre Dame Press, 1983), pp. 133–48, especially pp. 140–45, where Bok discusses authority and vulnerability in the relationship between listener and confessant.

11. Anatole France, *Le Lys rouge* (Paris: Imprimerie Nationale, 1958; originally published in 1894).

12. A simple illustration of the conflicts that may emerge between the researcher and the researched is provided by Nell Irvin Painter in her preface to the oral history she did with Hosea Hudson. Painter (p. viii) describes their disagreement over the book's title and author. Hudson wanted to appear in both, while Painter wanted to be recognized as the author. They finally settled on a compromise, and the book was published as *The Narrative of Hosea Hudson: His Life as a Negro Communist in the South* (Cambridge, Mass.: Harvard University Press, 1979), with Painter listed as author. An extreme case of a researcher's

appropriation of the speaker's life is discussed by Paul John Eakin in his foreword to Philippe Lejeune's *On Autobiography,* ed. Paul John Eakin, trans. Katherine Leary (Minneapolis, Minn.: University of Minnesota Press, 1989), pp. xvii–xix. The case involves Lejeune's changing reactions to Adélaïde Blasquez's book *Gaston Lucas, serrurier, chronique de l'anti-héros* (Paris: Plon, 1976). Initially, Lejeune judged this to be a masterpiece of ethnographic truth-telling, a belief somewhat shaken when he discovered that Blasquez had erased each interview with Lucas after transcribing it. There is, furthermore, the problem of Blasquez's representation, in her book, of her collaboration with Lucas as idyllically egalitarian, a representation that was exploded when Blasquez's publisher invited Lejeune to interview Blasquez for a video. Lejeune suggested that Gaston Lucas, who was still alive, should also be the subject of a video, but Blasquez replied that the living Gaston Lucas had nothing of value to say, for he truly existed only as the character that she, through her art, had created in her book. See also Lejeune's very interesting comments on the relationship between what he calls "the model" and the "ethnobiographer," in his essay "The Autobiography of Those Who Do Not Write," in Lejeune, *On Autobiography,* pp. 185–215.

13. Daphne Patai, "Ethical Problems of Personal Narratives, Or, Who Should Eat the Last Piece of Cake?" *International Journal of Oral History* 8, no. 1 (February 1987): 5–27.

14. This is the formulation used in a roundtable discussion entitled "Appropriation or Empowerment: Oral History, Feminist Process, and Ethics," organized by Sherna Gluck at the Oral History Association meeting in Baltimore, Maryland, 16 October 1988.

15. See Part IV of this volume for examples of how "return" and community involvement can, in certain types of action and advocacy research, be built into the project as ongoing features.

16. Liz Kennedy, at the roundtable discussion on "Appropriation or Empowerment: Oral History, Feminist Process, and Ethics," Oral History Association meeting, Baltimore, Maryland, 16 October 1988.

17. These problems are discussed with exceptional forthrightness in Sondra Hale's essay in this volume.

18. Patai, "Ethical Problems of Personal Narratives."

19. Agnes Hankiss, "Ontologies of the Self: On the Mythological Rearranging of One's Life-History," in *Biography and Society: The Life History Approach in the Social Sciences,* ed. Daniel Bertaux (Beverly Hills, Calif.: Sage Publications, 1981), pp. 203–9.

20. Maria C. Lugones and Elizabeth V. Spelman, "Have We Got a Theory for You! Feminist Theory, Cultural Imperialism, and the Demand for 'The Woman's Voice,' " *Women's Studies International Forum* 6, no. 6 (1983): 593.

21. Marjorie Mbilinyi, comments made at the conference on "Autobiographies, Biographies and Life Histories of Women: Interdisciplinary Perspectives," sponsored by the Center for Advanced Feminist Studies at the University of Minnesota, Minneapolis, Minnesota, 23–24 May 1986. A version of Mbilinyi's conference paper appears as " 'I'd Have Been a Man': Politics and the Labor Process in Producing Personal Narratives," in *Interpreting Women's Lives,* ed. Personal Narratives Group (Bloomington, Ind.: Indiana University Press, 1989), pp. 204–27.

22. Marie-Françoise Chanfrault-Duchet, "Narrative Structures, Social Models, and Symbolic Representation in the Life Story," in this volume.

23. As Calvin Pryluck puts it, "Ultimately we are all outsiders in the lives of others. We can take our gear and go home; they have to continue their lives where they are." Calvin Pryluck, "Ultimately We Are All Outsiders: The Ethics of Documentary Filmmaking," *Journal of the University Film Association* 28, no. 1 (Winter 1976): 22. I am grateful to Professor Mark Jonathan Harris, of the School of Cinema-Television at the University of Southern California, for sending me this article.

24. There are, of course, serious problems of possible bias, of which researchers have increasingly become aware. Marsha Darling, in "The Disinherited as Source: Rural Black Women's Memories," *Michigan Quarterly Review* 26, no. 1 (Winter 1987): 49, writes of the ways in which our very notions of what constitutes a legitimate "source" are shaped by method-

ological, conceptual, and political notions. Claire Robertson has also addressed these issues. See her "In Pursuit of Life Histories: The Problem of Bias," *Frontiers* 7, no. 2 (1983): 63–69. Despite her sensitive and sensible approach, Robertson herself engages in ethically questionable behavior when, according to her own account, while in Ghana working with an interpreter, Robertson deceived some of her informants about her increasing competence in the Ga language. As she explains: "On occasion, I found it helpful to pretend total ignorance of Ga because the informant was telling Mankah [the interpreter] things that she assumed I would not understand" (p. 64). For our purposes, what is significant about this statement is Robertson's apparent lack of awareness that this behavior raised ethical problems.

25. Jenny Bourne, "Homelands of the Mind: Jewish Feminism and Identity Politics," *Race and Class* 29, no. 1 (1987): 3.
26. Bourne, "Homelands of the Mind," p. 22.
27. Passages and lines of argument utilized in this essay first appeared in my "Ethical Problems of Personal Narratives" (cited above), "Who's Calling Whom Subaltern?" *Women and Language* 11, no. 2 (Winter 1988): 23–26; and in "U.S. Academics and Third World Women: Is Ethical Research Possible?" *Women's Studies in Indiana* 15, no. 1 (November/December 1989): 1–4.

IV

Community and Advocacy

The tension that ensues when we confront the incongruity of trying to do ethical research in an all too imperfect world has led some feminist scholars to devise alternative research models. Grounded in communities and carried into the academy by feminists who frequently started as activists, these models tend significantly to reduce the distance between researcher and researched. Projects that hold the promise of promoting unity of interest and long-lasting collaboration displace emphasis from the development of proper feminist research "attitudes" and individual modes of interaction, to the very structure of the research project itself.

Like many community-based projects, the Puerto Rican Popular Education program disscussed by Rina Benmayor represents both collective work done by the researchers and a collaborative effort in which the researcher joins with those whose testimonies are being recorded. Benmayor describes how the narrators, far from being merely "the researched," are engaged in an empowerment process in which the telling of their life stories is of immediate and measurable benefit not only to themselves but also to other members of their community.

Laurie Mercier and Mary Murphy, who also conducted their oral histories as members of a larger team, focus on the internal processes of such collective research. In assessing the Molders and Shapers project, they indicate some of the problems that can arise as a result of the varying relationships and identifications both in the community that is being researched and within the community that is conducting the research.

Although a sense of connectedness seems to be achieved more readily in collective community projects, individual researchers also try to bridge the gap between community and academy in various ways. Karen Olson and Linda Shopes each describes how her unique situation and background helped her negotiate the unequal social dynamics of interviews with working-class women. They also detail their efforts to address the issue of the researchers' larger social responsibility to use the stories with which they were entrusted in order to challenge prevailing stereotypes of working-class life.

Sherna Gluck, having set out to interview Palestinian women with the deliberate intention of using the interviews for the purpose of promoting their cause, illustrates yet another kind of advocacy. Whereas other researchers have expressed concern about their ability to forge a relationship with a community, Gluck, because she already shares a political agenda with the community she has studied, focuses instead on the potential contradictions between advocacy and scholarly practice.

The essays in this section explore concrete ways in which we can implement our commitment to do research for women and to establish closer links between oral history practitioners and the communities of women whose stories they collect.

10

Testimony, Action Research, and Empowerment:
Puerto Rican Women and Popular Education

Rina Benmayor

Over the past two decades, "minority" and feminist scholars have sought to challenge traditional disciplinary paradigms of social research. "Research for whom?" we have asked. "How is it conducted?" "Whose voice is privileged?" "Don't the 'researched' also interrogate the 'researcher?' " The concern to develop socially responsible research has forced us to question continually the relationship between investigation and the needs and rights of people. It has also forced us to rethink our research practices and our own motives for engaging in this activity.

This paper examines such questions through a program in action research in which "testimony," life history, and community play key roles.[1] It suggests ways to establish a closer relationship between scholarship and community empowerment, thus shifting the traditional locus of power and voice in research away from an exclusively academic base. It also calls for practices of collective investigation.

The El Barrio Popular Education Program is a community-based program of action research initiated by the Center for Puerto Rican Studies, Hunter College, City University of New York. The participants are predominantly Puerto Rican women who, because of historical circumstance and structural poverty, have not had access to schooling. The Program's primary purpose, then, is to promote empowerment through native-language literacy training and education of Spanish-speaking adults.

From the outset, it was clear that this Program would provide a much-needed service. In turn, direct involvement in a pedagogical project would allow for a more organic inquiry into the issue of empowerment. What is the empowering potential of literacy and popular education in the Puerto Rican community? How can culturally sensitive programs for social change be put in place? How do class, national, racial and gender identities serve or short-circuit the empowerment process? And how can community networks help translate individual empowerment into collective mobilization? These questions constitute the larger investigative agenda attached to the El Barrio Program.[2]

This paper highlights ways in which oral history practices contribute to transformation. When testimonies are generated in an organized, group context, they have the potential of impacting directly on individual and collective empowerment. They become more than empirical data and transcend their static destiny as archival documents. Social empowerment enables people to speak, and speaking empowers. At the same time, testimony, life history, and other forms of oral history research often lead to a reexamination of theory and method.

Concepts of "community" shape every aspect of action research. "Community" and "collective" are key to how and why this project was initiated, to its structure, research aims, and content, the positioning of the participants (including researchers), and the outcomes it has produced.

The El Barrio Program and its research component were conceived with the philosophy that investigation should be structured in ways that privilege reciprocity and mutual "returns" among community members and researchers. We contend that research has an obligation to create social spaces in which people can make meaningful contributions to their own well-being and not serve as objects of investigation.

This effort has had a profound impact on us as researchers. Our practice, too, is being changed. Power differentials between ourselves as researchers and the participants in the Program have not disappeared. Acknowledging this, we have struggled to develop an alternative practice based on relationship rather than detached observation, based on accountability, commonality and difference, "insider-" and "outsidership," and collective rather than individual work practices.

One final introductory note. At the Centro de Estudios Puertorriqueños, our concern with issues of power in research comes first out of a long struggle against the national, racial, and class oppression with which Puerto Ricans and other people of color have had to contend. Our understanding of gender oppression and the importance of its specificities is more recent. However, it is no less central. The educational process in the Program and our research practice are highly gender-marked: the majority of the participants and the majority of researchers are women.

A crucial part of the relationships we have established and of the empowerment process involves gender identity. This paper, however, does not argue for action research as a strictly feminist methodology. The aim is to challenge and change traditions of power and authority on multiple levels, an effort that recognizes the interdependence of oppressions and the need for shared strategies.

The Program

In 1984, the Centro de Estudios Puertorriqueños, Hunter College, initiated a Spanish-language adult literacy program in East Harlem, one of the oldest Puerto Rican neighborhoods in New York City. The initial purpose was to investigate the parent literacy practices of a community beset by high rates of school dropout. The need for adult literacy training became apparent, especially among first-generation migrants. Today, the El Barrio Program is a full-blown program in popular education, with beginning, intermediate, and advanced literacy classes in Spanish and one conversation class in English as a second language. Classes are held three days a week, each for a two-hour period.

The Program is located in El Barrio. It occupies one floor of Casita María, an early settlement house and the site of a well-known Hispanic senior citizens' center. Culturally and in class terms, the Program is perceived by the participants as an extension of the world in which they live. They often refer to the Program as a family and a second home.

An average of fifty students enroll voluntarily per year and are placed into classes corresponding to levels of literacy. Ninety-five percent of the participants are Puerto Rican women, from their late twenties to over eighty years of age.[3] The majority grew up in rural communities in Puerto Rico and arrived in the United States as young adults. They live on an average annual income of less than $5,000, which is well below the official poverty line. Seventy-six percent receive public assistance, and almost two-thirds are single mothers. Educational levels range from no formal schooling to some high school.

The staff consists of three teachers, a full-time counselor and a Program coordinator, and the Program director. Auxiliary staff includes college-student tutors and our research team. The immediate governing body is a Steering Committee composed of students, teachers, staff, and researchers. As a nonprofit organization, the Program has a Board of Directors.

Testimony and Empowerment Pedagogy

In "Affirming Cultural Citizenship in the Puerto Rican Community," we wrote:

> In the classroom, many participants find their traditional notions of education being challenged. Instead of the "banking" approach to learning in which the teacher periodically deposits information into the students' minds, the goal is to develop "critical literacy." The teachers organize their classes around socially relevant themes: gender relations, work, education, migration and social history. They encourage highly participatory and collective modes of interaction.[4]

Guided by a Freirian approach to empowerment pedagogy, the underlying premise in the Program is that personal experience serves as a critical basis for knowledge and skill acquisition.[5] Shared testimony in the classroom plays a particularly powerful role. Personal accounts generate group discussion and, from there, the words through which students learn to read and the topics about which they eloquently write.

This learning environment is both exciting and challenging, since it establishes a space in which participants are experts. "Testimonial" speech acts help foster strong peer identification, bonding, and a sense of collective. At the same time, this classroom atmosphere provides a validating framework for participants to "tell" their stories.

Instances like the following are commonplace. In the literacy workbook, which is entitled *Palabras de lucha y alegria* (Words of Struggle and Joy), students are asked to read dialogues, answer questions, and relate the subject matter to their own experiences. In one of the dialogues, the sentence "*Fuimos a una area bella y todos subimos la montaña*" (We went to a very beautiful spot and climbed the mountain), sparked a discussion of experiences with nature. A middle-aged woman related how she was raised in the mountains of Ecuador by a stepmother who abused her. She would often run and hide in the forest and became an extremely lonely child. As she described the beauty of her mountain refuge, tears of pain welled up in her eyes. The woman sitting next to her responded to this in a very direct way, putting an arm around her, as the rest of the class nodded and remarked how they understood. What began as a literacy exercise evolved into a moment of intense testimony and collective support.

Autobiographical essays, written as homework assignments, are an important part of the testimonial process in the classroom. They too foster solidarity, and move the discourse from individual to collective levels. As accounts are read out loud in class, participants come to realize that their circumstances are not unique, accidental, or the product of their own errors or "shortcomings."

As Rosa Torruellas has pointed out, "a critical turning point in the process of becoming literate is the ability to communicate one's thoughts and ideas in writing."[6] She notes that the women describe this practice as "*escribir de la mente*" (writing from the mind). The Program's pedagogy tries to foster an understanding of writing as a form of self-expression rather than as a mechanical skill. Even at the beginning level, the teacher discourages "copying." This is part of an effort to establish self-confidence and displace authority from the teacher.

"Writing from the mind" also links testimony to empowerment. A biographical sketch of one of the participants, based on a combination of life-history interviews, participant observation, and classroom compositions, illustrates this link.[7] In this sketch, Torruellas notes that when Mrs. Huertas enrolled in the beginning class four years ago, she signed her name with an X. Rural poverty and her caretaking responsibilities as the eldest female child had prevented her from attending school. She had reached adulthood without knowing how to read and write.

Illiteracy brought her embarrassment and frustration, as this account of her husband's courtship reveals:

> He would write to me, and my friend, who knew how to read and write, would read me the letters. She would also write them for me. . . . I would

tell her what to say but . . . I did not know whether she would write what I told her or if she would invent something else.[8]

Concern for her own children's education was an important catalyst in Mrs. Huertas's development. Her participation in her children's school won her the position of treasurer of her Parent-Teacher Association. She recalls with amusement how she had to memorize the accounts and give financial reports at meetings. "Oh God! I was treasurer of PS 121 and I didn't know how to read or write!"[9]

Finally, in her early forties, Mrs. Huertas joined the El Barrio Program. Now, she is in the advanced class and aspires to a high school equivalency diploma. She remarks that her educational development has become an important collective family experience. She says that she keeps a pad and pencil on her night table, and that after cleaning up the kitchen at night she likes to climb into bed to read or write. Her sons often help her with her homework, sitting around her while she works. They read and help correct her compositions despite their limited knowledge of Spanish, and they encourage her to continue. She regularly brings in compositions of her own inspiration, written at home, and shares them with her peers in class. One of Mrs. Huertas's expressed goals is to inscribe her life, to write her story "*de mi puño y letra*" (in my own hand).

Torruellas comments on how Mrs. Huertas has come to incorporate writing into her daily life as an important survival strategy. She has turned writing into an effective, sometimes cathartic vehicle for expressing her feelings and emotions. "*Uno se desahoga*" (It's a release), she says. The following poem is illustrative:

to be deeply loved
by someone gives you
strength
but to love someone
deeply gives you
courage
I'm not afraid to die
but I'd rather not be there
when it happens
but when I dream that
I'm alive, it seems like I'm dead
when I awaken.[10]

Esther Huertas's case highlights the therapeutic aspect of autobiographical writing. It shows how writing can inspire participants to create supportive niches for empowerment in their daily lives.

Testimony as a Research Tool

The therapeutic impact of self-disclosure taking place in the classroom has always been striking. This has led us to explore the potential of testimony as a research strategy to study the affirmative, empowering identities and practices of this marginalized sector of the New York Puerto Rican community.

We recognized that the classroom and the instances of self-revelation that it generated were limited sources of information for understanding the empowerment process. We needed to know more about participants' lives in the home and the community. Consequently, along with participant observation outside the Program, we began to collect extensive life histories.[11] These provide needed historical span and depth, a more extensive view of the past from which better to appreciate and evaluate the changes that are currently taking place in the lives of the participants.

Life histories also give us a sense of the issues and experiences around which identities are formed and a sense of how these may change over time. At the same time, we are witnessing the creation of a new version of the life story, whose content and expression is already marked by the transformations the participants are experiencing.

In collecting these life histories, we have come to realize how different this process is from the kind of oral history research the Centro had conducted previously. We had been collecting life histories in the New York Puerto Rican community for several years, as a way of creating a more well-rounded historical record and analysis of the Puerto Rican migration and U.S. "minority" experience. However, with the Popular Education Program, we recognized that action research has the potential to situate oral history differently. It also forces us to rethink many ethical and methodological practices.

First, the El Barrio Program established a different context for collecting oral history. Typically, we would undertake field searches for individuals scattered throughout the city, who would then be asked to engage their memories for a six- or eight-hour interlude in their lives. However, here we had a group for whom recounting life stories is an organic part of their coming together three days a week, thirty-two weeks of the year.

Second, the life history account could become more than a vehicle for documenting and interpreting the past. Life review and the act of telling one's story were active components in the process of transformation.

Third, the relationship between researchers and participants could, in fact, become much closer. Of the five researchers in our team, three have had staff and directive responsibilities in the Program, responsibilities that require their presence on an almost daily basis. As the lines blur between researcher and staff, trust and responsibility become substantially greater.

Fourth, instead of being "lone oral historians," hoofing it around the boroughs, we are an on-site team. And although the moment of the "interviews" is one-on-one, our process of study, analysis, and writing is collective, drawing on our various interdisciplinary perspectives, national and cultural backgrounds, and social experiences.

And *fifth,* action research generates a type of "return to community" that is qualitatively different from any we have produced before. Even socially committed research has tended to use a linear paradigm of "appropriation/ return." You extract data, interpret it, and *then* "return" it, in linear sequence. Our experience in East Harlem suggests that action research grounded in a specific community dynamic produces an entirely different outcome.

Rather than being a final stage in an "appropriation/give-back" paradigm, we have discovered that "return" is an ongoing and organic part of the entire Program. Participants do not depend on the research to get something back. By being in the Program, they gain literacy skills, knowledge, and dignity. When a woman moves from signing her name with an X to writing poetry, she has gained power. Similarly, when another is able to enroll in college, she has benefitted from the Program. Or when a participant finds that the historical content of the curriculum has broadened her knowledge, she has been enriched.

"Community" at the Center

We have found that the kind of research we are engaged in creates multiple layers of "return," allowing participants as well as researchers to become returners. "Community" is at the center of the entire endeavor and establishes a relationship of reciprocity throughout.

It is important to point out, here, the way in which we are using the term "community." A community, for our purposes, is not restricted to geographic location or national homogeneity. Rather, community

> consists of collective formations of individuals tied together through common bonds of interests and solidarity. What they lay claim to will vary according to the specific community, but includes such things as land, homes, beliefs, language(s), artistic expression, traditional or newly emerging practices, or anything else which is seen by them as defining qualities of who they are, what they want, and what they seek to be as a community.[12]

This definition of "community" focuses on dynamics of struggle rather than on static characteristics. The Program brings together a variety of identities and interests, sometimes complementary, sometimes conflicting. National/regional cultural identity constitutes a primary community in the Program. For most, there is a strong and unified sense of being Puerto Rican. There is also a shared Latin American identity that links the Puerto Rican members with the Dominican and Central and South American participants. And, in the context of the United States, *"hispano"* serves as a common frame of reference.

However, what makes national identity a priority, establishing it as a "community," is an acute sense of disadvantage based on being Puerto Rican or "hispano" in the U.S. context and the need for assertion in the face of this reality. Culture often becomes the rallying point. This is evidenced first in the fact that this is a Spanish-language Program. Other cultural manifestations are the festivities and celebrations, which are heavily marked by mostly Puerto Rican music, poetry, and food and dance traditions, and which include invited performances by musicians and dancers from El Barrio.

However, "community" in the Program is not only based on national or cultural affirmation. There is also an intense cognizance of shared conditions of poverty and class exploitation, an important part of which is the overwhelming stigma of being "uneducated." It is important to point out that the participants in the Program are among those of the Puerto Rican/Latino working class who have become most marginalized in recent decades. In the face of this, participants are quick to declare that they may be poor but they have their dignity. This assertion establishes a basis for confronting the daily difficulties of social and economic exclusion.

Class position is intertwined with issues of gender. The problems around which many women in the Program are mobilizing, albeit on an individual or domestic level, have to do with their particular daily life circumstances within the declining industrial context of New York City. Most are female heads of households and carry the burden of child-rearing by themselves; most have to deal with the indignities of being Welfare recipients and dependent on a range of poor social services. All face high levels of violence on the neighborhood streets, economic violence that excludes them and their spouses from participation in the labor force, and often domestic violence as well.

A sense of "community" around gender is present on one level, building on established practices of female culture in Puerto Rican and other Latin American contexts. However, participation in the Program is challenging women participants to deconstruct gendered ideologies of social roles and capabilities and to establish a more critical base of gender alliance.

Beyond these bonds and collective struggles, the Program itself constructs a particular community of women and men engaged in educational advancement. Its physical location in a Puerto Rican neighborhood, the ethnic, class, and gender composition of the participants, and the emphasis on collective, democratic practices of pedagogy all contribute to a strong sense of cohesion and group membership. *"La comunidad"* comprises all these dimensions, in varying combinations and degrees for each of the participants.

Consequently, "community" in the Program is created through common circumstances and common struggle. It builds on common histories and on bonds of national origins, class, and gender, and becomes more concretely expressed through the educational initiative in which participants are collectively involved. In this sense, we can say that the "community" created by participants in the Program is as much if not more responsible for empowerment as the contributions of teachers, staff, and researchers.

Community in the "Text"

The previous discussion of classroom testimonies and autobiographical writings show community and identity in action. Life histories also display the central importance participants attach to community at the level of discourse. In analyzing transcripts, we have found that the notion of "return to community" is actually embedded in testimonial accounts, giving them a raison d'être. This suggests that return is not merely the researchers' responsibility, but an activity that the participants themselves are deeply engaged in.

Mrs. Minerva Ríos's life history provides us with an example of how the relationship to community governs the telling of one's story.[13] Born on the Caribbean coast of Puerto Rico in 1905, Mrs. Ríos was eighty-two years old at the time of our interviews. At age sixteen, she completed the eighth grade, which for that time constituted a substantial educational achievement. What, then did this Program have to offer a woman who reads and writes fluently, who is not in search of better work opportunities or of an avenue to higher education? The role of memory was a key to this:

> At this Center they've had many programs and I've enrolled in them all. But, I think this Program is really extraordinary. Every writing assignment Felix [the teacher] gives us generates a memory. The other day he showed us a painting of women washing down by a river. Immediately, my mind flashed on the people washing on the riverbank [in my hometown], singing and washing in the river.[14]

After completing the life-history interview and observing her interactions in class, we came to the realization that the El Barrio Program offered Mrs. Ríos the opportunity to define and fulfill a special role within the collective, that of the "Historian." Her evocations of life on the island in the early decades of the century are more than just chapters in her chronology. They establish her as witness to and bearer of a bygone period of Puerto Rican culture.

Through these recollections, Mrs. Ríos affirms values that she perceives to have changed in today's world. A recurrent theme in her account of childhood is poverty tempered by the beauty of the physical environment: "Our lives were poor but happy because there was no violence."[15] The image of a carefree and wholesome past contrasts with a frequently expressed concern for her own physical safety today. She does not go out at night, she says, unless someone will pick her up and walk her to her door.

When speaking about the past, Mrs. Ríos continually refers to the issue of "*respeto*"—respect of children for parents, children for teachers, and parents for teachers—which, she laments, existed then but does not exist anymore:

> My mother was a very serious person who brought us up very strictly. We had to respect our teachers. I couldn't come home and complain about the teacher because she would tell me that the teacher was right. She'd take me to school, and in front of all the kids give me a spanking.[16]

School is another major theme of testimony. With great fondness and precision of detail, Mrs. Ríos paints a picture of a local, multigrade school house, where children of the rich and poor studied together. She tells us how colonial rule meant that teachers were often "imported" and that Puerto Rican children became well-versed in the major myths and chapters of U.S. history. However, there were no textbooks that included Puerto Rican history and Latin American history was not taught at all.

Mrs. Ríos arrived in New York in 1929, and then lived through the Depression. She eventually got a steady job in a commercial laundry, where she worked for forty years pressing cuffs and collars on men's shirts. The social programs of the Roosevelt period and unionization brought concrete benefits to her life. Consequently, she subscribes to the notion of socially responsible government, and to this day she sees federal programs as positive safety nets for the poor. Her own words are charged with didactic intent:

> At my age, I don't have any reason to continue studying, but I motivated my *compañeras,* giving them advice so that they don't abandon this important program and keep forging ahead. I told them about the time when these programs didn't exist. Today, we have to take advantage of all the opportunities the government offers through programs such as this one.[17]

Mrs. Ríos has often written compositions on these themes, and, as is customary, student writings are always read aloud in class. In a sense, participants' writings are produced for the "audience" of fellow classmates. However, there is an additional factor that shapes Mrs. Ríos's discourse. She writes for her *compañeras/os* in the Program, all of whom are younger and with whom she has a historical lesson to share.

Mrs. Ríos also wants her life history to be a legacy for future generations, in the form of a book. Hence, the life history interview has special value to her. Clearly, both written and oral formats provide meaningful platforms from which she imparts her knowledge and example to others. Far from being self-aggrandizing, her testimony is fundamentally instructive and designed to place the community rather than the individual at the center.

Other life histories attest to how individual experience is also framed within a discourse that goes beyond personal gain. Ana Juarbe has examined the history of Mrs. Belén Resto, a single mother who prides herself on never having received public assistance.[18] She had a high school education in Puerto Rico. However, she enrolled in the Program to gain some computer skills and reenter the job market after a sixteen-year absence. Yet after two years in the Program, she became a tutor in the children's after-school club at Casita María, and is now enrolled in her second year of college, pursuing Elementary Education credentials. Her life history does not focus on her own accomplishments. Rather, Mrs. Resto says: "I think if I achieve this [goal of becoming a teacher] in some way or another I can help my community. [The idea] is not merely to become a teacher, but to know how to teach, you know."[19]

In an article on Latin American women's testimonial literature, Doris Sommer suggests a particular relationship of Latin American women to community. She argues that in those texts "singularity achieves its identity as an extension of the collective." This, she states

> is consistent with existing cultural assumptions about the community being the fundamental social unit. . . . When the narrator talks about herself to you, she implies both the existing relationship to other representative selves in the community and potential relationships that extend her community through the texts. . . . The testimonial produces complicity. . . . Once the subject of the testimonial is understood as the community made up of a variety of roles, the reader is called in to fill one of them.[20]

This relationship between individual and community suggests new ways of "reading" and understanding women's testimonials. These speech acts, whether in the presence of a tape recorder or in the context of a classroom, interpellate the reader or listener. In this case, the listeners are the narrator's classmates and our research team, other members of her own community.

Community and the Politics of Research

Despite good intentions, many attempts to conduct culturally sensitive research still perpetuate the same subject position for the researched and the same individualistic, authoritative stance for the researcher. One important reason is that even "committed" scholarship is often initiated from academic rather than community contexts, and the objectives are more heavily, if not exclusively, weighted toward "scientific" or public policy rather than toward community agendas. Perhaps this suggests a need to decenter the investigative enterprise and its practitioners from an exclusive university base.

Doris Sommer's analysis, discussed above, also implies a community role for the interviewer/investigator. In our own case, we are better-positioned than most to develop structures of action research. We have the advantage of working in a research center that is deeply rooted in the Puerto Rican community, one that attempts to be accountable to it. This position confers on us a responsibility that, as Sherry Gorelick points out, goes beyond "giving voice."[21]

The El Barrio Popular Education Program has given us an unusually rich opportunity to experiment. In the first instance, the hope is to create a lasting institution that responds to ongoing community needs, and not one that exists merely for the purposes of research. Although the Centro de Estudios Puertorriqueños was responsible for establishing the Program, efforts are now underway to incorporate a leadership-training component that, along with the Steering Committee and Board of Directors, is a clear step in the direction of community self-management.

As the Program has developed, we have been challenged to reposition ourselves as participant investigators. Most of our research team members have had directive and coordinative responsibilities, doubling as Program staff. Others have engaged in daily classroom ethnography or served as classroom tutors and teacher aides. In this Program there is no such thing as the silent researcher who sits in the back of the room observing.

Of course, this leads to developing a more involved relationship between researchers and participants. This is enhanced by the fact that, for the most part, we are women interviewing women. Often, after finishing a life history, participants say, "When are you coming over again?" Or, "Come over and see me during the vacation," suggesting that after several sessions of divulging one's life story and sometimes rather intimate accounts, one would like to be assured that the interest is not merely temporary. The advantage to conducting research in an institutional context is that the Program allows for weekly, if not daily, contact and continuity.

Being a researcher in this setting also implies being a source of support. Julia Curry–Rodríguez addresses these expectations and ethical implications in another Latino community context, as a Chicana researcher working with Mexican migrant women.[22] While our involvement heightens a sense of personal responsibility and rapport with participants, the Barrio Program also provides a primary and organized context for support. It has a full-time counselor who is there to help participants deal with social service agencies, to provide emotional support, and to develop group solidarity. Consequently, responsibility and accountability are not left to the individual researcher to shoulder alone but rather are part of a collective effort.

Perhaps most striking is that the trust and reciprocal respect that characterize the majority of our relationships are ultimately based on an acknowledgement of a common objective of moving forward as a community. Even the most modest effort of documentation is deemed important to a community that has traditionally been denied a dignified public voice and historical recognition. Every individual we have approached for our oral history research over the years understands the importance of contributing the story of individual lives, "their little grain of sand," to the history of the Puerto Rican community in this country.

The common goal of community advancement contributes a great deal to mediating differences between investigators and participants in the Program. Each member of our team occupies multiple "insider" and "outsider" positions vis-à-vis the participants. In terms of gender, we are four women and one man. Ethnically speaking, we include Puerto Ricans, a Dominican, and a Sephardic woman raised in the United States and Latin America. Our class backgrounds range from poor, working-class to middle-class. We are mixed in terms of our racial characteristics and our experiences with discrimination. We include Puerto Ricans born and raised in New York and those born and raised in Puerto Rico. We range in age from mid-thirties to mid-forties. Some of us have children. We are academics from a range of disciplines and with different levels of community activism. We have varying degrees of Spanish fluency.

As Maxine Baca Zinn points out, regardless of shared ethnicity, gender, or class, a researcher enters each and every field situation as an "outsider."[23] We are acutely aware of points of convergence and unbreachable gaps between ourselves and the people with whom we are working. However, differences are mediated by the fact that we are part of a collective effort that has clear political and social goals. This allows for a greater sense of security on both sides.

In fact, the heterogeneity of our team—in terms of ethnic origins, class, educational levels, and gender—has stimulated rich collective analysis and debate. Each of us brings to discussions a range of perceptions, sensibilities, disciplinary backgrounds, and interests. We have the luxury of being able to test our ideas with each other on a regular basis and engage in collective study and preparation. Consequently, what we write is usually the product of previous exchanges in which our interpretations are collectively debated and refined. Moreover, we are attempting to share and corroborate our interpretations with the people about whom we write, difficult as this is.

Contrary to the way in which many alternative team research projects are structured in traditional academic settings, we have tried to draw on diverse strengths rather than on hierarchies of expertise.[24] This is reflected in our authorship practice, which does not distinguish research directors from research assistants. Our team combines expertise of different sorts, ranging from traditions of academic scholarship to community activism.

These are some ways in which our own practice has been influenced by accountability to the community of women and men who constitute the Program. Perhaps the most difficult part has been to explain effectively the nature of research and the specific goals of this project to people who have never before encountered this kind of work. Participants tend to describe life-history interviews in more familiar terms. Initially apprehensive about tape recording her life story, one woman later wrote in class: "This morning, at ten o'clock I had an interview. I felt very good. This is the first time I have ever been interviewed." Now, she calls our interviews "gossiping," which, on the one

172 / Rina Benmayor

hand, indicates a relaxed attitude toward her involvement and, on the other, a certain wonder about how this can be "research." Some participants interpret this research as "therapy," even though they have probably never visited a therapist. Other women continue to ask "What is this for?" Their most immediate frame of reference for an interview is the "face to face" interrogation at the Welfare office.

By way of addressing this dilemma and tempering the individualized nature of the interview, we organized a group meeting of the participants who had expressed an interest in being involved. Here we tried to explain the purpose of the research, its historical contribution to a collective story of the Puerto Rican experience, and the importance of leaving a legacy to future generations. We spoke of the more immediate need to counter the pejorative images of Latino culture that are held by common folk and policy experts alike. At this time, we also discussed methods, time commitments, and rights to privacy.

The second group meeting was held months later, as an evaluative tool. We were concerned to know what benefit, if any, participants derived from doing a life history, and what they liked and disliked about the process. Many stated that the process had been theraupeutic. One man eloquently said that this was the first time he had done a life review and that he became aware of past mistakes that he would never repeat. All agreed that they wanted to continue to meet as a group. However, the most poignant result was that the life-history interview, and a strong feeling of trust in the person conducting it, enabled one participant to recount a highly traumatic experience of childhood violence for the first time in her life. Having broken her life-long silence, she proceeded to recount the story to the group.

Conclusion

Situations like these remind us of the heavy responsibility of working with life history and of the importance of not working alone. Action research has the potential to reposition the researcher/subject power relationship in many ways. It creates a social space and a dynamic of reciprocity that give participants the power to make meaningful contributions to their own community. In the El Barrio Popular Education Program this is most readily visible through the human interactions that take place, day to day, in the classroom. By creating a space for testimony, literacy and empowerment are advanced.

The central role of community is also evident in the testimonial discourse, both oral and written. This suggests interesting new contexts for conducting oral history and related narrative research. Autobiographical writings are ways to inscribe oneself in the world and to leave a legacy to future generations. Moreover, the ways in which participants construct their life histories with didactic or exemplary intent suggest an organic connection to community and a responsibility to it. This invites us to look at text as well as context.

As researchers with a commitment to change, we must decenter ourselves from the "ivory tower" and construct more participatory, democratic practices. We must keep people and politics at the center of our research. This case study of the El Barrio Popular Education Program provokes thinking in a new way: privileging dynamics of reciprocity in which researchers and community members collaborate to strengthen collective returns to community.

Notes

This paper is based on collaborative research and analysis carried out by Rosa M. Torruellas, Ana Juarbe, Anneris Goris, and myself. Together with Pedro Pedraza, Jr., we comprise the investigative team at the Centro de Estudios Puertorriqueños, Hunter College, which is responsible for designing and carrying out this research. Many of the ideas presented in this paper are drawn from a lengthier, jointly authored article entitled "Affirming Cultural Citizenship in the Puerto Rican Community: The El Barrio Popular Education Program," which will be cited throughout.

1. Throughout this paper I make reference to oral history, life history, and testimony. I see these as interrelated terms: life history as a form of oral history, and testimony as the speech act that imbues life history with intent.

2. A fuller discussion of our investigation can be found in Rosa M. Torruellas, Rina Benmayor, Anneris Goris, and Ana Juarbe, "Affirming Cultural Citizenship in the Puerto Rican Community: The El Barrio Popular Education Program," in *Literacy as Praxis: Culture, Language and Pedagogy,* ed. Catherine E. Walsh (Norwood, N.J.: Ablex, forthcoming).

   In this paper, we observe that the participants in the El Barrio Program exemplify the fact that the vitality and creativity of marginalized communities are usually ignored by mainstream culture and social analysts. They show how, despite poverty and disadvantage, people do not passively accept their "fate," but actively search for ways to improve their personal and collective lives. These affirmative actions toward empowerment, we argue, are claims for a "cultural citizenship" based on human, social, and cultural values, rather than on legal rights.

   Cultural citizenship is a concept we have been developing with Chicano colleagues in the Cultural Studies Working Group of the Inter-University Program for Latino Research. In looking comparatively at empowerment processes in our communities, we note how disenfranchised peoples seek to alter existing relations of power in the home, the community, or the society. We are calling this the affirmation of cultural citizenship. Programs of action research like the El Barrio Popular Education Program permit a more grounded understanding of cultural citizenship and empowerment.

3. Enrollment in the Program is voluntary. There is a small number of women from other Latin American and Caribbean countries who have enrolled. In the past five years, only four or five Puerto Rican men have participated. Links between "workfare" and female-headed households may account for some of this imbalance.

4. Torruellas, Benmayor, Goris, and Juarbe, "Affirming Cultural Citizenship," ms. p. 6.

5. Paulo Freire, *Pedagogy of the Oppressed* (New York: Herder and Herder, 1972); Paulo Freire and Donaldo Macedo, *Literacy: Reading the Word and the World* (South Hadley, Mass.: Bergin and Garvey, 1987).

6. Torruellas, Benmayor, Goris, and Juarbe, "Affirming Cultural Citizenship," ms. p. 20.

7. The following interpretations are derived from Torruellas's lengthy biographical sketch of Mrs. Esther Huertas, which appears in Torruellas, Benmayor, Goris, and Juarbe, "Affirming Cultural Citizenship," ms. pp. 15–25.

8. Excerpt from the life-history transcript of Mrs. Esther Huertas, Oral History Archive #28, Centro de Estudios Puertorriqueños, Hunter College, New York, New York.

9. Oral History Archive #28, Centro de Estudios Puertorriqueños, Hunter College, New York, New York.

10. From a manuscript belonging to Mrs. Esther Huertas.

11. Ranging from three to ten hours in length and recorded in multiple sessions, these are loosely guided by an introduction of "Tell me about your life." This allows narrators to establish their own priorities and to construct their stories as they conceive them. In the course of the interviews, we try to weave in more specific questions regarding family and gender relations, work experiences, migration, discrimination, education, and support networks.

12. From "Concept Paper #4," Cultural Studies Working Group, Inter-University Program for Latino Research (1988), manuscript in progress.

13. The following portrait, derived from my longer interpretive biography of Mrs. Minerva Ríos, in Torruellas, Benmayor, Goris, and Juarbe, "Affirming Cultural Citizenship," ms. pp. 37–46

14. Excerpt from life-history transcript of Mrs. Minerva Ríos, Oral History Archive #27, Center for Puerto Rican Studies, Hunter College, New York, New York

15. Ibid.

16. Ibid.

17. Ibid.

18. This interpretation is based on a lengthier biography of Mrs. Belén Resto written by Ana Juarbe in Torruellas, Benmayor, Goris, and Juarbe, "Affirming Cultural Citizenship," ms. pp. 31–37.

19. Excerpt from the life-history transcript of Mrs. Belén Resto, Oral History Archive #29, Center for Puerto Rican Studies, Hunter College, New York, New York.

20. Doris Sommer, " 'Not Just a Personal Story': Women's *Testimonios* and the Plural Self," in *Life/Lines: Theorizing Women's Autobiography,* ed. Bella Brodzki and Celeste Schenck (Ithaca, N.Y.: Cornell University Press, 1988), pp. 107–30.

21. Sherry Gorelick, "Giving Voice is Not Enough: Problems and Promises of Feminist and Marxist Methodology," in *Gender/Body/Knowledge: Feminist Reconstructions of Being and Knowing,* ed. Alison M. Jaggar and Susan R. Bordo (New Brunswick, N.J.: Rutgers University Press, 1988).

22. Julia Curry-Rodríguez, "Reconceptualizing Undocumented Labor Immigration: The Causes, Impact and Consequences in Mexican Women's Lives" (doctoral dissertation, University of Texas, Austin, Texas, 1988).

23. Maxine Baca Zinn, "Field Research in Minority Communities: Ethical, Methodological and Political Observations by an Insider," *Social Problems* 27, no. 2 (December 1979).

24. Robert Blauner and David Wellman, "Toward the Decolonization of Social Research," in *The Death of White Sociology,* ed. Joyce Ladner (New York: Random House, 1973).

11

Confronting the Demons of Feminist Public History: Scholarly Collaboration and Community Outreach

Laurie Mercier and Mary Murphy

In November 1987, three hundred women, representing the class, racial, ethnic, age, and occupational diversity of Montana, gathered in Helena for a conference entitled "Molders and Shapers: Montana Women as Community Builders," which addressed the issue of women's voluntary work. The meeting resulted from several years of dreaming and planning, and hundreds of hours of unpaid labor. One component of the conference preparation was an oral history project. Supported by the Montana Historical Society and the American Association of University Women, the project produced forty interviews with Montana women involved in voluntary associations, and a publication, *Molders & Shapers, Montana Women as Community Builders: An Oral History Sampler & Guide*. A team of five women from four different cities implemented the various parts of the oral history project and publication.[1]

Eighteen months after the conference the five of us gathered around a friend's dining room table and, over coffee and cheesecake, reassessed our collaborative work. It was the first time we had been together since the project ended. Most of us had driven between seventy and three hundred miles to attend this meeting; and we squeezed in the time amidst the pressures of contract work, dissertation, legislative session, and writing-project deadlines. We were excited to see each other again, but also nervous about confronting the demons that had haunted the project: strained relationships, unrealized expectations, and some puzzlement and disappointment regarding the outcome of the project. We had never achieved a sense of closure about "Molders and Shapers," and we recognized that our future working relationships, our interests in public history, and our sense of professionalism demanded that we reevaluate our work together to put these demons to rest. We thought, too, that our insights might be useful to other women's collaborative efforts.[2]

Our discussion that evening centered around three major questions that we will explore in this essay: the promises and difficulties of a collective project; how our assumptions—about working together and about women's voluntary work—affected the project's design and implementation; and the challenge of combining scholarly work with public outreach.

We had been studying, teaching, and writing Montana women's history since 1980 or earlier. Some of us had worked together on other ventures, and we all frequently shared our findings from oral history and archival research on an informal basis. Through our various projects and studies we had independently begun to recognize the contributions of women who had previously escaped our attention: the women across the state who had labored quietly in clubs, churches, associations, and neighborhoods to improve Montana's cultural, economic, and civic life. These community-builders were rarely heralded in local history books or honored in county courthouse niches, yet their work had laid the foundation for libraries, parks, hospitals, school lunch programs, and shelters for abused women. As feminists, we had often scorned volunteerism on a theoretical basis, criticizing the system that undervalued women's labor and expected their charity to solve major social problems. Yet we ourselves had spent countless volunteer hours lobbying in support of women's political and economic issues, protesting nuclear proliferation and intervention abroad, and exploring people's untold stories in our public history work. Designing the Molders and Shapers project became an exercise in praxis. We were forced to reevaluate our theoretical approach to women's historical community-building in light of our own political activities and feminist beliefs. We began to see this work not merely as unpaid, unrecognized labor, but as the outward expression of women's commitment to supporting and changing neighborhoods and communities, and, at times, to challenging oppressive institutions as well.

We found few materials about women's community-building in Montana's libraries and archives. However, years of Women's History Month celebrations, community exhibits, university seminars, and other public programs had legitimized the study and interpretation of women's experience and had heightened interest in women's history. Some club women, recognizing the importance of their group's work and history, had stashed away records in basements and closets; others had asked us how to preserve and write about their history. The confluence of our historical research, our own volunteerism, women's interest in their history, and our desire to document more of that story finally led us to tackle an oral history project chronicling the role of Montana women as community-builders.

We formed our collective during Women's History Month in March 1987, while we were brainstorming over lunch—a common launching place, we suspect, for many other women's projects. Two of our members, along with various women's organizations, had already begun planning a conference, scheduled for November 1987, that would bring together women from across Montana to explore the role of women community-builders. The upcoming state centennial had sparked interest in women's history, and planners sought to channel that into a reflective, productive meeting. A wide variety of women's groups reacted enthusiastically to the idea of a conference, and the Montana Committee for the Humanities and the American Association of University Women pledged funding. We recognized a double opportunity to satisfy our own intellectual curiosity about women's voluntary work and to provide a forum in which to present our findings and stimulate further study. By the time we left the restaurant, we had committed ourselves to organizing an oral history project that would survey women's voluntary work across the state. We would present the results and offer "how-to" workshops at the conference, hoping to give women the tools to initiate their own documentary projects. On reflection, we realized that our actions mirrored those of the women we subsequently studied: we came together in response to a need; we did not worry initially about how we would finance the project; we were not concerned about what each of us could commit or contribute—we just decided that this project needed to be done and we could and would do it. We also unthinkingly substituted enthusiasm and the bonds of friendship for a coherent work plan, and we failed to involve the women we hoped to inspire in the planning process.

Why did five women living in four different Montana cities agree to work collectively on such a project? It did not make logistical sense considering our lack of resources, but because there are so few of us working in women's history in Montana, we have had to overcome the barrier of physical distance to escape intellectual, emotional, and political isolation. We relished the exchange, support, and feedback that would accompany such a collaborative effort. We also knew the project would demand economic and personal sacrifices. Only one in our group was fully employed; others were committed to completing a dissertation, lobbying for a state women's political group, writing an opera and book, and finding editing work.

While two members of our group concentrated on arranging conference details, three of us conducted oral history interviews and agreed to produce a booklet that would feature excerpts from the interviews and provide guidelines for groups wishing to conduct similar projects. From the outset, even with some institutional and grant support, it was clear that such an ambitious project would rely on our volunteerism more than on outside generosity. Prospective collectives should realize that even with volunteer labor there are numerous costs connected with any kind of oral history project and public program, and those costs should be carefully budgeted in the planning stage. We begged and borrowed whenever possible. The member who worked as oral historian for the Montana Historical Society allocated some of her budget to help support the interviews and also supplied tape recorders, a computer, and transcribing assistance. Another member arranged for a benefactor to underwrite the costs of the publication.

We worked independently but came together every few months to discuss conference progress and the interviews. In retrospect, we should probably have narrowed the scope of our project design. We intended to survey community-building in its broadest sense—political and union activism, work in churches and clubs, cultural activities of ethnic groups, and informal networks among neighbors and friends. But we had just eight months to complete forty or more interviews on a part-time, sporadic basis. If there was any one factor that caused problems with the quality of the project, it was the imbalance between what we set out to do and the time we budgeted. That miscalculation prevented us from evaluating interviews, redesigning questions, and locating narrators who could provide key perspectives.

There were other complications: midway through the project, the Native American interviewer hired to assist with the project fell seriously ill and had to discontinue her interviews. This meant that our pool of interviews would lack an important Native American component. As the time drew near to produce the publication, a personal crisis engulfed the collective member who had agreed to write the overview essay and who had in her possession the majority of the interviews. Her crisis became ours, aggravated by her inability to describe her problem to the rest of us, and by her immediate coping mechanism of dropping out of sight. With only a month left before the conference, the collective had to take drastic action.

Each of us suspended other responsibilities and we met in Helena for a week of concentrated work. We tracked down our missing member and convinced her to join us, and she began to pick up the pieces of the work she had abandoned. But we also felt like her "jailers," a feeling we resented as much as she did, and we worked in silence that week. The conference deadline forced us to work quickly and intensely, and there was no opportunity to express anger or to seek an understanding of what went awry. We chose to sacrifice process to production. Yet we did not forfeit all principles to turn out a product. We contracted with a woman-owned typesetting business to prepare our mock-up for the printer, and we employed one of the few unionized print shops in the state to produce the publication. We met deadline after deadline with just minutes to spare, and taxed the good will of the producer, typesetter, and printer. One hour before the Molder and Shapers conference began on November 13, 1987, our printer arrived with enough booklets to supply conference attendees. It is not an experience or method we recommend.

We succeeded because we believed the project should take priority over personal difficulties. We were willing to bail out one of our members, and temporarily give up our individual projects to help the group accomplish its goals. This was an advantage of collective work. Nevertheless, our failure to establish clear guidelines, expectations, and responsibilities of work at the beginning of the project led to a tyranny of structurelessness and robbed us of many of the joys of collaboration. Had we articulated and discussed our assumptions of each other's contributions, had we allowed more time, and had we built in some contingency plans, we would have prevented later misunderstandings, frustrations, resentment, and anger.

It was not until our gathering a year-and-a-half later that we were able to talk about the experience. We concluded that collective projects offer enormous advantages. Collectivity pools talents; it pushes ideas and interpretation to new levels of clarity through challenge and debate; and it offers a framework ideally suited to feminists committed to encouraging women's growth and work. We remained convinced that collaboration is the most stimulating, supportive, engaging, and rewarding kind of work. We suggest that groups learn from our mistakes and insist on devoting time at the beginning of a project to laying out explicit ground rules and to discovering each other's strengths, weaknesses, and actual willingness to do particular work in order to minimize, as much as possible, the effects of the inevitable crises that are a part of all our lives.

These requirements demand a brutal honesty—with oneself and with one another. We all have a hard time saying no: there are so few of us doing this work; we are charged by each other's ideas and insights; and we are flattered to be asked to participate in projects of interest. But, we must at times rein in our idealism, or at least recognize that the projects that *should* be done or that we *want* to undertake are not possible given our other responsibilities. We need to learn to be more frank and to accept each other's frankness. For example, in an oral history project, we need to state clearly, "I will interview eight women in this community because it fits in with my current research," or admit, "I will contribute ideas and do some interviews, but I really can't write anything." The other members of the collective need to hear and respect those limits.

Collaboration does not necessarily imply that all will share the same tasks equally; it means that the group reaches consensus about who will do what, based on individual skills and interests. In the end, if we have been honest about each other's capabilities, we can appreciate what each has contributed, rather than castigate someone because she has not completed an assignment. Even with delineated responsibilities, unanticipated crises arise, especially for those of us doing this kind of community history work for little or no money. Every collective ought to have contingency plans for just such emergencies— they will happen.

Prospective collaborative projects must recognize what a major role economics can play in creating a crisis. Our member's flight from her commitments revealed something tragic about the nature of women's history work. In retrospect she realized that she had become paralyzed at the beginning of work on the booklet, not because of writer's block, as the rest of us had believed, but because of her outrage that she would not be paid for her labor. Our project just happened to be the straw that broke the camel's back. She was frustrated because she was trained in women's history and passionately cared for her work, but could not make a living in the field in Montana. Institutions, groups, and individuals had a long history of expecting her to do this work for nothing. The satisfaction of working with other women on an interesting topic offered some reward, but, as we had heard from so many of our narrators, and as she so tellingly demonstrated, enough was enough. Intellectual stimulation, after all, does not put bread on the table.

During our reassessment, we discussed the fact that our failure to read more critically the literature on voluntary associations affected the design of the oral history project. We planned to include a wide range of women's groups in our study, to interview women of color and working-class women, as well as the typically more visible, white, middle-class club women. The questions we developed, however, were based on our research in the scholarship on voluntary associations, which is a literature that with few exceptions documents a white, middle-class experience.[3] We did interview women from a variety of working-class and ethnic groups, but we tried to fit their experiences into a model constructed from a past that had little to do with their lives or concerns. In retrospect, this was a serious flaw in our process. Oral history projects usually put a priority on collecting interviews, not on critical review, and ours was no exception. Because we did not stop to evaluate the interviews midway through the project, we did not alter our questions or seek different narrators, actions that might have yielded a more accurate picture of the diversity of women's voluntary work. It is possible that the design of our questions channeled women's responses into previously established categories and did not allow them to define community-building in their own terms.

Nevertheless, as with nearly all interviews, narrators managed to tell their own stories despite the obstacles presented by interviewers. We found that ethnic and working-class women often came together because of the immediate cultural and economic needs of their ethnic group or class, rather than to support activities defined as community needs by elite-sanctioned, middle-class groups. Ethnic women formed lodges to preserve their language and culture or to obtain practical benefits such as insurance. Native American women gathered together to make star quilts for give-away ceremonies important to their communities. Working-class women joined union auxiliaries to support their husbands' efforts to gain better wages and improve the lives of their families. Bowling leagues and craft clubs fostered working-class solidarity. Low-income and disabled women founded groups to fight power company shutoffs and threatened cuts in the state's general assistance. The efforts of these groups frequently ran counter to the aims of "civic improvement" efforts that sought to make more tolerable the inequalities of society, yet did little of substance to make society more humane.

Although we tried to recognize class and cultural differences, our own training, and our intention to document and celebrate the voluntary work of all women, hindered our understanding of other kinds of important community work not included in the mainstream of women's voluntarism. Even in traditional club settings, working-class and ethnic women had different agendas from their middle-class counterparts. At the Molders and Shapers conference, one black participant noted that "our goals were different from the white women's clubs. Our motto was 'lifting as we climb.'" She recalled, "We had to learn to value ourselves." African American women, confronted by racism as well as sexism, organized to meet the needs of black communities and to combat society's negative stereotype of the black female. Had we scheduled a review of our interviews midway through the project in order to analyze the voices we were collecting, we would have reformulated some questions, pursued other lines of inquiry, and moved to some other conclusions more rapidly. For example, we could have inquired about culturally different approaches to community service, probed more carefully the motives of middle-class volunteers, measured relations between women of different classes and races, and examined why middle-class women sometimes rejected their class interests to work for fundamental economic, social, and political change.

Another problem in the design of the oral history project was our selection of narrators. Even with ethnic and working-class organizations, we tended to approach women who were officers and leaders because they were most accessible or because they were often the long-term members. We had two sets of questions, one that focused on the history of the group, and one that sought the individual's history as a volunteer. Our original plan was to create a body of interviews representative of woman's role as community-builder. Upon review, we realized that our collection of interviews was heavily weighted with associational leaders, and perhaps not representative of general members' experiences. In our evaluation we also speculated that because our interviews were so tightly focused on our topic, we may have created a skewed impression that club work occupied an enormous proportion of these women's lives. Had we phrased our questions differently, or put them in the larger context of a life-history interview, we might have discovered more about the relative importance of various groups at different times in women's lives and how voluntary work fit into their life cycles.

Our self-criticism also led to dissatisfaction with the language used to elicit responses, a language that failed to allow a truly multicultural and class-based analysis of women's community-building. We even wondered if we could adequately interpret responses based on some questions that turned out to be far more puzzling than we realized. We recalled, for example, that many women did not understand the question, "Do you consider yourself a feminist?" Several women who had worked actively in community organizations to improve the status of women were confused by the terminology. One woman interpreted "feminism" to mean "feminine" and answered as if the interviewer thought she was afraid of "masculine," political work. Others still held negative images of "bra-burning feminists" that belied their own work on behalf of women. Our term "community-building" confused other narrators. These examples illustrate how interviewers and narrators may operate in different spheres of language, even while sharing the same class, culture, or political ideology. One benefit of a collective project is the recurrence of this phenomenon among several interviewers, allowing analysis to reveal the flaws in the substance of the questions, rather than assuming that misunderstanding flows from one interviewer's personal style. Had we listened to or discussed each other's interviews early in the project, we might have been able to discern a common dynamic between the questions we asked and the stories we heard. We could have attempted to discover a language that we, as scholars, could have used more effectively to allow women of all classes to respond in their own language.

Both at the time we were assembling the booklet and upon reexamination, we realized that our process of selecting oral excerpts was flawed. Again, time constraints precluded each of us from reading all the interviews and developing some interpretations that we could test and discuss with the collective. The principal interviewer would make a first cut, and then provide us with a pool of excerpts from which to select representative samples to include in the guide. However, that first winnowing meant that only one of us was deciding which quotations were potentially significant. Because we knew and respected each other's work, because we shared the same political orientation, we assumed that our interpretations would probably be the same. As we discovered, that was not necessarily the case. In our rush to complete the project, we tuned out the polyphony that is the core of a truly collaborative enterprise. In the future we would know to schedule more time for collective scrutiny and debate at this stage of the process.

The Molders and Shapers conference was a huge success. The atmosphere of the conference was electric—one could feel the excitement in the air as women described and applauded each other's voluntary work. The oral history project was well received, but while we accomplished our goals of recording untold stories and publicly disseminating them, we discovered that our enthusiasm was not enough to propel women to carry on in their own communities the work we had begun. At the end of the conference, just a few participants raised their hands when they were asked how many would pursue a project on the history of their associations. After all, these were busy women. They would return home to care for families, lobby for comparable worth, and staff the food bank and clothing co-op. They could afford a few days to attend a conference where they came together with women who had similar visions for their communities and listen to lectures and panels by women who had studied women's groups. They did not, however, have the time, energy, or desire to commit to the "passive" work of recording and evaluating women's stories. Nor, perhaps, was there a sense that documenting their voluntary work was that important. Again, we had operated under an assumption that all we had to do was provide affirmation and the appropriate tools for recovering their pasts, and women would be ready to begin.

We knew of many feminist scholars who studied and interpreted the lives of women, but we had hoped to spur nonacademic women to record their own history. We knew of women's scholars who had worked in communities, done interviews, and involved women in the interpretation of their past, but the scholars remained the authorities. We wanted to take our work one step further and empower women to take an active role in the interpretive process. We thought we could provide examples and train and encourage women to seize the initiative to do their own history. However, there were serious flaws with our "democratic" impulses.

We had assumed that women *would* want to carry on such work, that the success of the Molders and Shapers conference and the examples of our interviews would inspire them to continue this work in their own communities. Our expectations were naive and clashed with the aims of this volunteer community. Women had asked for the conference. They supported the idea of bringing together women like themselves from around the state to discuss and analyze their history as community-builders, and they requested workshops on how to record oral history interviews, to preserve photographs and records, and to write club histories. Although women sought education about history and about history-making, their interest did not imply a commitment to go back to their communities and undertake history projects.

Our experience and our commitment to public history led us in an inappropriate direction. We believed a truly "public" project would involve community members in the creation and interpretation of their history. On reflection, we realized that we needed to rethink the meaning of our responsibilities to "return to the community." How should feminist scholars involve communities in the production of their history? How do historians avoid making assumptions about how women want to contribute to that production? Of central importance is the involvement of the community in the planning process. In our case, we did listen to volunteer women express their desires to learn more about their past and place in history, and we recognized a dearth of historical materials that prompted us to launch an oral history project to correct the imbalance. But it was naive of us to assume that these women would want to become historians. Even though many of the representatives of groups with whom we met expressed interest in pursuing documentary projects for the centennial, they could not commit the labors of their colleagues. Community women were perfectly willing to help us create interviews, and they were pleased that they were the subject of our attentions. Nevertheless, we were seen as professionals validating their experience and history. That was not their job, nor could they justify the time to embark on a history project when other needs seemed more pressing.

Feminist scholars and public historians must recognize that not only is a division of labor in community history projects acceptable, it is often preferred. It is in fact the way voluntary groups have operated for decades: divisions and committees organizing to cater to members' specific interests and energies, the parts of the whole making different contributions to club projects. As historians, we recognized the importance and value of women's voluntary work and sought to record, interpret, and publicize that history as our contribution to community-building. As feminist historians, we recognized the importance of women's history in our own lives, in shaping our sense of worth and ability. We hoped to share that experience with other women. We also believed there could be a utilitarian side to this project. Having realized the crucial role of women's voluntary work to the well-being of communities, and having heard over and over in our interviews stories of the decline of voluntary groups, we thought that focusing public attention on women's organizations and having women record their own rich past might reinvigorate a flagging movement. We learned that people gain inspiration from a variety of sources, and that the heart of voluntary work lies in a love of the task and belief in its importance. We loved doing women's history and believed in its power; the women we interviewed loved and believed in their work. We could work collaboratively, but it was presumptuous to think that all women would or should become historians.

Realizing this, we reevaluated the Molders and Shapers conference and oral history project in a different light. The collective's conference organizers had produced and mailed follow-up newsletters soliciting comments from participants, and from those responses they became convinced that our efforts had been successful. They believed the conference and oral history project did affect women's lives, but perhaps not in ways we expected. A black participant from Bozeman had organized some of her records from the Montana Federation of Negro Women's Clubs and presented a sack-lunch seminar on black women's clubs in Montana; some women's groups in Missoula and Butte donated their records to appropriate archives; and a woman who had not completed high school remarked that because she liked being with women who had ideas, she had decided to go back to school. These examples showed us that we needed to measure our success in a variety of ways, not only by the number of oral history projects that sprang from the conference.

Comments from the postconference survey revealed that Molders and Shapers had made an impact in three general areas. First, it had helped women change their sense of themselves and of other women. One woman remarked that she had a new "feeling of sisterhood, of pride in women past and present." Initially, we had been disappointed by reports that women were interviewing their sisters, mothers, and grandmothers, because we had hoped that women would organize oral history projects around their associations and reach beyond traditional family interviews. We realized, however, that these interviews were important for developing an understanding of women's personal histories and their relationships with the women closest to them—and perhaps they would be but a first step to a wider curiosity about women's history. As another participant commented, "I will be able to do an oral history with my own mother, sister, grandmother. I plan to use oral history in my classroom and also to teach an awareness of women in Montana history."

We received evidence that the conference in fact had had a revitalizing effect on community work. Many people commented on how hearing about their history renewed their commitments to volunteerism: "To put the value of volunteerism in an historical perspective has been of great value to me in my present efforts—I feel rededicated!" "It made me realize that the work I have accomplished in the community is more important than I ever believed or was given credit for. . . . [It] made me decide to continue to follow through and stick to my beliefs because I know it is for the betterment of the community and it is time to dissolve the 'old boy network' that is running this town into the ground." Another participant remarked, "This conference has been an upper to me and a reinforcement of my belief that Montana women played a big role in the growing of the state. It is time that these facts came out of the closet and we are recognized for our place in history."

Finally, through the conference and oral history booklet, women learned what it is that historians do, just as through our interviews we became educated and respectful of what club women did. Many groups that had been conspicuously possessive about their records began donating them to archives, thus demonstrating a personal trust in us, and an understanding of the need to make their work public if it was to be recognized and perhaps continued. Others realized that their "ordinary" lives were of interest to scholars: "I learned to see the extraordinary in the ordinary daily life." And one woman commented upon the bridge-building between scholars and nonacademics: "I see women coming together again, a recognition by feminists of contributions of ordinary women and less polarization [between the two groups]."

Although the club women did not seize on our proposal to launch their own oral history projects, they did participate actively in Molders and Shapers. They were willing narrators and enthusiastic conference participants, and they subsequently took steps to preserve and shape their history by donating records to archives, interviewing family members, and continuing their own work. The making of history became a joint endeavor—between us as professional historians and them as willing providers of raw materials who had come to recognize the importance of preserving and writing their history, even if they did not carry out that final step. In this sense a process of mutual legitimization and education occurred. We also learned that it is impossible to predict how women will internalize and later act upon the information historians present.

As we worked through our concerns during our evening meeting in 1989, we were saddened by the fact that a lack of financial support was causing the disintegration both of our work together and of the cumulative body of knowledge about Montana women's history that we shared. Our collective echoed many of the complaints of the women we had interviewed. Economic necessity had forced several of us to make decisions that would take us out of the state or out of the profession. One member viewed our meeting as an end to an era, representative of the fallout from the "destructuralizing" of the history movement in Montana—due to economic hard times and changing priorities in the university system and at the state historical society. In a larger context, it was a microcosm of the diminishing support for community and women's history in the Reagan Era. We wondered if we would collaborate again, especially since, having worked through the collective's problems, having shared painful confessions and warming affirmations, having come to know each other's strengths, talents, and weaknesses, and having come to a new analysis of our role in community projects, we believed we could probably work more closely than any other five women in the region. We concluded that for brief periods of time, collectives like ours can form, function, and accomplish consequential feats for a cross-section of women in a state like Montana, but that over the long haul not even hardy souls with the best intentions can afford to continue without some sort of institutional assistance. As women's groups and women scholars struggle to preserve the hard-won gains of the 1970s and fight the erosion of the 1980s, we need to lobby state institutions and granting agencies to support public history that focuses on women's lives.

Our findings in the Molders and Shapers project may have revealed more questions than answers, but we explored new territory in the history of women's voluntary associations, and we began to rethink earlier conclusions and methods for interpreting and presenting that history. We also learned how to insist on an appropriate process for collaborative work. We had begun our final meeting with tension, frustration, and disappointment; throughout the course of a sometimes painful discussion we confronted our own assumptions about history, community work, and our collaborative enterprise. By the end of the evening, despite our worries about the future, some of us began to talk excitedly about overcoming financial obstacles and the barriers of distance in order to work on new projects and to implement the ideas we had generated that evening. Some of us had come to the meeting swearing never again to work on a collective endeavor. But we exorcised our demons and came away groping for a project that might bring us back together. In spite of the pitfalls, we realized that collaborative work taxed each of our talents to its measure and returned that effort manifold. Like all women community-builders, we may have had some regrets, but we knew the rewards of accomplishing good work in good company.

Notes

1. Laurie Mercier of Helena, Mary Murphy of Butte, and Diane Sands of Missoula were the primary interviewers for the project. Alice Finnegan conducted additional interviews in Anaconda. Linda Peavy and Ursula Smith, of Bozeman, organized the conference. Sands, Murphy, Mercier, Peavy, and Smith wrote *Molders & Shapers*. Patti Borneman, administrative assistant for the Montana Historical Society's Oral History Office, was responsible for transcription and production. The interviews are available to researchers at the Montana Historical Society.

   The authors would like to thank Linda Peavy, Ursula Smith, Diane Sands, and Patti Borneman for their insights into the Molders and Shapers project, and for their encouragement to us when we proposed writing this essay. We extend a special thanks to Anastatia Sims for her critical reading of the draft and her thoughtful comments.

2. We gratefully thank Jennifer Jeffries Thompson, who offered her home and her support for our session together.

3. Major works in the field of women's voluntary associations include Karen J Blair, *The Clubwoman as Feminist: True Womanhood Redefined, 1868–1914* (New York: Holmes and Meier Publishers, Inc., 1980); Mary Ann Clawson, "Nineteenth-Century Women's Auxiliaries and Fraternal Orders," *Signs* 12 (Autumn 1986): 40–61; Jill Conway, "Women Reform-

ers and American Culture, 1870–1930," in *Our American Sisters,* ed. Jean E. Friedman and William G. Shade (Boston: Allyn & Bacon, Inc., 1976); Arlene Kaplan Daniels, *Invisible Careers: Women Civic Leaders from the Volunteer World* (Chicago: University of Chicago Press, 1988); Nancy A. Hewitt, *Women's Activism and Social Change: Rochester, New York, 1822–1872* (Ithaca, N.Y.: Cornell University Press, 1984); Jacquelyn Dowd Hall, *Revolt Against Chivalry: Jessie Daniel Ames and the Women's Campaign Against Lynching* (New York: Columbia University Press, 1979); Wendy Kaminer, *Women Volunteering: The Pleasure, Pain, and Politics of Unpaid Work from 1830 to the Present* (Garden City, N.Y.: Anchor Press, 1984); J. Stanley Lemons, *The Woman Citizen: Social Feminism in the 1920s* (Urbana, Ill.: University of Illinois Press, 1973); Theodora Penny Martin, *The Sound of Our Own Voices: Women's Study Clubs, 1860–1910* (Boston: Beacon Press, 1987); Susan A. Ostrander, *Women of the Upper Class* (Philadelphia: Temple University Press, 1984); Mary P. Ryan, *Cradle of the Middle Class: The Family in Oneida County, New York, 1790–1865* (New York: Cambridge University Press, 1981); Anne Firor Scott, *Making the Invisible Woman Visible* (Urbana, Ill.: University of Illinois Press, 1984); and Margaret Gibbons Wilson, *The American Woman in Transition: The Urban Influence, 1870–1920* (Westport, Conn.: Greenwood Press, 1979).

There is as yet no comparable body of work relating to black or other minority women, although in 1974 Gerda Lerner published an essay, "Early Community Work of Black Club Women," in the *Journal of Negro History* 59 (April 1974): 158–67, and in recent years scholars have begun to address this lacuna. See, for example, Marilyn Dell Brady, "Kansas Federation of Colored Women's Clubs," *Kansas History* 9 (Spring 1986): 19–30; Lynda F. Dickson, "Toward a Broader Angle of Vision in Uncovering Women's History: Black Women's Clubs Revisited," *Frontiers* 9, no. 2 (1987): 62–68; Paula Giddings, *When and Where I Enter: The Impact of Black Women on Race and Sex in America* (New York: William Morrow, 1984); and Cynthia Neverdon-Morton, *Afro-American Women of the South and the Advancement of the Race, 1895–1925* (Knoxville, Tenn.: University of Tennessee Press, 1989).

12

Crossing Boundaries, Building Bridges: Doing Oral History among Working-Class Women and Men

Karen Olson and Linda Shopes

In oral history, as in other intellectual practices, feminist methodology has frequently been driven by the concept of sisterhood, the idea that women as a group share certain similar life experiences and social roles. While this concept of unity among women is useful in delineating a sexual politics and building a body of work that acknowledges women's voices and contributions, it often understates differences among women, particularly the critical differences of class and race. Admittedly, different groups of women are broadly "covered," often with considerable passion, sensitivity, and insight, in the growing body of feminist writing, including that which relies upon oral history. What is often missing, however, is an explicit analysis of "different" as also meaning unequal. Mere awareness of the diversity of women's experience does not adequately address the fact that social differences are most often grounded in social relations marked by asymmetries of power.[1]

Our own thinking in this direction, while indubitably shaped by our commitment to an egalitarian social order, has been pushed considerably by the process of interviewing working-class women and men in conjunction with the research projects described below. Our interviews have led us, first of all, to certain insights into the complex web of power relations within which individual lives are embedded and into the links connecting the social identities of gender, class, and race and ethnicity. Second, we have had to confront the problems of an interview structure that is inherently unequal, as we rather privileged researchers interview people who are less so. Finally, because an interview methodology, more than other forms of inquiry, blurs the line between "research" and "life," we have been moved to consider, perhaps more carefully than we otherwise would have, the way we use our interviews and, more broadly, the connections between our work and the social context within which we have undertaken it. We shall discuss each of these issues in turn.

I.

For both of us, oral history has proved an especially challenging form of inquiry. Narrators' accounts have led us to confront our own feminist biases and to rethink women's history in less categorical, more dynamic terms than we had been using.

Karen Olson

My current research is an ethnographic study that explores class, race, and gender in the steelmaking community of Dundalk, Maryland, in the historical context of the decline of the Sparrows Point plant of Bethlehem Steel over the past two decades. The initial purpose of my study was to understand how feminist consciousness is experienced and expressed in a blue-collar community, and my research plan consisted of interviews with adult women between the ages of thirty and fifty. I had no intention, and certainly no desire, to interview men, but my informants persisted in steering me away from preconceived notions of a separate female world to their own conceptualization of their reality as inescapably intertwined with that of their husbands. Central was the fact that their husbands, all steelworkers, worked swing shifts. Work at the plant was, and still is, organized around three shifts—3 P.M. to 11 P.M., 11 P.M. to 7 A.M., and 7 A.M. to 3 P.M.—and the shift men were assigned to changes, or swings, every seven days. This means that a man could not be relied upon to be present for a regular evening meal, for Little League games, or for child care while his wife worked or went to school. As I tried to imagine what it must be like to negotiate a satisfactory marriage under those conditions, it became clear that in order to accomplish the feminist goals of my research I would have to know more about the men who live with the women I am studying.

My decision to interview steelworker husbands was based, then, on the insistence of wives of steelworkers that many of the decisions they made for themselves about homemaking and child-care responsibilities and about work outside their homes were constrained by the particularly demanding regimen that dictated the work life of their steelmen husbands. Interviews with steelworkers revealed that they brought to their family life an understanding of "manliness" shaped by the environment in which they labored.[2] In a mill characterized by extremes of heat and danger, the men who do difficult manual labor rely on physical strength and an insensitivity to feelings of discomfort in order to tolerate their jobs. Steelworkers must accept from superiors commands that confirm their powerlessness to control the environment in which they often spend sixty or seventy hours every week. The power they do assert is expressed in individual demands for respect and personal autonomy that are confined to the social arena they share with coworkers—who are subjected to practical jokes and casual insults—and wives and children—who are subjected to imperious efforts to control their behavior. Manliness is thus understood by steelworkers as the ability to endure hard physical labor and debilitating working conditions in exchange for financial control over the households they head and the prerogative to "blow off steam" at home and to choose recreation for themselves in lieu of sharing responsibility for household maintenance.

Racial conflict is never far below the surface as white steelworkers vacillate between blaming supervisors and blaming their black coworkers for the cloud of discontent that floats continually around the mill. For the families of black steelworkers, the dimension of race adds another layer of inequality to an already complex hierarchical structure. Black men must continually devise defensive strategies in order to survive the hostility of white workers who resent the competition for jobs that black steelworkers represent. For the wives of black steelworkers, the conventions of manliness that are endemic to work in steel are confounded with the issues of black manhood that result from ubiquitous racism.

The process of doing oral history interviews with steelworkers and their wives thus led me to several unanticipated insights about gender, class, and race. In this steel community, the demands of the workplace impinge on family life in especially powerful ways. Husbands bring to their families the constraints of an erratic work schedule and a concept of manliness based on the "toughness" of the steel industry. Their wives maneuver around these constraints by adapting to the work schedule and tempering the emotional hardness of their husbands' lives. Racial tension adds a dimension of combativeness to men's lives; for both black and white men the constant nagging racial strains are one more way in which the job affects the home. While none of this is very surprising information, when it is encountered in oral history research about working-class women's lives it forces the recognition that the study of women needs to be the study of gender relations, which in turn are inextricably linked to the relations of class and race.

Linda Shopes

My own work in oral history points in the same direction as Olson's, though it leads to conclusions less about the way gender, class, and race divisions create a matrix of unequal social relations, and more about the way a similar triad works to construct a social identity. My research is on Baltimore's canning industry; I am interested in the way this major industry operated to help shape the social life of the city from its development in the mid-nineteenth century to its demise one hundred years later. A portion of the story lies outside of living memory; for the early decades of the twentieth century, however, when the tasks of food preparation had become almost exclusively the province of Polish women, over half of them married, oral history interviews are a critical source. I am interviewing a number of women and a few men, now in their seventies and eighties, who as young children worked in the canneries with their mothers or other female relatives. All grew up and many still live in the area of the city known as Fells Point, an old waterfront neighborhood where many of the canneries were located.[3]

Although my training in women's history had alerted me to differences between working-class women and the middle-class women who dominate the literature, I nonetheless found myself initially approaching interviews with assumptions about the primacy of gender in women's lives, assumptions that derived from a feminist historiography grounded in the study of native-born, white, middle-class women. This historiography does acknowledge its class specificity and cautions against a facile application of its insights to other groups of women, but it generally does not see aspects of self other than gender as problematic. As a result, aspects such as class position and racial and ethnic identity are treated as if they were of secondary importance for women and not intrinsic to the female experience.[4] This perspective was considerably challenged as informants recalled their mothers' and other female relatives'—and in some cases their own—work in the canneries. The phrase interviewees typically used to express women's relation to cannery work is "it was their whole life." Women's work is rarely perceived in such terms; if anything, "family" is invoked as women's "whole life." The use of this phrase to refer to a work experience became a clue that the content, structure, and rhythm of cannery labor helped shape a social identity that could not be adequately explained by conventional gender-based analyses grounded in middle-class women's lives.

As it has been described to me, cannery women worked purposefully, getting up at 4 A.M. during the peak of the season and, goaded by piecework wages and bosses' expectations, they worked until the day's crop was packed, sometimes as many as twelve or thirteen hours. They coped with the strain and weariness of this regimen in a variety of ways, including requiring children's assistance both at home and in the canneries and maintaining disciplined personal habits. Until the 1940s, when a few canneries were organized by labor unions, cannery women did not engage in any concerted, collective action to change the conditions of what by anybody's reckoning was messy, exhausting, boring, and poorly paid work. But the women did not let the canneries completely run them over: they would work at whatever cannery had the best produce, would take food home for their families, and would on occasion refuse to work on a religious holy day or past noon on Saturday. Husbands, themselves often marginally employed, did not object to their wives' working nor did their wives have to seek their permission. Economic necessity precluded giving the matter much thought, and the money the women earned was used for family essentials. Although better-paying, more regular work was available in neighborhood factories, they went to work in the canneries both because they were women and because they were Polish. Working at a site just a few blocks from home and paid piecework wages, they could integrate cannery work with household responsibilities: they would come home to fix breakfast for family members, bring babies to work with them, setting them in a basket or box by their work station, and direct older children—who had easy access to the canneries—in the execution of household chores. And as immigrants, unfamiliar with the rhythms of factory labor and with the English language, they seemed to find a certain security in the quasi-agricultural work of the canneries and in being among a group of women like themselves.[5]

Thus the canneries, by employing women at minimally skilled, low-paid, difficult jobs, by providing them with a measure of flexibility to maintain family responsibilities, by allowing a certain ethnic segregation, shaped among them an identity that was simultaneously female, working-class, and ethnic. In this way cannery work became "their whole life." To argue thus is not to suggest that this identity was free of the power inequalities Olson discusses. Employers, of course, had more than a hand in shaping these women's experience—they knew a cheap source of labor when they saw it. And certainly husbands never brought their babies to work with them. Women's cannery work was clearly part of the larger social economy of the city. But the point here is that as an explanatory framework for a life experience, gender functions not as a singular, unitary category, but as one inextricably bound to class and ethnicity. Oral history, of course, is not the only source that leads historians to rethink their assumptions; nor is there any inherent reason why it must do so. But as a person narrates a life story, and the account wends its way through the accumulated details of a life, social categories are exploded: the subject becomes an actor in simultaneous, multiple roles that do not conform to easy generalizations.

II.

While the content of our interviews was leading us to new insights into the multiple social roles of working-class people, the interview process was forcing us to confront our own social roles as interviewers, particularly the imbalance of power in the interview relationship. Indeed, inequality is embedded in the interview structure: it is we, after all, who seek out our interviewees for their stories; they do not approach us with the knowledge that they may have something valuable for us to record, nor do they seek our stories for their research or "for the record." Moreover, as educated, academic women we have been afforded—at least in the eyes of the larger society—higher status, greater access to resources, and consequently more power than the working-class people we interview. Yet, reflecting on our own behavior, we have found that the choice of research projects related to our "personal," subjective selves has enabled us to diminish some of the social distance between us and our interviewees, at least in the here-and-now of the interview.

Karen Olson

Because I am on the faculty at Dundalk Community College I have found interviewing men and women associated with Bethlehem Steel less encumbered by class differences than if I taught at an institution removed from the community by geographic and social distance. The college was created in response to the desire of this working-class community to make college degrees and professional careers accessible to its children, and the college has the reputation of being responsive to the values and aspirations of Dundalk residents. For better or worse, the community college environment lacks the competition over scholarly research endemic to universities and avoids the rigid divisions that typically separate teachers, students, and administrators. Dundalk Community College professes an especially egalitarian ethos, expressed most emphatically, perhaps, by the fact that its Professional Development Program includes every college employee, thus blurring distinctions between professionals and nonprofessionals. Teaching in this atmosphere has enabled me to establish collegial relationships with employees at the college—administrators, faculty, secretaries, maintenance crews—who live in Dundalk and who are connected in a variety of ways through relatives, neighbors, and past history to the steelworker families I am researching. Although I do not live in Dundalk, virtually all of my interviews have been set up either directly or indirectly through contacts with people who know me through the college and can recommend me as someone who shares a commitment to the well-being of their community.

It is perhaps self-evident that in order to study steelworkers it is necessary to understand the process of making steel and to be appreciative of that work. Yet the fact that many informants express surprise and gratitude when I do demonstrate such interest is a measure of the insensitivity of the larger society to the value of industrial labor. One informant who left Dundalk to attend a middle-class suburban college reported her dismay that students and the faculty alike expressed disdain for "grits" who wore "blue jeans and flannel shirts and did dirty work." These middle-class Baltimoreans argued quite seriously that blue-collar work was unimportant in the age of the computer and should be minimally remunerated. The popular media perpetuates such stereotypes, referring to Dundalk as "Dumdalk" and "the armpit of the country." Hence members of the community are understandably on the defensive. My own quite simple statement that I find the community interesting and admirable causes much of the defensiveness to evaporate.

Because my training is in anthropology as well as in history, the format of my interviews is more a dialogue than a series of questions presented to informants, and in our conversations I feel free to interject comments about myself. Informants are more willing to reveal their own experience when they learn that I have shared many of the family problems that plague them—a father who was chronically unemployed, a son whose adolescent acting-out included run-ins with juvenile services, a troubled marriage that ended in divorce. Self-revelation is particularly important with black informants who have no reason to assume that I, as a white woman, am sympathetic to the problems blacks have negotiating a white world. Because I was a staff member of the Student Non-Violent Coordinating Committee when my son was born in 1965, he was delivered in the segregated black annex of an Atlanta hospital. This item from my own biography perhaps helps black interviewees to reveal more detailed experiences of racial tension and discrimination. In these ways, revelations about my own life have worked to diminish the social distance between my interviewees and myself.

Linda Shopes

When I initially contact an interviewee I identify myself as a teacher at the University of Maryland Baltimore County, a recognizable institution to most, where grandchildren, or the grandchildren of friends, may have been enrolled. And as we discuss how I am to find an interviewee's home, where I usually conduct the interview, I tell them I live "near the stadium," another familiar landmark. Thus they have two ways of locating me in relation to their own world.

Within the interview, I find myself presenting a personal style that helps overcome social distance. Most of the people I interview are of Polish descent. So am I. When I tell them this in the small talk that precedes the interview—and I am surprised by the enthusiasm with which I do so since "being Polish" has never been much of my conscious identity—we both like it; it creates a familiar bond. In fact, many of the women I interview are not unlike my female relatives. While I am not especially close to these relatives, I have a general sense of their experiences and attitudes: I know that they like neat clothes, that they demand clear speech, and that they value hard work, thrift, personal propriety, and religious devotion. I am able to affirm those preferences in the course of an interview—in the way I dress, talk, and respond to their accounts. Nor is this behavior especially calculated; it is quite automatic—a self emerging from my background that helps reduce distance and create trust.

Furthermore, as interviewees tell me stories of dogged labor with little return, of lives profoundly circumscribed by poverty and family responsibilities, of efforts to create order and pleasure, I am not surprised by my sympathetic response—this *is* where my sympathies lie. I am surprised, however, that I am able to maintain sympathy when they speak of matters that "I"—apart from the interview—am rather critical of, for example maternal sacrifice and religious devotion. At these times the power of the personal interaction overrides my critical judgment. I explain this response in part by the fact that those I interview are at least a generation older than I, and I am responding to them with a socialized respect for my elders. Yet in my "real life" I am not especially respectful to those older than I, nor am I uncritically sympathetic to my female relatives. So I am led to understand interviews as highly framed encounters, not governed by the rules of ordinary interaction. The peculiar intimacy available to strangers who share an important experience seems to create in at least some interviews a social space where normal power relations perhaps get blunted.[6]

As researchers, then, we both find it useful to affirm certain commonalities—a shared social milieu, common ethnic bonds, similar life experiences, even the mutual effort to "do" the interview—as a way of equalizing the interview encounter. More generally, we have found that the posture we strike in an interview, the intent and the commitments we bring to it, invariably shape the interpersonal dynamic and so can contribute to a more egalitarian encounter. Our own critique of the inequalities present in the larger social and political world that we all inhabit as citizens are undoubtedly communicated to interviewees who choose to hear them in our questions, our asides, our sympathetic affirmations. At times we and the people we interview become allies in a common critical endeavor. Olson's interviews with women and their steelworker husbands, for example, frequently become collaborative exercises in analyzing the dynamics of shift work, as we jointly speculate on its benefits to the company and its toll on workers' families. In interviews of this sort there appears to be a strong commonality of purpose and consciousness shared by the interviewer and the people being interviewed.

Judging from the kind of intimacy achieved in many of our interviews, it would be easy to assume that we have overcome the barriers of class and gender differences. But it is important not to be seduced by this sense of mutuality and so avoid a critical evaluation of the interview process. All interviewees create meaning, construct a self, and negotiate power in an interview; the question is how the people we interview are doing these things vis-à-vis a relatively more privileged, well-educated researcher. Richard Sennett, in *The Hidden Injuries of Class,* has written of how some working-class people he interviewed sought his approval by articulating progressive ideas about race relations.[7] We have had similarly awkward experiences with interviewees: a former cannery worker struggling with feelings of embarrassment at having worked at such a "low class" job; another seeking to "boost" the image of the local Polish community; a steelworker visibly uncomfortable when asked to talk about his personal experiences.

Yet we also wonder if, in our own sensitivities to inequality, we indulge ourselves a bit and perhaps overestimate our own privilege, even our own importance, in the eyes of the people we interview. Most, in fact, seem not especially overwhelmed, intimidated, or impressed with us at all. If we assert power by inserting ourselves into their world unbidden and asking for their stories, they also assert power by gratifying or denying our request. If we define the terms of the inquiry by asking the questions, they also define it by answering the questions as they wish. They are, after all, a self-selected group and so are perhaps those with the strongest sense of self, who are publicly available, and for whom a frank account of aspects of their lives is not especially threatening. And, like all interviewees, we suspect, they too "get" something out of talking with us: the satisfaction of "helping you out" as they often phrase it, a sympathetic ear for the stories they take pleasure in telling, a chance to be heard, to air grievances, to work over and perhaps seek reassurances for certain decisions, and, yes, to complain.

And so the problematic embedded in the class dynamic of our interviews seems especially difficult to pin down. Nonetheless, it is there, emerging in different ways in interviews with different people, reminding us that it is inaccurate to generalize about "the working class," which, like every social group, differs along other dimensions of self. Olson, for example, finds that some of the people she interviews, perhaps assuming that she shares certain middle-class prejudices about "the character flaws" of working-class people, tend to hide or even lie about such personal behavior as drug use or excessive drinking during an initial interview session. Some interviewees are also apologetic about the kind of work they do, the homes they live in, the cars they drive. Their social worlds and styles of life overlap enough with Olson's that they are perhaps drawn into uneasy comparisons with her. Shopes, who interviews people more removed from her in age, income, and lifestyle, and who is not a participant in their community, does not come up against these responses. However, these very differences do seem to account for the reverential tone in which the people she interviews frequently talk about their parents: "My parents, I don't know how they did it"; "My mother, she was a good woman"; "When I think about what they went through . . ." These seem to be more than personal expressions of filial devotion: interviewees seem genuinely moved by—and still not quite accommodated to—the vast differences between the near subsistence-level circumstances of their parents' lives and the comfortable middle-class lives enjoyed by their own children and grandchildren. Shopes, a representative of that middle class, perhaps not unlike their own children, evokes these implied comparisons, is to be instructed in them, and is perhaps being told to appreciate them.

A similar posture, evident in both content and tone, runs through both our interviews. People strive to tell us about their experiences with considerable thoughtfulness, detail, and nuance. They seem concerned that we "get it right," that they give an accurate account. And this seems to us more than an effort to be a good interviewee. Many self-consciously articulate the difficulties of working-class life, the strain of long hours, the constant, nerve-fraying efforts to make ends meet. In so doing they are implying a comparison with the more middle-class lives they see around them. Some have told us directly: "Put that in your book," or "That will make a good story." And Shopes's interviewees, for example, vigorously contest middle-class interpretations of child labor, asserting that "it didn't hurt us any."

It seems then that the people we interview are quite aware of class differences in this society and also know that the middle-class world we represent does not understand or respect their way of life. They see their role in the interview as instructing us about those differences so that we can then communicate them to the middle-class audience of students, readers, and policy-makers they presume we have access to. Thus the interview relationship might properly be understood as a triangular one: the interviewee, us, and the larger society. If the larger society is the ultimate recipient of the insights of the interview, then, in terms of this model, the researcher is cast in the role of mediator. The informants we interview assume that we know the necessary procedures for setting the public record straight. They enter the interview hoping that our academic role will provide the means for injecting their own worldview into the elusive arena of public knowledge. This may be precisely where class differences are most poignantly revealed in the interview structure, in the assumptions or hopes of the women and men we interview that because we have greater social power than they do, we will be able to change public consciousness in ways that will make the experiences and agency of working-class women and men more visible and important to society at large.

Thus we are led to believe that our interviews are not so much records of facts that are more or less true—although they are that—but social texts, records of a social interaction situated within the context of class relations in the larger society. Thinking of interviews in this way allows us to avoid a too-facile assertion of the leveling created within an admittedly intimate interaction. Perhaps more important, it prevents us from so objectifying the interviewee as an "other" that we ignore the dialogic nature of the interview itself.[8]

III.

By entrusting us with their stories, working-class informants have given us the responsibility of presenting and interpreting their lives in the arenas of public discourse to which they themselves have little access. Acting on this responsibility conscientiously challenges many of the conventions of normal academic practice. Those who "study down" generally transform the experiences they have recorded into commodities of personal privilege: a job, tenure, increased professional prestige. The *contents* of the work may or may not contribute to a respectful, nonstereotypical view of those studied. But, as a social fact, it typically helps recreate a hierarchy of privilege. Traditionally, anthropologists who study "primitive people" in exotic places have been most guilty of and, admittedly, also most sensitive to such practices.[9] But developments in the historical profession in the last two decades, including the burgeoning oral history movement, have put us in a similar position. The politics of the 1960s has affected the profession in what are undoubtedly positive ways. Like anthropologists, historians have begun to "study down": they have become acutely sensitive to the diversity of social experiences in the past and have sought a variety of explanations for them. And, like anthropologists, historians now face the problems endemic to "studying down," including the temptation to exaggerate the exotic, the heroic, or the tragic aspects of the lives of people with little social power.[10] Simultaneous with its interest in a more socially diverse past, the history profession has itself become more open to social diversity. While equity does not prevail, more women and minorities are practicing historians than ever before. Indeed, it is they/we who are frequently doing the "studying down" out of deeply held personal and political commitments. And many have sought to articulate and act on those commitments outside the academy.[11]

At the same time, however, countervailing trends have worked against diminishing the distance between the scholar and the public, and have in fact discouraged scholars from assuming public, or civic, responsibility for their work. The academic labor market has become much more competitive since the 1960s; so, likewise, has the academic subculture. To survive in that subculture, members must talk with their peers, not with their public. This process, it must be emphasized, is embedded within the structure of the academic community; it is not the personal fault of individuals, but an integral part of the system of evaluation, tenure, and promotion that has evolved with a labor surplus in the academic marketplace. Given the competitiveness of the academic enterprise, professional credibility often necessitates that we abandon social commitments and frame our work in theoretically complex arguments that invite collegial appreciation. The danger here is one of which we are all aware: the predominance of academics who are themselves alienated from the world they study by the language they use and the professional identities they have created.[12]

Informants who have been systematically excluded from such professional privileges as money, jobs, status, prestige, and scholarly authority challenge us to avoid the standard academic practice of turning life stories into commodities of privilege. But, given the structure of the academic marketplace, of the knowledge industry, and of the media within which public discourse takes place, finding ways to do this and arenas in which to do it continues to challenge us. For us, one of the avenues for opening up possibilities of linking our work and the larger public has been the choice of research projects located in our home communities where we have ongoing personal and social commitments. By researching subjects that are close to home, we have a greater opportunity—and perhaps feel a greater urgency—to communicate what informants have told us.

Both of us have attempted to make those links in ways that are modest but perhaps helpful as examples of what is possible. Shopes has found that a general interest in the local angle of her work offers opportunities for inserting what she is learning about cannery workers into certain public arenas—a local museum requests a tour of the cannery district; a library, an informal talk; a popular publication, a short article. More broadly, her specific interest in cannery workers has logically extended outward to include other aspects of local social history, and for these, too, a public audience exists. The most exciting example of this is an alternative history tour of Baltimore undertaken in collaboration with other local historians. Presented on occasion during the last several years, and currently in production as a book, this tour visits working-class and black communities and sites of labor unrest in the city, thereby countering the sanitized view of Baltimore's past that has developed along with the recent tourist trade. Because the former cannery district in Fells Point is currently undergoing massive gentrification and upscale development—a process that many residents have vehemently if futilely fought—there is ample opportunity in this segment of the tour, to contrast, and link, past to present.[13]

Thus, for Shopes, the frequently invoked caveat among oral historians of "return to the community" becomes not so much a return to the specific community of cannery workers she has interviewed, but an effort to return what she has learned from them to the broader civic community. Because each of these efforts at return is directed toward a specific, often very mainstream audience, it remains a challenge to maintain a focus on the larger issues of inequality, power, and social relations without losing the audience. It is even more difficult to avoid usurping interpretive authority and turning these broadly educational activities into one more version of the "expert" telling the "public" what she knows about local history, essentially extracting illustrative quotations out of context to support her own analysis or to provide some colorful anecdotes about working-class life. In an effort to solve this dilemma and handle her role as mediator, Shopes has found it important to return again and again to her interviews, listening for subtleties in point of view and interpretation that often lie below the surface of the words. These interviews become the basis of her presentations. Sometimes, for shorter accounts, she chooses to adopt the reporter's ploy of description, acknowledging her reliance on interviews but nonetheless presenting a rather seamless account of working-class life. This sort of "authoritative summary" is perhaps justified by the effort to remain true to the "spirit" of the interviews. On other occasions, when there is time to frame the presentation more explicitly in terms of class, extensive quotes from interviews are used to enable interviewees to describe and interpret their experience; authorial intervention comes by juxtaposing the perspective of the interviewees with that of the middle class, either contemporary commentators on cannery workers and their community or current assessments of working-class life. Yet there is no guarantee—other than a good-faith effort—that these quotations are not in some ways taken out of context. Indeed, the problems of presentation remain real: Shopes must negotiate her own conceptual and aesthetic preferences in terms of both the interviewee's narrative voice and the audience's expectant ears.[14]

An additional problem, of course, is the value of these broadly educative activities in effecting any sort of meaningful change. They are all essentially "one-shot deals," with no effort at follow-up or sustained interaction. Here Olson's work, because it is firmly grounded in an institutional setting, is perhaps more effective.

The connections between Olson's oral history interviews and a larger commitment to social change occurs primarily within the context of Dundalk Community College. Colleges and universities are notorious for casting their scholarly nets afar and ignoring the communities in which they reside. Working-class community colleges commit analogous sins by providing their brightest students with upward mobility opportunities that motivate them to leave the community and reject their working-class roots. Bringing research on the steel industry back to Dundalk Community College has been a mechanism for encouraging instructors as well as students to see this working-class community as an area rich in valuable intellectual and social resources. Olson has set up a series of public forums and faculty development workshops that encourage instructors to use the Dundalk community and the Sparrows Point steel mill in their design of student assignments and in their own scholarly research. The series has included two extended visits by Mark Reutter, author of *Sparrows Point: Making Steel—the Rise and Ruin of American Industrial Might,* who talked about his own use of interviews to build his argument about the decline of steelmaking in America.[15] Olson's use of students and college employees as sources of interviews and research data has reinforced the principle that the role of the college is to enable residents to understand and change their community rather than rise above it.

Olson's research on class, race, and gender consciousness has also been directly relevant to the work of the Faculty Council and the Multi-Cultural Affairs Committee in designing institutional systems for mediating sexism, racism, and class prejudice in the instructional program and support services of the college. Oral histories provide valuable documentation of the potency of community prejudices as well as the complexity of their motivation and consequences. Informants who have particularly insightful perspectives on class, race, and gender have been asked to speak to faculty and student groups in forums that allow Dundalk students to analyze and address the social inequities that sabotage the cohesiveness of their community. In this way the continuity between Olson's political commitments, professional affiliation, and research focus make it possible for her oral histories to feed back quite easily into an institutional setting that serves as a vehicle for social change in the Dundalk community.

Only by being citizen-scholar-activists rooted in a community over an extended period of time do we have the opportunity to develop the networks, the political insights, and the credibility that may enable our research to be useful in a process of social change. By doing work where we have personal commitments, our academic contributions are more likely to come out of a personal, creative, politically engaged self, one that has a social—and not simply academic—purpose.

For the feminist scholar, participating in a diverse community as a politically engaged self can mean many different things. All of us make the best decisions we can—within the contours of our own particular life trajectories—about how most effectively to invest our intellectual energies in the process of social

202 / Karen Olson and Linda Shopes

change. Economic security and personal fulfillment are not to be scorned, for academics or anyone else. But we have more than most, and what is imperative for a feminist methodology is that we seek to use our relative privilege in ways that subvert existing power relations. To do this, we need to structure important conversations between ourselves and the communities we study, actively to seek public arenas for our work. This requires a civic, not just an academic life, requires that we "dig where we stand," and that we stand on ground thoughtfully mapped to mark the contours of power, inequality, and conflict in the social realities we research.

Notes

1. The best discussion of the historical literature that addresses the differences among women appears in Nancy Hewitt, "Beyond the Search for Sisterhood: American Women's History in the 1980s," *Social History* 10, no. 3 (October 1985): 299–321. Hewitt frames the problem and provides a thoughtful discussion of the issues in a historiographical context. For some examples of the historical literature that documents diversity among women, see Kathy Peiss, *Cheap Amusements: Working Women and Leisure in Turn-of-the-Century New York* (Philadelphia: Temple University Press, 1986); Elizabeth Ewen, *Immigrant Women in the Land of Dollars: Life and Culture on the Lower East Side, 1890–1925* (New York: Monthly Review Press, 1985); Paula Giddings, *When and Where I Enter: The Impact of Black Women on Race and Sex in America* (New York, W. Morrow, 1984); Deborah Gray White, *Ar'n't I a Woman?: Female Slaves in the Plantation South* (New York, Norton, 1985); and Mamie Garvin Fields with Karen Fields, *Lemon Swamp and Other Places: A Carolina Memoir* (New York, Free Press, 1983).

2. There is only a sparse, though growing, body of work on masculinity. For discussions of middle-class men and masculinity see John Higham, "The Reorientation of American Culture in the 1890s," in *Writing American History*, ed. John Higham (Bloomington, Ind.: Indiana University Press, 1970), pp. 73–102; Margaret Marsh, "Suburban Men and Masculine Domesticity," *American Quarterly* 40, no. 2 (June 1988): 165–86; E. Anthony Rotundo, "Body and Soul: Changing Ideals of Middle-Class Manhood, 1770–1920," *Journal of Social History* 16 (Summer 1983): 23–38; and Peter Gabriel Filene, *Him/Her/Self: Sex Roles in Modern America* (New York, Harcourt, Brace Jovanovich, 1975). For a historical appraisal of manliness in working-class communities, see Sean Wilentz, *Chants Democratic: New York City and the Rise of the American Working Class, 1788–1950* (New York: Oxford University Press, 1984).

3. For an occupation that has employed a large segment of the female labor force, cannery work has been until recently a much ignored subject. Two recent studies of California cannery workers have begun to redress this imbalance: Vicki L. Ruiz, *Cannery Women, Cannery Lives: Mexican Women, Unionization, and the California Food Processing Industry, 1930–1950* (Albuquerque, N.M.,: University of New Mexico Press, 1987), and Patricia Zavella, *Women's Work and Chicano Families: Cannery Workers of the Santa Clara Valley* (Ithaca, N.Y., Cornell University Press, 1987). The best published description of women in the Baltimore canneries is in Marie Obenauer, *Working Hours, Earnings and Duration of Employment of Women Workers in Selected Industries of Maryland and of California*, Bulletin of the Bureau of Labor, no. 96 (Washington D.C., U.S. Government Printing Office, 1911).

4. The classic statement of the importance of women's sphere in female identity is Carroll Smith-Rosenberg, "The Female World of Love and Ritual: Relations between Women in Nineteenth-Century America," *Signs* 1 (Autumn 1975): 1–29; see also Nancy Cott, *The*

Bonds of Womanhood: Women's Sphere in New England, 1780–1835 (New Haven, Conn.: Yale University Press, 1977). Two important challenges to this perspective are Dolores Janiewski, *Sisterhood Denied: Race, Class and Gender in a New South Community* (Philadelphia, Temple University Press, 1985), and Elizabeth Fox-Genovese, *Within the Plantation Household: Black and White Women of the Old South* (Chapel Hill, N.C., University of North Carolina Press, 1988).

5. For a full discussion of Baltimore cannery women see Linda Shopes, "Women Cannery Workers in Baltimore, 1880–1943" (paper delivered at the Seventh Berkshire Conference on the History of Women, Northampton, Massachusetts, 21 June 1987).

6. Much of our understanding of the interactional nature of interview situations has been shaped by the theoretical work of Erving Goffman; see especially *The Presentation of Self in Everyday Life* (Garden City, N.Y.: Doubleday, 1959) and *Interaction Ritual: Essays on Face-to-Face Behavior* (Garden City, N.Y.: Anchor Books, 1967).

7. Richard Sennett and Jonathan Cobb, *The Hidden Injuries of Class* (New York, Knopf, 1972), pp. 141–50.

8. On the oral history interview as a communicative event, see Eva McMahan, *Elite Oral History Discourse: A Study of Cooperation and Coherence* (Tuscaloosa, Ala.: University of Alabama Press, 1989); Judith Modell, "The Performance of Talk: Interviewing Birthparents and Adoptees," *International Journal of Oral History* 9, no. 1 (February 1988): 6–26; Peter Friedlander, "Theory, Method and Oral History" in *The Emergence of a UAW Local, 1936–1939: A Study in Class and Culture* (Pittsburgh, Pa.: University of Pittsburgh Press, 1975), pp. xi–xxxiii; Ronald J. Grele, "A Surmisable Variety: Interdisciplinarity and Oral Testimony," in idem, *Envelopes of Sound: The Art of Oral History* (Chicago, Precedent Publishers, 1985), pp. 156–95.

9. The precarious position of postcolonial ethnography has forced anthropologists to grapple with the complex issues of "studying down." See, for example, Laura Nader, "Up the Anthropologist—Perspectives Gained from Studying Up," in *Reinventing Anthropology,* ed. Dell Hymes (New York, Pantheon, 1969), pp. 284–311; and James Clifford, *The Predicament of Culture: Twentieth-Century Ethnography, Literature, and Art* (Cambridge, Mass.: Harvard University Press, 1988). For a discussion of the importance of understanding the processes of power in present-day cultural systems, see Eric R. Wolf, "American Anthropologists and American Society," in *Concepts and Assumptions in Contemporary Anthropology,* ed. Stephen A. Tyler (Athens, Ga.: University of Georgia Press, 1969).

10. The difficulties inherent in academic analyses of working-class people in historical studies is discussed in John Clarke, Chas Critcher, and Richard Johnson, eds., *Working-Class Culture: Studies in History and Theory* (London, Hutchinson, 1979).

11. The decision by some professionally trained historians, both inside and outside the academy, to publish nonscholarly oral history accounts of the social experience of nonelites can be viewed as a politically motivated effort to broaden the audience for such work; insofar as these accounts challenge social stereotypes and are themselves also about efforts at progressive social change, they can also be seen as efforts to contribute to social change. See, for example, Theodore Rosengarten, *All God's Dangers: The Life of Nate Shaw* (New York, Avon, 1974); Nell Irvin Painter, *The Narrative of Hosea Hudson: His Life as a Negro Communist in the South* (Cambridge, Mass.: Harvard University Press, 1979); and Sherna Berger Gluck, *Rosie the Riveter Revisited: Women, the War, and Social Change* (Boston, Twayne, 1987).

Several long-term projects designed to link history—often via oral histories—to the process of community empowerment offer especially exciting possibilities for socially engaged historical work. Among the most notable are the New York Chinatown History Project at the Center for Community Studies, Inc., 70 Mulberry Street 2/F, New York, N.Y. 10013; and the Centro de Estudios Puerterriqueños, Hunter College, City University of New York (see Rina Benmayor's essay in this volume). For reflections on this sort of historical work, see Jeremy Brecher, "A Report on Doing History from Below: The Brass Workers History

Project," in *Presenting the Past: Essays on History and the Public,* ed. Susan Porter Benson, Stephen Brier, and Roy Rosenzweig (Philadelphia, Temple University Press, 1978), pp. 267–77; and Linda Shopes, "Oral History and Community Involvement: the Baltimore Neighborhood Heritage Project," in Benson, Brier, and Rosenzweig, eds., *Presenting the Past,* pp. 249–63.

12. For a discussion of integrity of purpose in the academy see Immanuel Wallerstein, *University in Turmoil: The Politics of Change* (New York: Atheneum, 1969); Edgar Z. Friedenberg, "The University in an Open Society," *Daedalus* 99 (Winter 1970): 56–74; Salvador E. Luria and Zella Luria, "The Role of the University: Ivory Tower, Service Station, or Frontier Post?" *Daedalus* 99 (Winter 1970): 78–83; and Derek Bok, *Beyond the Ivory Tower: Social Responsibilities of the Modern University* (Cambridge, Mass., Harvard University Press, 1982).

13. This tour, and the process of putting it together, is described in Elizabeth Fee, Sylvia Gillett, Linda Shopes, and Linda Zeidman, "Baltimore by Bus: Steering a New Course Through the City's History," *Radical History Review* 28–30 (1984): 206–16; the book version of the tour, tentatively entitled *Touring Baltimore: A New Look at Our Past,* is to be published by Temple University Press in 1991.

14. On the problem of authority in the public presentation of historical material, see Michael Frisch, *A Shared Authority: Essays on the Craft and Meaning of Oral and Public History* (Albany, N.Y.: State University of New York Press, 1990).

15. Mark Reutter, *Sparrows Point: Making Steel—The Rise and Ruin of American Industrial Might* (New York, Summit Books, 1988).

Advocacy Oral History:
Palestinian Women in Resistance

Sherna Berger Gluck

The sheer importance of rendering women visible—casting them as agents as we simultaneously documented their oppression— seduced feminist historians into believing that our scholarly work was inherently political and of undeniable value for women. Somewhat innocently, we believed that the lofty goal of transforming knowledge about women into accessible texts was sufficient, and we did not preoccupy ourselves with the use that might be made of our work.

This innocence was lost definitively as a result of the Sears-EEOC debacle, when feminist historical scholarship was introduced by Sears as part of its defense against charges of sex discrimination.[1] The controversy still raging over this courtroom drama has forced many of us to be more attentive to the implications of our research. Thorny questions raised by this case, coupled with long-standing doubts about the use of stories of living women for the production of knowledge, have driven many feminist oral historians to construct projects that more directly and immediately benefit the women who are researched.

Like many scholars, my political beliefs have played a crucial role both in my choice of research topics and in my commitment to make my work accessible to working-class women like those whom I interviewed. Although I tried to convince myself that I was succeeding in integrating politics and scholarship, I was left with nagging doubts. I continued to be plagued by the question of how my public interpretations of the lives of the women I interviewed was of benefit or value to them.

It was only after going to occupied Palestine*, and eventually constructing an advocacy oral history project that directly linked my use of women's oral history to my political activity, that these doubts were eased, if not fully erased. Now, in contrast to my earlier concern about having my scholarship

---

* In 1948, when Israel declared independence in advance of the schedule approved by the 1947 U.N. partition plan, Jews constituted 35% of the population of historic Palestine. Granted 55% of the land by the partition plan, they acquired another 15% of the land as a result of the 1948–1949 war. After the 1967 war, Israel occupied the remaining areas of land of historic Palestine: the West Bank and Gaza, and annexed East Jerusalem. In November 1988, the Palestine National Council (of the PLO) declared the independent state of Palestine (with the borders to be determined through negotiation). When I refer to the occupied territories, to occupied Palestine, or simply to Palestine, I am referring to the West Bank, Gaza, and East Jerusalem.

reflect my political commitments, I have to grapple with the potential contradictions between my political advocacy and my scholarship.

For a variety of complex reasons, including the Talmudic tradition in which I had been raised and which had fostered my social consciousness, I had long been an opponent of Zionist expansionism. But it was only after the Sabra and Shatilla massacres in Lebanon in 1982 that I publicly criticized Israel. Five years later, after the beginning of the *intifada,** I became an active, outspoken advocate of Palestinian self-determination. To have a greater understanding of the situation in Palestine and to be more effective in my advocacy work, I joined other Jews from the United States in an eyewitness tour of the West Bank and Gaza in December 1988. During our travels together, we talked with, and I interviewed, Palestinians in the occupied territories as well as progressive Israeli peace activists.

As a feminist activist and scholar, I had a long-standing interest in women's liberation movements and in the development of both "women's consciousness" and feminist consciousness.[2] Initially I planned to document the role played by both Palestinian and Israeli women in resisting Israeli occupation. Although I believed that this project had an intrinsic scholarly value, I was particularly interested in using the materials I gathered to educate the feminist public in the United States on the Palestinian question, and to convince them not only of the absolute legitimacy and justice of the Palestinian struggle for self-determination, but also of the need for action. The other side of the coin was my advocacy of feminism. I had been encouraged by Palestinian friends in the United States to pursue my oral histories with women in Palestine, among other reasons, to help fuel the internal discussion there on women's liberation.

The direct linking of political advocacy and women's oral history posed new problems for me. Where previously my interviews with women were guided primarily by a commitment to give them a voice—or rather, to make their voices heard—now I was going to be using those voices much more deliberately to advocate on their behalf. The typical concerns of a feminist scholar about authenticity and mutuality had preoccupied me in my earlier work. I had also sought to bring to my work critical questions that ultimately shaped the interview process and extended the parameters of the narrative. The oral history became, then, both a personal account defined by the narrator and a historical document that was shaped by my intervention.

In interviewing women in a highly volatile political situation, and one in which I at least partially shared a political agenda with my narrators, could I bring my usual critical interviewing skills to bear? Could I continue to shape the interviews for broader historical purposes and avoid becoming a mere

---

* The *intifada* refers to the Palestinian uprising against the occupation that began on 9 December 1987. It was the first sustained mass resistance within the occupied territories since the struggle for national liberation was launched in the 1960s.

conduit for political platforms? Would the very process of mutuality to which we aspire in most women's oral history projects undermine my ability to function as a scholar? With the political reality of occupation uppermost in the minds of Palestinian women, could I probe and prod without arousing their suspicion or undermining their trust, so that I could create an authentic— or at least a fuller—life history?

The dual goal of maintaining my scholarly integrity at the same time that I used my scholarship for overt and immediate political purposes led to a host of questions and problems that still perplex me. It is these on which I will reflect in this essay, and not on the problems emanating from my role as an outsider, my use of interpreters, or my limited time with the women and the somewhat "unnatural" circumstances in which the interviews took place.

The Evolution of an Advocacy Oral History Project

My initial intention to study both Palestinian and Israeli women who were resisting Israeli occupation of the West Bank and Gaza was quickly modified, as a result of the limited amount of time I had to conduct interviews and also because of my heightened political sensitivities. Observing and, to some extent, experiencing the daily reality of Palestinian lives under occupation, I came to understand more profoundly the "trap" of symmetry. The meaning of fighting Israeli occupation is not the same for Palestinian and Israeli women, and attempts at symmetry merely blur the distinction between occupied and occupier and deflect attention from the basic injustice experienced by the Palestinian people. This is not to deny the oppression of Jewish women in Israeli society, nor to denigrate their role in opposing occupation. Although they might make common cause with Palestinian women, the material conditions and daily realities of their lives are simply not parallel, and neither is the jeopardy they face for organizing against the occupation.

Because the collection of Palestinian women's oral histories both for purposes of advocacy and for those of historical documentation had such apparent value, the initial interviews conducted during my first trip were somewhat spontaneous and were not part of a clearly defined research plan. It was over the subsequent five months before my second trip, and during the interim before my third trip, that I broadened and sharpened my inquiry: to study the expression of Palestinian "women's consciousness" within the context of the *intifada* and the nationalist movement, and to explore the development and expression of consciousness about their own oppression, i.e., feminist consciousness, among women at the grass roots level.

The initial interviews were conducted with the national leaders of the four women's committees.[3] Together, these committees, especially the three progressive ones, form the core of the movement for women's liberation and provide an avenue for women's nationalist activity in the West Bank and Gaza. In these early interviews with highly educated and politicized women, the creative tension between advocacy and scholarship became immediately apparent.

These women knew that I could serve as a medium of communication with the U.S. public. After all, this was both their goal in talking with me and my goal in interviewing them. But I wanted more from them than the recitation of the injustices of occupation, the worthiness of their cause, and the structure and programs of their committees. I wanted also to hear about the development of their own consciousness, about any conflicts they might have had with men in the nationalist struggle, and the self-conscious compromises they might have made in order to forward the nationalist movement. This meant pushing them.[4] To do so, however, meant running the risk that they might see me as a "first world feminist" who was insensitive to their situation. It might also make them distrust me as an advocate, which, in turn, could close off access to other people and to the range of information I needed to be a well-informed spokesperson in the United States. The problem of monitoring ourselves in order to maintain trust and continued cooperation probably arises any time an interviewer engages in mutual exchanges with the narrator, but it is a particularly acute problem in interviews with political activists, and especially in the context of advocacy oral history.

In any event, good interviewers do try to help their narrators construct the interview in their own terms. Indeed, the best oral histories are those that achieve a balance between the narrator's agenda and the interviewer's agenda—agendas that are, at times, disparate. I encountered several barriers to achieving the kind of balance necessary for creating a full, rich life history. First and foremost is the daily reality of occupation and the immediacy of the political struggle, which makes personal questions about their pasts seem ridiculous. For instance, questions about early childhood were viewed as irrelevant, except when these questions evoked memories like those of the childhood game of "guerrilla fighters-Israeli soldiers"—the Palestinian equivalent of cowboys and Indians. As a result, although less immediate aspects of life did have to be explored if I were to represent these women as more than merely romanticized cardboard heroines, I often felt foolish asking about things that were not transparently related to the current political situation. As an advocate, and not merely a "dispassionate" scholar, I monitored myself more carefully and, in the process, lost some of the freedom to explore my usual wide-ranging life-history questions.

Second, the fact that these women were living under military occupation meant that it was risky to record information on the more personal aspects of life that I would normally explore. Because all political organizations are outlawed and most political activities are subject to severe punishment, how could I, for instance, openly ask about the development of their political awareness and activities or about their political affiliations? Although many of these narrators would know how to protect themselves from dangerous disclosure, I could not risk my credibility by venturing into these aspects of their personal history. At some level, I was always aware of the perception that they held of outsiders, so tellingly articulated by one of the male political activists in the village where I did extensive interviewing on my third trip: "There are three kinds of visitors: collaborators, merchants, and friends."

Finally, the reluctance of some of the more ideological leaders to pursue lines of personal inquiry evoked memories of my experiences interviewing American women who were former members of the Communist Party. The Marxist repudiation of personal biography and fear of exaltation of individual experience often resulted in oral histories that focused primarily on political issues, ideas, and programs.

In my conversations and interviews with over two dozen women in the course of my three trips, only rarely was I able to overcome the barriers to obtaining a personal life history. In spite of these problems, and in spite of the fact that individual consciousness is rarely revealed through the recitation of a political platform, an examination of the subtlety of language and the occasional contradictions between personal expression and a political line provided me with important clues.[5] For instance, even in the context of a relatively controlled presentation, with an emphasis on the primacy of the national struggle, one leader revealed at least her own underlying feminist consciousness and commitment by repeatedly adding the phrase "and personal self-development" to the much more restrictive line delivered by her colleague in a joint interview. What these occasional interjections also suggested was that there was an active debate within the nationalist movement about women's liberation.

Ultimately, variations in awareness of and adherence to ideology, as well as individual quirkiness, did yield revealing material both from urban, educated leaders and from their less educated village counterparts. Occasionally, I was able to gain insights into the ways that conflicts within the rigidly patriarchal family laid the foundation for the development of feminist consciousness. The clashes between the changing expectations of young women and the old patriarchal values that were the cornerstone of traditional Palestinian society were common occurrences, and cut across political lines.

These conflicts were perhaps more evident and dramatic among those who had achieved higher education both in the West and in other Arab countries. In some cases, the very issue of access to higher education triggered a confrontation, as in one instance where a sixteen-year-old daughter embarked on a hunger strike that was to last two weeks after her father refused to send her to the university. In another instance, it was the realization that her father had created a will leaving nothing to her—in fact, a violation of Islamic law, which gives daughters one-half the amount given to sons—that led a thirteen-year-old girl to launch a rebellion and a verbal war that continues to this day, a dozen years later.

For the less educated women who form the rank and file of the women's committees at the level of the village and refugee camp, it was both the conflict with patriarchal authority and the collusive partnership between daughters and their traditional mothers that often paved the way for change. This was evident, for instance, in the case of two sisters who are active in the local women's committee and who work in the production project run by the committee in their village. In contrast, for a woman from another village, it was the clash between traditional values and the total powerlessness of her mother that had heightened her feminist consciousness.

This village activist recounted, in the most intensely personal and emotional of the oral histories I collected, how her mother had been unable to fight her father and the weight of tradition. As a result, twelve years ago Samira was forced to marry her orthodox Muslim cousin, despite the fact that her family had earlier agreed to her marriage to a partner of her own choice. Samira's personal resistance to her husband's religious dictums was supported and strengthened by her involvement in the women's committee. Today, following the path of least resistance and belying her own feminist consciousness, she wears *sharia* dress, covering herself with a scarf, a long skirt, and long sleeves. But she leaves the house at 7 A.M., doesn't return until early evening, and goes from village to village organizing other women on their own behalf as well as for the nationalist struggle. Her authority in the house, despite her husband's attempts to control her, is abundantly clear.

Both my interview with Samira and my observation of her daily life in the home were a result of an evolving research plan that was designed to accommodate my dual roles as scholar and advocate. I had certainly gathered sufficient information in my initial interviews with the leadership of the women's committees to effectively reach out to the American feminist community and educate them about the Palestinian women's fight for national and social liberation. As a scholar, however, I felt compelled to explore the extent to which less educated women in the villages and refugee camps subscribed to the official platforms of the committees, as well as the extent to which their participation in the local committees reflected a consciousness about women's social condition. Ironically, by pursuing these scholarly interests, I not only increased the historical value of the oral histories, but I also expanded my role as an advocate.[6] By more carefully selecting and broadening my choice of narrators, I was collecting material that could be of immediate use to the committees, both for recruitment and publicity and in their ongoing assessment of their grassroots work.

The major purpose of my return trips to Palestine (a three-week stay in June 1989 and a four-week visit in December/January 1989–90) was to interview village committee members. Regardless of my personal sympathies, I tried to make it clear that I was not aligned with any one committee, and I did succeed in enlisting the cooperation of all four committees. However, because of their greater consciousness of and efforts to mobilize international support, it was the three socialist-feminist women's committees who hosted me most of the time and made arrangements for me to spend time in villages, including overnight stays in some villages and one refugee camp. During my third visit, I concentrated on a single village, staying there overnight with members of two of the committees and returning repeatedly for daytime visits with women active in each of the four committees.

Despite the language barrier, I was warmly welcomed into the homes of the women and into their committee centers.[7] And perhaps because of the language barrier, I was able to become a more acute observer of behavior and relationships. For instance, when an English-speaking man and a half dozen young non-English-speaking men joined us in a Gaza refugee camp to talk about the political situation, my host—a leader of one of the local committees who wore a modified form of modest dress in public, and who spoke only a few words of English—sat with us and engaged in the discussion (as it was translated into Arabic), often disagreeing vociferously with the men. As far as I could observe from both her body language and her heated delivery, she held her ground. And she also seemed to be accorded great respect by the men, a concrete example of the changing relationships between men and women that many of my narrators had mentioned and that I repeatedly observed during my stays in peoples' homes.

Indeed, it was in becoming a temporary member-guest of their communities that I gained the deepest insights into the views of women's liberation held by grassroots activists. Samira's authority in the home, mentioned earlier, was demonstrated both in the fight to control the television channel, and in how she ordered the entire extended family out of her quarters so that she could have complete privacy to record her interview.

On another occasion, in a different village, it was while we sat around the table in their copper-enamel workshop chatting that I began to understand more profoundly the consciousness of the young women of the group. It was the end of a full day, during which I had interviewed many of them on an individual basis. The English-speaking member of the committee at whose house I was to spend the night had just returned from her job at the committee headquarters outside Jerusalem, and she joined us at the worktable. After exchanging news of the day, including a story of the ridiculous efforts made by Israeli soldiers to remove a Palestinian flag from the electricity wires, the conversation turned to my life in the United States.

In response to my invitation to ask me questions, the four young women inquired about my age. The exchange that followed was very telling—perhaps more so than anything they had said directly in the interviews. They expressed incredulity at the fact that I was as old as, or even older than, many of their mothers. They attributed the fact that I didn't look as old to my engaging in work outside the home. Each of them, and in different ways, repeated this explanation. When I suggested that perhaps their mothers looked older because of their large families (from the interviews, I learned that they each had ten to twelve children), and because they had brought up their families under the hardships of occupation, these explanations were shrugged off and the women returned to the fact that I worked.

The younger, unmarried women of the group talked in their interviews about wanting to continue to work outside the home after marriage, even when their children were young. A new mother, who was on temporary leave from the workshop, planned to return when her daughter was six months old. The centrality of work in their visions of the future was clearly evident in the interviews I had recorded. But during their interchange with me, what became even more obvious was that they viewed "productive work" as an avenue for personal fulfillment and social liberation. In their oral histories, they emphasized their attraction to the committee for nationalist reasons, but this informal session revealed that they subscribed to what is a classical socialist-feminist analysis of women's liberation, and one that is at least implied in the platform of the committee to which they belonged.

In the interviews with grassroots activists, I faced many of the same problems, with perhaps a different twist, that I experienced earlier in interviewing the committee leaders. It was not just that they all had a political agenda or that the purpose of my interviews was political, but that the daily reality of occupation was what was uppermost in their minds. How could it be otherwise, what with helicopters whirring over their villages at night, roadblocks impeding their freedom of movement, and the ever-present expectation of pre-dawn raids by the Israeli army? Certainly, they could understand my interest in the roles of women in the *intifada*, and it made sense to them when I asked about their ideas of the relationship between men and women, their expectations for the future, or their hopes for the role of women in a future Palestinian state. They seemed to answer these questions freely and with candor.[8] Through careful questioning, and sometimes through more direct observation of their lives, I was able to go beyond the political line. But only rarely did I feel free to ask the kinds of questions that would have yielded an in-depth life history. I was constrained by the factors I have already mentioned—above all, by the repressive political conditions that made it risky to record personal information—and by the rather unnatural circumstances in which I conducted the interviews.[9] The patterns of visiting, particularly the group visits with outsiders interested in their political situation, were not conducive to recording life-history interviews. The artificiality of sitting alone in a room in the house with the narrator and a translator—not to mention the imposition on other family members when the room had to be vacated—was an additional impediment. As a result, my interviews themselves took a different shape. When I could, I conducted truncated, individual life histories that were relatively short and more focused on their evolving consciousness and involvement in the women's committee. At other times, I conducted short group interviews with the most active members of the committees, seeking their reasons for joining the committee, their personal plans, and their vision of the Palestinian state and women's roles.

Much like an anthropologist, I have been at the mercy of events, including the availability and willingness of all groups to receive me with equal enthusiasm—something that my advocacy and resulting relationships with particular Palestinians in the United States might, in fact, have limited. In the evolution of my research and my role, I have been made more acutely aware of how oral historians who are documenting contemporary events must also be part anthropologist-sociologist. For while we are gathering materials for future historical purposes, we are also engaging in contemporary analysis and in the dynamics of both interpersonal and political relationships.

The Dilemmas of Public Presentation

One of my goals in collecting Palestinians women's stories is to bring the issue of their national and social liberation to the attention of the American public. Because I am not simply a propagandist but also a scholar-advocate, I have had to construct, self-consciously, my public presentations and continually assess how to present my materials. Although we *always* pick and choose our illustrations and regularly make decisions about how to talk to different audiences, most scholars find refuge in a supposed stance of neutrality and do not openly acknowledge how they shape and mold their material. By clearly espousing a cause and by using oral histories to strengthen my argument, not only was I exposing myself more than most scholars, but I also had to confront, personally, the potential contradictions between the two roles—scholar and advocate—I was trying to combine.

Perhaps the major dilemma I faced was how to speak about the differences among the various women's committees. I had no intention of suppressing material, but neither did my advocate role make me feel free to discuss all the nuances of ideology that separated the groups. Although they all espoused the social as well as the national liberation of women, the extent to which they wholeheartedly embraced women's liberation as an *integral* part of the nationalist struggle varied, both among national leaders and grassroots activists. Would even implied criticism of the level of feminist analysis and consciousness of any of the women's committees make some "first world" feminists question why Palestinian self-determination should be supported if women's liberation was not a priority? Presenting the intricacies of the differences between the groups might confuse the issue and work against my aim of educating an American feminist audience about "Third World feminism" and its frequent embeddedness in national struggles for self-determination. Furthermore, it would also undermine my own commitment to the fragile unity of the Palestinian women's movement.

The advocate role also directly impinged on the solution to my dilemma.

Because of the complex network of political alliances and factions, my work with Palestinians in the United States and in occupied Palestine could be jeopardized if I was viewed as a partisan of any *single* women's committee. There was, of course, also the question of loyalty. I felt that it would be a betrayal of my Palestinian hosts to make invidious comparisons between the groups. Yet it is necessary to question continually whether glossing over the differences between the groups might not be intellectually dishonest and a violation of scholarly standards. This dilemma about the face we put on our material is one that oral historians working in living communities regularly encounter, and it is certainly a standard problem for anthropologists.

In trying to find a solution to how to present my materials, I began to recognize that I might not always be able to combine seamlessly the dual roles of scholar and advocate. The task I had to set for myself, then, was how to have my advocacy/politics and my scholarship continually inform each other, even when I chose to emphasize one or the other to a specific audience. To more general audiences that I was trying to educate about the Palestinian cause, by both speaking and writing, my research would form the basis for my discussion, but I would not put forward lengthy, detailed analyses of the complexities of the Palestinian women's movement. Although this oversimplification might obscure differences among the groups, I would certainly not deny them, and, when appropriate, I would explain how the groups differed in both ideology and strategy.

To feminist scholars who are more cognizant of the complexities of Third World feminism, particularly in the context of national liberation struggles, I could paint a fuller picture. It would be meaningful to provide an analysis of the variations among the groups, including an explanation both of how these are reflected at the level of activity and of the implications of these differences for women in a future Palestinian state. The advocacy promoted in this scholarship would be more akin to the less immediate advocacy in which most feminist historians engage, i.e., the effort to transform our understanding of women's experience, at the same time that it would also introduce the Palestinian cause, at least as subtext.

The decision to give different emphasis or weight to the two roles in varying contexts is primarily a personal and instrumental solution, and is probably not that different, in fact, from the quiet choices we all make when we extend the presentation of our scholarship beyond academic circles. In trying to combine the roles of scholar and advocate, however, these decisions, as well as the choices of narrators and interview methods, must all be subjected to closer scrutiny. It is essential that we examine the possible conflicting demands of the two roles at *each* stage of the process, at least identifying the difficulties and trying to resolve those that we can. Ultimately, after peeling away the various layers of the problem down to an essential core, we may be faced with contradictions between the two roles that cannot be resolved, but only acknowledged.

Oral History as an Agent of Change

Several avenues of social change have been opened through the oral history process in which I have been engaged. The voices of the Palestinian women have served to raise the consciousness of Americans about Palestine and of Palestinians in the United States about feminism. Additionally, the questions I asked of the women during the interview process encouraged them to think about women's issues in a different way.

Dialogue with North American feminist audiences has encouraged their deeper understanding of the implications of feminism in the Third World, and an acknowledgment—even from Zionist women—of the daily reality and political conditions governing the lives of Palestinian women, in particular. My talks and the ensuing audience exchange frequently have resulted both in a reassessment of positions on the Palestinian question and in a revision of the concept of global feminism and what constitutes women's issues. On occasion, members of the audience have been moved to action: to writing on behalf of Palestinian political prisoners, or to donating to a book fund for the women's committees.

Palestinian men and women in my audiences, on the other hand, often are forced to confront their own political contradictions. Palestinian American youth, for instance, and Palestinians who emigrated to the United States prior to the *intifada* are, by and large, considerably less progressive in their social outlook than are the men and women who are living under and actively resisting occupation. Within that immediate context, and as a result of the changing consciousness and roles of women there, contemporary Palestinian feminism has not only taken shape, but also has begun to seep into the larger debate.

With rare exceptions, that process has not yet taken place in the Palestinian community in the United States. Indeed, because talk of women's liberation *appears* to threaten traditional values—the idealization of which often constitutes the primary expression of nationalist consciousness for Palestinians here—there is resistance to discussing the oppression of Palestinian women. At most, if it is acknowledged at all, it is clear that this discussion is viewed as peripheral to, and even a subversion of, the question of Palestinian self-determination. Accordingly, feminists are usually viewed as out of touch with, if not downright insensitive to, the real needs and aspirations of Palestinian women—as if there were no Palestinian feminists. The words of active, nationalist feminists from Palestine, on the other hand, make it clear that the simultaneous struggle against national and social oppression is legitimate.

When there has been a large number of Palestinians in my audience, the question of women's reproductive roles, especially, has generated heated discussion. The Palestinians are then moved to reevaluate their own position on the issue as a result of hearing about the attitudes of the leadership of the women's movement, which, by and large, advocates women making their own choices. Although the committees, through their programs, attempt to empower women to make their own decisions, they do urge women to have no more than four or five children. Their attitude stands in sharp contrast to many older, leading nationalist women who still believe that women have a revolutionary obligation to have ten children in order to give Palestinians an edge in the demographic war with Israel.

Through my use of their words about the future, their roles as mothers and workers, and the breakdown of patriarchal authority, Palestinian women have been able to reach past their circumscribed borders and speak to a wider audience on behalf of their liberation. They have been able to challenge, if not immediately to expand, the consciousness of both Americans and Palestinians in the United States so that feminism becomes incorporated into the political discourse on Palestine. My advocate-scholar role has enabled me not only to play a dual role, on two issues—feminism and Palestinian self-determination—but also to practice this role facing two directions: toward the United States and toward Palestine. Through my questions, which, of course, are shaped by my own feminism, the Palestinians whom I interviewed have been encouraged to extend their internal dialogue about women. For example, after several repeated returns to the village where I did most of the interviewing during my last trip, one of the women commented: "Your questions are good; they make us think about these things." Apparently there had not previously been extensive discussion among the women in her committee on the role of women in a future Palestinian state. After I had interviewed a few of them and asked this question, they decided that this was a highly legitimate issue to which they had not given enough thought, and they subsequently held a group discussion on the topic. In contrast to the traditional "scientific model" that condemns a result such as this and labels it as something that contaminates "our subjects," we, as feminists, applaud this kind of interactive effect of our research. Although there is always the obvious danger that outsiders, through the use of their own cultural referents, might be practicing just one more form of cultural imperialism, the reactions of the women I interviewed demonstrated that they viewed questions such as these as relevant, and that they were able to translate them into a meaningful form for their own use. On the other hand, as a result of the interactive process and the questions they asked me, I was forced to reexamine many of my own assumptions and gained a deeper understanding and appreciation both of Palestinian feminism and of its essential embeddedness in the nationalist struggle.

Conclusion

My role as an advocate for Palestinian self-determination made my task of interviewing easier in some respects and more difficult in others. On the one hand, within the very volatile context of the *intifada*, and given the way that Israelis have sometimes used outsiders as collaborators, my credentials as an advocate made me trustworthy. Each group (if not the individual women with whom I met) even if they had advance, outside information about my work, questioned me about my activities and my beliefs. Showing them photographs of demonstrations organized by two groups to which I belong, as well as the statement from our feminist solidarity group (Feminists in Support of Palestinian Women), further bolstered their faith in me. Ironically, their trust, coupled with our shared political commitments, inhibited me from conducting full life-history interviews, with the emphasis on personal biography. Within the political context of Israeli occupation—a fact that loomed large in their daily lives—it was foolish of me to have expected to be able to do this. Long-term participant-observation would be the only natural way to achieve this end—though I wonder what contribution I would be making to their daily political struggle by this method, and I am sure they would have these same doubts.

Because of both their political self-consciousness about the significance of the women's committees and their awareness of outsiders' interest in women's issues, my own feminism and research agenda on women's changing consciousness could be accommodated, to some extent, in the interviews. Nevertheless, this did not change the basic dynamics of the interview nor did it promote the feeling of intimacy—albeit, in reality, a rather imbalanced one—that so often characterizes feminist oral history. There were moments, of course, when a close connection as women was made—for example, in our mutual recognition of, and resulting joking and laughter about, men's recalcitrance in assuming household responsibilities.

On only one occasion, and probably because of the depth of her pain and despair over her personal situation, was there the kind of intimacy in the interview situation that led to a more personal account of the life of a Palestinian woman. Samira, to whom I referred earlier, huddled with my interpreter and me over the one source of heat in the very chilly room, a small electric heater. There was something symbolic about our postures: the group huddle and the ability to share her story seemed to give Samira the warmth and support she so desperately needed. Her oral history—one of the few that was intensely personal and more like a life history—provided me with rich insights and examples of how women in her situation negotiated the rather perilous terrain of a life that daily challenged her feminism. Despite the tremendous value of her account, I have not been comfortable using her story in the context of my advocate-scholar role. I am plagued by the feeling that I am objectifying her. In other words, my experience as an advocate-scholar, which had the effect of transforming my oral histories from more personal stories to accounts of primarily political experiences, heightened my sensitivity to using the intimate details of women's lives. Although I am optimistic about finding an appropriate feminist way to use her story in a more scholarly arena, I cannot overcome the feeling of voyeurism I would have if I were to use this material in my more general political presentations. The dilemma I face in using material like Samira's in public presentations, as well as my concern about promoting an understanding of Palestinian feminism on its own terms—which is muddied, I believe, by detailing the intricate differences among the groups—perhaps points to an advantage of separating the roles of scholar and advocate, at least in the presentation of our work. Even if we resolve the problem by using our materials differently in the two arenas, this does not mean that we should abdicate our responsibility to maintain scholarly standards, on the one hand, or political advocacy, on the other.

The effort to combine the roles of scholar and advocate may present us with a host of perplexing questions that feminist scholars do not normally face. An advantage, however, is that by combining the two roles we are often able to reap the reward of observing the direct impact of our work. As feminist oral historians, we will not all make the same choices, nor are we all tempermentally suited to playing more direct advocacy roles. Yet we must all remain sensitive to how our scholarship might undermine our ethical principles, to how our political beliefs affect our scholarship, and to potential uses to which our scholarship might be put. Concern about these issues need not immobilize us, however, but merely make us self-conscious about our research process, including the ways and the forums in which we present our work.

Regardless of how we choose to do research *for* women, it is important that we stand by each other and fight the forces of the academy that delegitimize advocacy scholarship and would have us abdicate our social responsibilities as feminists. Research *for* women, including advocacy scholarship, has forwarded the cause of women's liberation and, on occasion, has even led to reforms that have helped to alleviate the pain of at least some women. Above all, advocacy scholarship keeps us rooted in the social movement from which we sprang. It retains the potential for informing the movement and for activating the academy.

Notes

1. Because of the controversy over this case among feminist historians, it has been extensively documented, including the publication in *Signs* 11 (1986): 751–79 of several of the briefs and offers of proof. See also Ruth Milkman, "Women's Studies and the Sears Case," *Feminist Studies* 12 (1986): 375–400. And for a particularly poignant discussion of how scholarship can be used for purposes that are anathema to its producer, see Alice Kessler-Harris, "Equal Opportunity Commission v. Sears, Roebuck and Company: A Personal Account," *Radical History Review* 35 (April 1986): 57–79.

2. I am using "women's consciousness" to mean consciousness of women themselves as a group, and an awareness of their own power and of the collectivity that is derived from their traditional roles. This stands in contrast to a consciousness about their own oppression, which is feminist consciousness. For an excellent analysis of the power and meaning of women's consciousness, see Temma Kaplan, "Female Consciousness and Collective Action: The Case of Barcelona, 1910–1918," *Signs* 7 (1982): 545–66.

3. The four women's committees are: Federation of Women's Action Committees; Union of Palestinian Women's Committees; Union of Working Women's Committees; and Women's Social Work Committees. These committees developed in the late 1970s and early 1980s. All of them work in both the villages and refugee camps as well as in the urban centers. Their

activities are fairly similar, but their level of commitment to women's liberation varies, even by their own admission. Although the three socialist committees are more inclined to describe themselves as feminist, most Palestinian women activists shy away from the label because of its connotation of cultural imperialism. For an excellent discussion of this general problem, see Janet Afary, "Some Reflections on Third World Feminist Historiography," *Journal of Women's History* 1, (1989): 147–52.

4. In talking about interviewing people who are advocates of a cause—the limited sense in which he uses the term advocacy oral history—William Lang, in one of the few articles on the subject, discusses this same problem. See his article, "The Dangerous Waters of Advocacy Oral History," *International Journal of Oral History* 8 (1987): 199–204. In contrast to my point of view, however, he is ultimately critical of crossing the line between sympathetic interviewing and what he calls polemical oral history (pp. 201–2).

5. All initial interviews with the leadership were conducted in English. Although this placed the narrators at some disadvantage, I do not think that the kind of clues I found in their sometimes conflicting ideas were mainly a function of their level of competence in the English language.

6. Howard Green's "Critique of Public History," *Radical History Review* 25 (1981): 164–71, raises important issues about the advocacy in which public historians engage, particularly as policy advisers. To the extent that the oral history work with Palestinian women described here was also intended to supply them with materials to analyze further their own movement and activities, it conforms to his plea for historians to "enable people to participate in an ongoing struggle for the redefinition of authority in their own lives and in the larger culture" (p. 170).

7. Because the village women and the women in the refugee camp spoke virtually no English, I had to be accompanied by an English-speaking member from the committees' central offices. For the most part, these translators provided only approximate translations, and, on my return, a Palestinian friend provided literal translations of the interviews and commentaries on the exchange. Although I am greatly indebted to all the women in Palestine who assisted me, I am unable to acknowledge them formally by name, since this could place them in jeopardy.

8. For this I am relying on my U.S. translator's assessment, based on both a critical listening to the tapes and an understanding of the culture. I wish to thank Michel Shehadeh for his assistance, and acknowledge his valuable insights. He has pointed out that the women might have been more eager to talk about the *intifada* and the role of women in the uprising because that experience empowered them, in contrast to discussions about their past experiences and their daily lives.

9. Although nothing that was told to me was technically illegal, both my narrators and I were aware of the risks of having their accounts recorded. We agreed on the measures I should take to protect the tapes.

Afterword

The essays in this volume highlight the ways in which feminist oral history, in interrogating other discourses as well as its own assumptions, has produced a spiraling effect: from each successive turn on the spiral, the view is similar but also different. While the concept of research by, about, and for women continues to be a powerful impetus for feminist oral history, our understanding of this tenet has been transformed, leading us to new perspectives on the objectives of our research and on the connections between researcher and researched. This transformation has caused us to alter our habits of eliciting, listening to, and analyzing women's words. We have learned that we need to establish relationships with our narrators that do not veil the real distance between ourselves and them. Conversely, we have explored alternatives capable of decreasing this distance somewhat, and resulting in closer collaboration between the researched and the researcher. We have also given far greater attention to the limitations and potential uses of our research, and this, in turn, has led to the creation of research projects and products that take these constraints into account.

Neither the sometimes quite harsh appraisal of the feminist research model nor the critique of the older oral history work with its implicit assumption of an unproblematic meaning behind women's words is intended to denigrate the task of collecting these words. The great strength of oral history lies in the ease with which all kinds of voices can be recorded by all kinds of researchers. No longer does the "record" depend upon a scholarly consensus on the choice of lives to be counted as significant. The democratic potential of oral history must not be obscured by our examination of the complexity of the oral history process, nor by our attempts to refine the craft. Professionalization, however, not only is the consequence of the growth of specialized knowledge and skills; too often it serves as a mechanism of control and legitimation, and, as such, should be approached with skepticism. The tendency to engage in academic debate can inhibit the recuperative work of oral history, work that is still necessary if women are to be both visible and audible. We must not be lulled into the belief that the mere doing of this kind of work is likely to bring about social transformation, but even less should we give in to the scholar's doubts by demeaning the powerful contribution that oral history can make to the process of change.

Ironically, the process of recording oral histories and then making them accessible removes us ever further from the original source: the speaker. But it is the words that must first of all be recorded, for these provide us with the basis for all our scholarly endeavors and with the possibility of popular production.

In affirming that the work must come first, before criticism, analysis, and utilization, we are brought back to the arguments of the first group of essays in this collection, essays that aim to improve our capacity to listen and to comprehend. As we have seen, the interview process is itself an interaction of immense complexity, one in which both group and individual characteristics play defining roles. The interpretation of texts, as well, demands a multilayered approach, comprising analyses of mythical, political, historical, social, and linguistic elements. Thus we find our work enriched by new perspectives made available by social history, ethnography, and discourse analysis, among many others. Sophisticated readings can be accomplished, as several of our contributors have demonstrated, without losing their firm grounding in a particular reality.

What the essays in this volume reveal is that there is not merely one appropriate methodology, nor one type of research project, that all scholars should rush to duplicate. No blanket prescription will help us; we need, rather, to engage in self-critical examination of our practices and to go on to develop a range of models from which to select our procedures according to the needs of specific, and often unique, research situations. It is possible to be temporarily immobilized by an awareness of serious problems in the oral history process, whether these relate to procedures, or to ethics, interpretation, or politics. For such an awareness does undermine the very ease and apparent naturalness that lie at the heart of oral history work: human beings conversing. Alternatively, researchers can decide to ignore these problems for the sake of proceeding unimpeded. But a third path is possible, and this is indicated, in their several ways, by the essays in this book. This path shows us how to get on with our work even as we reflect on its procedures and its uses and take steps to change these where needed. In this connection it is important to stress that our commitment to greater critical awareness of the techniques on which oral history depends should in no instance lead to an effacing of our narrators while we analyze primarily ourselves.

Despite the traps in which feminist scholars have sometimes been caught as we have attempted to translate—too often with a heavy hand—the principles of feminism into appropriate research practices, these same principles have also given us the impetus to concentrate on our work in a critical spirit, and to draw from other disciplines and mold their resources to our needs. The long-term value of oral history will surely remain what it has been from the beginning: the expression it gives to our abiding interest in, and sympathy with, other lives, times, and places.

By questioning both the conventional truths and the feminist wisdom that have shaped the various stages and moments in the oral history process, the essays in this volume, in their individual agendas and their collective impact, can, we believe, contribute to the development of an informed feminist practice of oral history.

Index

Contributors

Sherna Berger Gluck coordinates the oral history program at California State University, where she also teaches women's studies. Gluck's early book on U.S. suffragists, *From Parlor to Prison* (New York: Vintage, 1976; reprinted: New York: Monthly Review Press, 1985), was one of the first products of women's oral history scholarship. Her methodological article on women's oral history is still used widely, especially in women's history. Gluck's research has focused on the development of women's consciousness, on women and work, and on working-class feminism. Her most recent book based on oral history is *Rosie the Riveter Revisited: Women, the War and Social Change* (Boston: G. K. Hall, 1987; and New York: New American Library, 1988). She is currently working on the topic of women's liberation in occupied Palestine.

Daphne Patai is Professor of Women's Studies and of Portuguese at the University of Massachusetts at Amherst. In addition to articles in the fields of oral history, Brazilian literature, utopian fiction, and women's studies, she is the author of *Myth and Ideology in Contemporary Brazilian Fiction* (Rutherford, N. J.: Fairleigh Dickinson University Press, 1983) and *The Orwell Mystique: A Study in Male Ideology* (Amherst, Mass.: University of Massachusetts Press, 1984). Patai's most recent book, an oral history of Brazilian women today, is entitled *Brazilian Women Speak: Contemporary Life Stories* (New Brunswick, N. J.: Rutgers University Press, 1988). Her next oral history project will be a study of contemporary Brazilian feminism, 1975–1990.

Kathryn Anderson is an Associate Professor of Speech Communication at Fairhaven College and Director of Women's Studies at Western Washington University, in Washington. She received her Ph.D. in Speech Communication from the University of Washington in 1978 and has been speaking and writing on women's oral history for more than fifteen years.

Rina Benmayor is Research Director of Cultural Studies, Center for Puerto Rican Studies, Hunter College, City University of New York (CUNY). She received her Ph.D. in Romance Languages and Literatures from the University of California at Berkeley. She has recently been concentrating on Puerto Rican women's oral histories and has spearheaded a special series of articles on the topic in the *Oral History Review* (Fall 1988), including her own "For Every Story There Is Another Story Which Stands Before It."

Katherine Borland is a doctoral candidate in folklore at Indiana University, Bloomington, currently conducting fieldwork in Nicaragua on the relationships between literacy, folklore, and nationalism. She is the author of "Horsing Around with the Frame: The Negotiation of Meaning in Women's Verbal Performance" (1990) and "Spoken to Written Language: Thoughts on the Evolution of Consciousness," forthcoming in *Constructing Rhetorical Education: From the Classroom to the Community.*

Marie-Françoise Chanfrault-Duchet received her Ph.D. in Linguistics and Literature in 1984 from the University of Tours (France), where she now teaches in the French department. She has published numerous articles on oral history, most recently: "Dire les relations sociales en milieu rural: la mémoire collective comme medium," in *Historia y Fuente Oral* (1990). She is currently at work on a book entitled *The Interdisciplinary Analysis of the Life Story.*

Gwendolyn Etter-Lewis received her Ph.D in Linguistics in 1985 from the University of Michigan and is currently Assistant Professor in the Department of English at Western Michigan University. She is the author of a number of articles on African American women and language, and is at work on a book about African American women's oral narratives. Her informants for this book are sixty to ninety-five years of age and graduated from college between 1920 and 1940. In 1989–90 she was a Ford Foundation Postdoctoral Fellow.

Sondra Hale holds a Ph.D. in Anthropology from the University of California, Los Angeles (UCLA), where she now teaches Women's Studies. She has published many articles on Sudan and on African and Middle Eastern women, including "The Politics of Gender in the Middle East" (1989), and "Women's Culture/Men's Culture: Gender, Separation and Space in Africa and North America" (1987). She is currently writing a book on gender, Islam, and the state in Sudan.

Dana Jack received her Ed.D from Harvard in 1985 and a Master's in Social Work from the University of Washington in 1972. She has worked extensively in psychological counseling and is the co-author, with Rand Jack, of *Moral Visions and Professional Decisions: The Changing Values of Women and Men Lawyers* (Cambridge University Press, 1989). She is currently at work on a book entitled *Silencing the Self: Women and Depression.*

Laurie Mercier received her Master's degree in history from Memphis State University in 1980 and was oral historian at the Montana Historical Society,

1981–88. She is currently a public historian in Pullman, Washington, and a Ph.D. candidate in American Studies at Washington State University. She has published many articles about Montana women and workers, and, with Mary Murphy and others, coauthored *Molders and Shapers: Montana Women as Community Builders, An Oral History Sampler and Guide* (1987)

Kristina Minister received her Ph.D. in Speech Communication from Northwestern University in 1977. She is on the faculty of Midway College in Kentucky, where she teaches communication and is director of the Women's Studies Program. She has directed numerous readers' theater productions, worked on a number of Arizona oral history projects, and is investigating the narrative construction of self.

Mary Murphy received her Ph.D. in history from the University of North Carolina, Chapel Hill, and is currently on the faculty of the History Department at Montana State University. With Laurie Mercier and others, she coauthored *Molders and Shapers: Montana Women as Community Builders, An Oral History Sampler and Guide* (1987). She is one of six coauthors of the prize-winning book *Like a Family: The Making of a Southern Cotton Mill World* (1987).

Karen Olson is Professor of History and Anthropology at Dundalk Community College in Baltimore, and a Ph.D. candidate in American Studies at the University of Maryland, College Park. She has produced a seven-part videotape series entitled *An Introduction to Cultural Anthropology* (1977–80). Her article "Old West Baltimore: Segregation, Black Culture and the Struggle for Equality" will appear in a collection of essays on Baltimore history directed at a nonacademic popular audience, forthcoming from Temple University Press.

Claudia Salazar is a doctoral candidate in Speech Communication at the University of Illinois, Urbana-Champaign, currently conducting fieldwork in Brazil. She is the author of several essays on women and language, including "Unruly Women: Deconstructing the Women in Development Discourse," in *Knowledge Explosion: The Impact of Feminist Scholarship in the Disciplines.* She served as the guest editor of a special issue of *Women and Language* (1988) on the Third World, gender, and communication.

Linda Shopes is an Associate Historian at the Pennsylvania Historical and Museum Commission. Her article here, ironically, represents the conclusion of her work in Baltimore, where she lived for twenty-three years. A Ph.D. candidate in American Studies at the University of Maryland, College Park, she is the author of "Beyond Trivia and Nostalgia: Collaborating in the Construction of Local History" (1984) and a co-editor of a forthcoming book on Baltimore history.

Judith Stacey received her Ph.D. in Sociology in 1979 from Brandeis University, and is Professor of Sociology and Women's Studies at the University of California, Davis. The author of *Patriarchy and Socialist Revolution in China* (University of California Press, 1983) and numerous articles on socialism and feminism, she has also written widely on family politics. Her most recent work is *Brave New Families: Stories of Domestic Upheaval in Late Twentieth Century America* (Basic Books, 1990).